Bringing the House Down

Bringing the House Down

A Family Memoir

DAVID PROFUMO

JOHN MURRAY

First published in Great Britain in 2006 by John Murray (Publishers)
A division of Hodder Headline

The right of David Profumo to be identified as the Author of the Work has been asserted by
him in accordance with the Copyright, Designs and Patents Act 1988.

I

Extract from 'In Praise of Limestone' from *Selected Poems* by W. H. Auden and extract from
'Annus Mirabilis' from *Collected Poems* by Philip Larkin are reproduced by kind permission
of Faber & Faber Ltd.

Every effort has been made to contact all copyright holders of material reproduced in this book.
If any have been inadvertently overlooked, the publishers will be pleased to make the necessary
arrangement at the first opportunity.

A CIP catalogue record for this title is available from the British Library

ISBN-13 978-0-7195-6608-0
ISBN-10 0-7195-6608-8

Typeset in 11.5/14 Monotype Bembo by Servis Filmsetting Ltd, Manchester

Printed and bound by Clays Ltd, St Ives plc

Hodder Headline policy is to use papers that are natural, renewable and recyclable products and
made from wood grown in sustainable forests. The logging and manufacturing processes are
expected to conform to the environmental regulations of the country of origin.

John Murray (Publishers)
338 Euston Road
London NW1 3BH

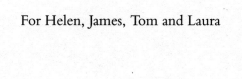

For Helen, James, Tom and Laura

Contents

List of Illustrations

All photographs courtesy the author unless otherwise credited

SECTION I

1. Commander Robert Hobson, my maternal grandfather
2. My mother, aged three
3. Valerie Hobson, promoting *Werewolf of London*
4. Boris Karloff and Valerie, in *Bride of Frankenstein* (Universal Studios)
5. Laurence Olivier and Valerie, in *Q Planes* (Carlton)
6. John Mills with Valerie in *Great Expectations* (J Arthur Rank)
7. Portrait of my mother taken during the Blitz
8. Valerie in *Kind Hearts and Coronets* (Ealing Studios)
9. Tony Havelock-Allan and Rex Harrison
10. Matthew Smith and Augustus John discussing Smith's portrait of Valerie (Westminster Press)
11. Dinner at the Royal Command Film Show (London News Agency)
12. Valerie inspects the troops on a visit to Bromley (Kentish Times)
13. Valerie and Jack at the Chelsea Arts Club Ball (courtesy of Tatler)
14. Herbert Lom and Valerie after a performance of *The King and I*
15. Valerie and Jack in a nightclub
16. Jack prepares to carry his bride over the threshold (Belgrave Press Bureau)

SECTION 2

So, when one of them goes to the bad, the way his mind works
    Remains comprehensible: to become a pimp
Or deal in fake jewellery or ruin a find tenor voice
    For effects that bring down the house could happen to all
But the best and the worst of us . . .
                                    W. H. Auden, 'In Praise of Limestone'

So life was never better than
In nineteen sixty-three
(Though just too late for me) –
Between the end of the *Chatterley* ban
And the Beatles' first LP.
                                    Philip Larkin, 'Annus Mirabilis'

. . . L—d! said my mother, what is all this story about? . . .
                        Laurence Sterne, *The Life and Opinions of*
                                    Tristram Shandy, Gentleman.
                                        vol. IX, ch. 33

I

Ghost Net: an Exordium

NOTHING IS SO uncertain as the past. It hurtles away from you, like phosphorescence glimmering in the wake of your boat as it speeds through the night. We like to think of time as a convenient formulation that prevents everything happening at once, but cause and event are forever commingling, like the Möbius strip you effectively cause if you spin the wheel and head back into the spread of your own wash.

So it goes. Graham Greene began his novel *The End of the Affair* – a title quite apt at this juncture – 'A story has no beginning or end: arbitrarily one chooses that moment of experience from which to look back or from which to look ahead.' I could claim this book has been forty years in the making, but, as it is a collective family memoir, the stories really begin further back than that. In its present form, it was discussed for a longish time, but if I have to stick my compass point into some place chronological from which to describe the succession of arcs, it will have to be the morning of 4 July 2001, when I strapped myself into the co-pilot's seat of Mi-2 helicopter number RA-23380 on the banks of a river on the Kola Peninsula in Arctic Russia.

There were eight of us aboard, off to fish a nearby water. Twenty minutes later, as we came in over the gorge, the pilot lost control in a massive downdraught, and his machine was thrown suddenly towards the ground. Crash and burn, I thought, in a brief instant of synaptic calm. This is how it ends. I had time to turn and see Volodya's face – a cartoon mask of nemesis – and then, as the rocks rushed up to meet us, we both shouted obscenities before we hit.

The chopper crashed on to its nose in a welter of extreme metallic noise. It slid along its starboard side for fifty yards, creating a debris field of snapped fuselage and sheared rotors. Below me, an exhaust caught fire, but the crewman – despite having broken his hip – saved the day by crawling in with an extinguisher. There was a moment of caged terror in the smoke, with screaming, the bitter reek of fuel, and bodies flailing against each other. I was the first to be hauled up into the light, and I tumbled out on to the ground, stayed to assist, was waved away, and, blood streaming down into my eyes, ran clear for my life.

If you had to be in a helicopter crash, I suppose this was the one. It was almost a miracle that nobody was killed. There were broken hips and collar-bones; one man had the skin taken off his back. We waited ten hours for any rescue operation, Russia being what it is. My ex-RAF room-mate, who had a punctured lung, felt the internal haemorrhage and, holding my hands, said he thought he wasn't going to make it. I was lucky, and had only sustained broken ribs and a minor head-wound. Leaving him with his son, the chief guide, I marched purposefully off, fell over a tussock, and passed out in the grass.

Later, we walked round the wreckage in disbelief. The pool where Mother Russia had involved us in such a close geological embrace was called Paradise – *Et in Arcadia ego.*

There was plenty of time for thinking, in those 'golden hours' before anyone came. I will not pretend that I began to see God's handiwork in each dew-kissed flower (there was precious little of that around), but I was aware I had been brought down to earth, and I was delighted to be alive. Leaning against my bag, I realized this would have seemed a stupid way to have died – writing a travel article about field sports – and with a cold, queasy flush, something that shrunk my scrotum and made me hug myself in a pathetic reflex, I saw that I had been taking a lot for granted. Later, sharing a bottle with the only other man not to have been airlifted to hospital in Murmansk after our evacuation, I wondered precisely what unfinished business there might have been, had we gone up in the expected fireball.

One answer that formed, before the vodka kicked all reason into touch, was a project I had been discussing with my mother before she died in 1998: to write a book about my parents. My father was less sanguine about the idea, but she had left behind an autobiography that covered her life up until the day I was born. Neither of them had wanted anyone else involved except their only child, and since nothing but brief capsule biographies of either of them had ever appeared in print, I felt for the first time a faint sense of responsibility. Even in the aftermath of the prang, snoring with relief in my bloodstained fleece, I never for one moment supposed this was a book without which the world could not survive, but when I returned to the (newly welcome) family fold, I found I was convinced it was on my list of things to undertake, along with as much drink, rock-and-roll and home-based fishing as might be feasible.

I have always toyed with the prospect of being a procrastinator, but that bucolic sage H. D. Thoreau has an apophthegm which now, at the age of fifty, I find hard to ignore: 'The youth gets together his materials to build a bridge to the moon, or, perchance, a palace or temple on the earth, and, at length, the middle-aged man concludes to build a woodshed with them.' Well, at least I've now got plenty of room to store the family timber.

My father was the Secretary of State for War who resigned in 1963 during what is now generally known as the Profumo Affair. When they married in 1954, however, it was my mother who was the more celebrated of the two. As Valerie Hobson, she had featured in more than forty films, and was a star of the West End when they became engaged. She retired from show business shortly before I was born, so I never saw her on stage; the pictures in this book will attest to her glamorous appearance, and I shall not risk any reproof similar to the scorching remark made by Talleyrand, when a blade at the Napoleonic court harped on too fulsomely about his mother's beauty – '*C'était donc monsieur votre père qui n'était pas beau?*' With her auburn hair and dark grey eyes, Valerie Hobson did indeed appear arresting throughout her life; it would seem I have inherited the darker, mobsterish looks of the Profumo males. I used to joke about our Mafia physiognomy, and when I learned there was a scion of the family in New Jersey who was actually importing olive oil from Sicily, I was hardly surprised (all I'm inferring is, we are an enterprising family).

One impetus for this book was therefore to restore my mother's story to an encysted version of events – I'm talking about the early sixties, now – since her professional achievements have been so marginalized that she has been consigned to a walk-on role in the brief, but more lurid, saga on which the world's media has understandably chosen to fix. The events surrounding my father's resignation are of course a *sine qua non* of this account, but its principal aim is to explain who my parents were when they met, and how (partly for my sake) they stayed together, despite a liaison exposed in full limelight, and its intense afterburn. The affair that really concerns me is their love affair, which endured, in however adulterated a form, for the rest of their life together. It seems to me that this is well worth trying to understand, because (as Larkin also wrote), 'What will survive of us is love.'

My parents co-operated with my efforts after a fashion – I dislike the pompous shorthand of 'giving it their blessing' – but it was never conceived of as being their 'version of events'. It is my version. It does not aspire to 'set the record straight', nor to be read as history. It is scruff-order – rather than full-dress – biography, with no pretence to being official or definitive. It would also be absurd for me to affect an Olympian detachment, and it is almost entirely subjective.

I subscribe to George Bernard Shaw's maxim, 'If you cannot get rid of the family skeleton, you may as well make it dance.' Let's just say that, like one or two other characters in this story, I'm also doing it for the money.

By the time I formally embarked on any research, my father was in his late eighties and had already been hospitalized twice with strokes (though from the enthusiasm with which he pursued his social life, you would scarcely have known it); inevitably, then, our interviews fluctuated according to the vigour of his memory (which I think was always selective, at the best of times). In earlier years, neither of us had felt ready to engage in this sort of thing, and even so he could be a tricksy interviewee, having forgotten none of the seasoned politico's ploys when under fire (both of my parents were cunning extroverts, and knew their respective audiences). In the winter of 2004, we went to Downing Street where my father was to receive an award for his decades of charity work, and a radio interviewer asked him, 'Can you tell us why you're in here today?' He smiled and nodded, 'Well, you know, it's snowing outside.'

When I began studying the lives of my parents – whom I am going to designate by their initials, J and V – I was precisely the age my father was when disaster struck them. It may be that this made me more sympathetic to how they both behaved, particularly in the aftermath of the resignation (or the 'Great Fall', as V had it in her journal). I was impressed by the complete absence of bitterness or self-pity on my father's part; one evening, looking through some photographs together, as an *aide-mémoire* – they were of one of his audiences with the Lion of Judah – he said, 'I *have* enjoyed my life.'

Being a collective memoir, this book is made up predominantly from resources within the family. Because of the size of what I grandiosely refer to as 'the archive' – dozens of ledgers and albums containing cuttings and ephemera, boxes of sporadically kept journals, diaries and letters – I have not had to indulge in much gumshoe work, nor have I Holroyded around after every last clue. Although I did once fancy myself as an academic, my greatest feat was perhaps deciphering my father's handwriting, so nearly illegible as to make the average doctor's script look like an illumination from the Book of Kells. Both my parents' lives were amply documented – V's first press cutting dates to when she was four – and this made my task much easier, like a commissionaire having a cab rank on his doorstep. At times, though, the sheer volume was dispiriting, and I would stare at the material wishing, by some process of psychic osmosis, it could be downloaded into my understanding by its mere proximity.

The book was written in our Scottish home, up a Perthshire glen, at the huge partners' desk my grandfather (just before he died) gave my father when he first took his seat in Parliament in 1940. Until quite recently, J always worked at it himself, and in the drawers he had methodically stowed the things he loved and needed – Plant Finder handbooks, a large magnifying glass, boxes of rose and violet crème chocolates, ball-point pens with naked women on them. The leather top is of scuffed and ancient oxblood, and, if you narrow your eyes, it resembles an aerial view of fire. There have been several occasions when, up here in my mountain eyrie in the small hours of the morning, a keen wind clattering in the chimneys, I have sat, head in hands, confronting all the paperwork and feeling lost for words, and heard those little goblin voices whispering, from the margins of the room, that this was all folly – indeed, I would have welcomed the arrival of some homunculus who might, Rumpelstiltskin-like, have offered to spin all this straw into gold.

Biographers – or 'lifewriters', as the term now is in certain circles – are notorious for growing proprietorial about their subjects, and of course with your own parents the rules of engagement can become peculiar. Many families generate their own mythologies and develop a fondness for their legends, and I have tried not to let inconvenient facts too often puncture our familiar anecdotes. I cannot vouch for the absolute accuracy of these narratives, some of which might be little better than hearsay, and I expect there are mistakes, some of which may be deliberate. Certainly I have not gone out of my way to be scrupulously fair to anyone, so in that respect, at least, I hope this essay is true to life.

Such an artificially intense involvement with everything concerning Jack and Val was – as may readily be imagined – at times quite complicated. To be the first person ever to read my father's war diaries, to unravel the fears and escapades of a young man sitting in a caravan some sixty years earlier, and then to call him up in extreme old age and discuss some detail, was an unusual opportunity (and connecting those two characters was central to my task). There were occasions when I was strongly aware of my mother's presence, too, perhaps especially when, one evening in Scotland, I was going through a box of her diaries and a book suddenly detached itself from my library wall and sent the shelf below cascading from its banjo hooks on to the floor. The fallen books were all my reference volumes about the Profumo Affair, and what had felled them was my mother's copy of the script of one of her earliest films, *Bride of Frankenstein*. That seemed like a fair cop.

So now, a million keystrokes later, I probably know more about J and V than they ever did about one another. The process has involved some precarious moments, but *in fine* it has, rather than anything else, affirmed to me their underlying ordinariness. I'm not exactly suggesting my father was the man on the Clapham omnibus (he would have tended to take a cab) but he strikes me at least as *un homme moyen sensuel*, rather than some *lusus naturae* from a freak show. My mother was distinguished by her good looks and professional success, no doubt, but her marital vicissitudes were scarcely unique, though literally writ large. Whatever else I may have done, at least they have now been written down.

Still and all, this has not been a case of '*Tout comprendre, c'est tout pardonner*' (surely, as Auden pointed out, one of the most misleading of commonplaces): in many ways they were not the easiest of parents to have, but then I was probably not the paragon of filial obeisance that my powerful capacity for self-delusion has somehow suggested during the interim. Unlike most writers, I was already rather fed up with some aspects of my subject before I even put pen to paper – the media coverage, in particular – but I was fortunate in never becoming bored by the central characters, though my sense of humour, often quite Stygian, may have darkened a couple more clicks. I suppose my favourite discovery was a (hefty) solicitors' bill dated April to October 1963, for 'Professional Charges relating to Your Affairs during this period' – that sounded worryingly plural – and the moment when, struggling out of his car on that same, snowy Downing Street evening in 2004, my father announced to the policeman, 'Oh dear, I'm afraid my pants are falling down' – the paradigm of a Whitehall farce.

Somewhere near the centre of this account lies the turbulence generated by the events of 1961–3. Bertrand Russell once posed the question, 'How long is an event?', and possibly the best answer is that given by a desperately under-prepared student, asked in his Oxford viva to enumerate the consequences of the French Revolution: 'I think it's too early to tell.' Whereas the latter-day imbroglios of public figures tend to be tempests in teacups, the thing that is known as the Profumo Affair (or, in casual synecdoche, merely 'Profumo') has become embroiled in the churning lava lamp of history.

When the cosmologist Edwin Hubble was trying to measure Red

Shift, he needed to establish certain stars which could furnish a light intensity constant enough to act as comparables: he called these his Standard Candles. Our family débâcle has effectively become a Standard Scandal, against which the valency of any subsequent affray among the *classe politique* – Lambton, Thorpe, Parkinson – can be measured. As recently as 2004 I was amused to see the complications of David Blunkett referred to as 'Profumo-Lite'. My project, then, arrives faintly pre-fabulated. In the popular imagination of anyone who remembers it at all, our family *affaire* has practically become a modern folk tale (though of course there are plenty of folk who would have precious little idea what I'm talking about). Naturally, it still looms largish for us, and the half-life of those events seems preternaturally long, but it's strange how it has become a forty-year wonder, down-page news, perhaps, but perennially the little black dress of scandals.

It has morphed into a brand name, a cottage industry. Quite apart from the *bibliotheca scandalosa* of publications, fictional or otherwise, our name has inspired a rock band, a nightclub, and a gossip column in a carp-fishing magazine. In 1989, a production company made a family movie – *Scandal* – in which the part of my father, depicted *in flagrante* in a facsimile of the parental bedroom, was played by a famously homosexual actor in a toupee of almost taxidermal implausibility, who went on to portray Gandalf and Widow Twankey (the actor, Ian McKellen, I mean, not the hairpiece). At four in the morning, one beats in vain at the psychotherapist's door.

On the last day of February 2006, I visited my father's flat to show him the manuscript of this book that I was finally delivering to the publisher; he clapped his hands in delight over the breakfast table, and said we must have a celebratory glass of champagne. A week later, I was awoken in our London house at five in the morning by a clattering noise downstairs, and I found a bookshelf had tumbled from the wall and thrown a stack of my interview notes all over my desk. Just before one o'clock, my father suffered another stroke, and later died in hospital, with me holding his hand. He was ninety-one.

I had hoped to publish this book during his lifetime, and, although I read extracts aloud to him during work in progress, he never did get to see all of it. Beyond the adjustment of several tenses, I have undertaken only minimal rewriting after his death. He knew this was not going to be mistaken for a hagiography, and he seemed unconcerned by the image of him I was presenting. In later life, I think he found people's curiosity about him amusing rather than irksome; on what was to prove his last 'public' appearance (at Sir Edward Heath's memorial service, in November 2005), as I was manoeuvring him in a borrowed wheelchair to a fairly prominent position in Westminster Abbey, I remarked to him on how many of the great and the good were assembled in the congregation. 'Ah, yes,' he replied in a stage whisper. 'The great and the good . . . and *us*.'

Ghost nets are long snares, constructed from virtually invisible monofilament nylon, that commercial fishermen anchor offshore to enmesh groundfish by their gills. Sometimes they tear free of their moorings, and begin to drift around the ocean currents, assuming a life of their own. They entrap species indiscriminately, sinking beneath their weight until the catch rots or is devoured, then rise again from the sea floor to resume their damaging progress at random, sometimes for many years.

I may have a penchant for histrionics, but it seems to me the sorry saga of the Profumo Affair has been like this. It bobs up and down, catching people this way and that, and I'd like to see the day that someone lugs it out of the water and chucks it on a fire.

On New Year's Eve 1947, my mother attended the Chelsea Arts Club Ball at the Royal Albert Hall, Kensington. It was a fancy-dress occasion, and she went as Madame Récamier, attired in an Empire dress borrowed from her current film studio. Even from this point, my parents' versions differ, but it seems that V's husband, Tony, was in tow, reluctantly accoutred as a toreador, and that Valerie Havelock-Allan (as she then was, in the eyes of the law, though surely Valerie Hobson to others present) was on the dance floor with one of her many male admirers when a policeman muscled in on the proceedings and informed her that she would have to move her car, as it was causing an obstruction.

This was John Profumo, a Tory politician who had lost his seat in

Kettering after the war but was one of the party's more charismatic candidates. He was at that stage stepping out with the widowed Duchess of Kent (Princess Marina), but had had his eye on V since the première of her recent film, *Blanche Fury.* That evening, J and V ended up in a private box, drinking champagne. At that stage – and good for them – I was a long way from their thoughts. It was exactly seven years later that they married.

When I was born, in 1955, to my mother's indignation J informed my young half-brother Mark that I had come down from heaven in a helicopter. Given his preoccupation with the Ministry of Civil Aviation at the time, one can appreciate this fable. It was lucky, considering the Russian whirlybird, that my own story didn't end up being a neat version of that, in reverse.

II

Expectations

I T HAS BECOME somewhat hackneyed to describe the weather
during which a person is born, but in the case of Babette Hobson
(as she was initially known) it is of some relevance, as she was
delivered, prematurely, on the quayside at Larne in Northern Ireland
during a tempest, the boat in which her mother had been crossing the
Irish Sea having been hit by a German torpedo. This was Saturday 14
April, 1917. The family clothes had all been lost, and she was practically a 'sackcloth baby'.

Dr Killen of Sandy Bay removed the caul which surrounded my
mother's head, and it was worn in a pouch round his neck by my
grandfather, Bob Hobson – then a naval commander in charge of a
flotilla of minesweepers – as a charm against drowning. The baby was
small and weak, would not take milk properly, and was partially sustained by chicken essence being massaged into her body.

The Hobson ancestors were from County Waterford, but left in the
eighteenth century to try for a fortune in the sugar plantations of the
West Indies. Settled in the Leeward Islands as administrators and
lawyers, they prospered reasonably, one becoming Attorney-General,
another the Provost Marshal of St Vincent. Bob's immediate family
was sizeable – he was the youngest of thirteen children, his own father
an army captain, a biological success if nothing more. The Navy was
chosen because funds for education had understandably run scarce,
and you could be apprenticed in a ship from a very young age. Bob
was ten when he sailed as a 'snottie' to Zanzibar and the China Seas,
first aboard HMS *Edgar*, then HMS *Philomel*. The crew used to divert
themselves with cockroach races, sticking a candle on the back of each
insect, before scooping them overboard, winner and losers alike.

I never did meet either of my grandfathers, but, despite the loyal and affectionate description of Bob in my mother's account (she always managed to stick up for the men who let her down), I think he was a feckless, charming, sentimental, hard-drinking sailor with blue eyes and a penchant for gambling. It's always reassuring when this sort of stuff turns up as you scoop your net hopefully around the family gene pool.

He was twenty-four when he met Violet Hamilton-Willoughby, who had been friendly with one of the brothers. She was six years younger, with the milky complexion and russet hair she was to pass on to their daughter. They married in April 1905, the certificate stating that Violet's deceased father, Claude Arnold, was a 'Clerk in Holy Orders'. In fact, she had been adopted from the local vicarage by some wealthy parishioners named Hamilton, and had appended the Willoughby part for status at a later date.

Midshipman Bob was penurious but perpetually full of schemes. For their honeymoon, he took his young bride off to the Klondike, where his brother Freddie (one of several black sheep in the Hobson flock) was dwelling in a clapboard hut, with a baby and an invalid wife. Fortune nimbly evaded the Hobson brothers. They upped sticks from Toronto, Alberta, Winnipeg. Seriously ill with pneumonia in the territory of the Siouan tribe, Vi was saved by a native medicine woman, and her husband was made an honorary chief (well, that was the story he liked to tell his daughters, brandishing the pipe of peace he supposedly was given at his initiation ceremony, though that was of little use in putting bread on the family table). My grandmother used to impress me, though, with her description of the squaws washing their lovely black hair in horse urine.

It was never an easy marriage. Booze and gambling were early features, and after a final warning Vi borrowed the train fare and resolved to leave Canada for good. Bob bestrode his horse and raced alongside the track, 'shouting for her at each carriage'. She only alighted at the next stop when he threatened to gallop in front of the engine. At least I can trace where any histrionic genes kicked in, hatted, booted and spurred. She only agreed to stay with Bob if he gave up drink and returned to England. 'This he swore with great solemnity,' according to my mother's account. He was commissioned in the Royal Navy at the start of the Great War, and tussled with temptation for many years – my grandmother would not even allow liqueur chocolates in the house. In the end, 'perhaps thinking the advent of a second war in one lifetime exonerated him from his promise, he made up for lost time' in the late 1930s.

He never lost his gift for the blarney, at any rate. His love letters, often signed 'Bobkin' or 'Smutkin', are frequently apologies for poor behaviour – 'I am such a silly fool, I said things I never meant . . . I'm an old rotter and you have given your life to a selfish old beast – but he worships you.' They seemed to do the trick, however, and I do not think he was so dissolute that he ever countenanced abandoning his family; he was just not very skilful at making decisions. I won't pretend I don't feel an affinity with this minor swashbuckler, hopeless entre-preneur, and overall dreamer, despite the fact that our paths never actually crossed (excepting, perhaps, now, as I skip blithely back across the unpeeling family wake, my state-of-the-art outboard throwing up a great rooster-tail of spray; I'm sure Commander Hobson and I would have enjoyed several, agreeable pink gins somewhere around the final dock).

There followed a safe, comfortable but unsettled childhood. In effect it was years before they had a proper home and Bob took his two daughters – there was an older girl, Patricia, whom my mother claimed was always the prettier one – to stay like cuckoos in the resi-dences of several relations. Their welcomes varied from warm to brittle. Some houses had rooms free by virtue of wartime deaths, and their first such billet was with an Uncle Harry, in Brighton. Here, at the age of four, Babette began dancing classes, and received the first of her notices in the press, for the portrayal of Cupid in the Great Hall of the Dome in the Brighton Pavilion (1921). Although there was no family precedent for it, her choice of career had already been made; but inevitably there was a falling-out on the home front, and it was time to move on.

In the village of Greenford, just outside London, were two married aunts. The Otters lived at Stanhope Park, and were childless; across the green dwelled the Lawrences, with five children, a nurse, and four servants. Nona Otter was married to an Edwardian trencherman who worked in the Stock Exchange; she was a diminutive, skittish woman, five feet tall and with thinning hair that she concealed beneath a gypsy-style scarf. There was plenty of room in that house – on the top 'nursery' floor there was a forbidden suite containing Cousin Nellie, who had taken to her bed some twenty years previously, after being jilted at the altar. This Miss Havisham took all her meals on a tray, and was inclined to roam the house when others were asleep; the only time young Babette saw her was when the old lady was being carted out in her coffin.

It was a plush ménage, in a modest, leafy way, with a billiards room and servants' quarters. The cook was known as Nanny Strutt. She was not a nanny, but was a Strutt – the scion of a genteel Norfolk family, but born on the wrong side of the blanket. 'Her minute private means', wrote my mother, 'distinguished her greatly from the other servants.' The groom and coachman were less than pleased with Bob's decision to keep his spider monkeys in their stables – he had trained them to answer nature's call into their cupped hands, and fling their faeces into the face of the nearest person. Vi doted on a fashionable marmoset – 'Baby' – which spent most of the day on her shoulders, and slept in a knitting basket.

The Hobsons were poor relations, and Babette was mortified when, picking a pear in the walled garden, she was informed by the gardener that she must not eat it until it had been weighed, and 'invoiced to Mister Bob'. It was the first, unwelcome reek of an adult world beyond the secret garden. At the age of seven, she began to feel guilty that she was causing problems for her impecunious father, and vowed openly to become rich as soon as possible, to protect her parents; 'sometimes the frustrations of waiting to grow up were so great that I don't remember being a true child at all.'

Across the fields, with a distant view of Harrow, was The Cottage, home to Lord and Lady Lawrence. Aunt Dolly had married a benevolent soldier with walrus moustaches, the inarticulate grandson of a Viceroy of India. She was imperious and spectacular, with bright red hair, but she was also, in my mother's later view, 'a bitch'. She patronized the shy and modest Vi, and was sarcastic about the daughters. One day, they saw her sporting their mother's favourite brooch

– two coral cherries, with jade leaves. Bob had been obliged to give it to his sister when she had settled yet another gambling debt.

There was a mulberry tree in the garden, where the pale, gangly, bashful Babette would go to hide. Thirty years later, she was invited to open an Odeon cinema on the site of her aunt's garden, and in the foyer was a basket of logs with the written invitation that patrons help themselves – 'Mulberry wood. Burns sweetly.'

Next, they became paying guests in a former rectory in Cosham, Hampshire, home to two Misses O'Shea – one ninety, the younger sister only eighty-six – who were teetotal, vegetarian homeopaths, devoted to croquet.

Babette was plain-looking and developed a tomboy style, as she felt her father was disappointed he had never managed a son – 'I was pasty-faced, all angles, with mouse-straight hair, and my eyes were too big. The brace on my teeth made my mouth enormous. I was a real gumdrop.' They moved to Southsea, where her mother quietly took up work in a milliner's shop, and her father had a heart attack.

It was her dental problems that set my mother off on the Start-Rite-sandal road to stardom. In a Wimpole Street waiting-room she overheard two ladies discussing auditions – somebody named Cocky needed dancers for *White Birds* at His Majesty's, one-thirty that very day. Nanny was wheedled into walking her to the bottom of the Haymarket, and for the first time she was stage-side in a theatre. She had no appointment card, music or shoes, but instructed the elderly pianist, Miss April, to begin Rubinstein's 'Romance'. Impresario Charles Cochran asked her age, and she lied that it was ten. He told her he needed to see her mother on her return, because she had some talent – 'I don't know how much yet, because you're so young.' Next week, at a meeting in his Bond Street office, he recommended to Vi that her daughter should begin classes at RADA, under the tutelage of Kenneth Barnes. They stored the family belongings, and moved back in with the Otters.

My grandparents were trusting and otherworldly, and knew nothing whatsoever about the world of professional acting. There had been no evident source for tuition fees, should their simian daughter be accepted at the Academy – Bob even called her 'Mokey' because she was so skinny and clung to him like a pet. The Commander, whose income at that time seems to have derived from the buying and restoration of mediocre antiques, had absolute faith that all would be well. On Christmas Eve he took his girls to tea at Gunter's in Berkeley Square, then shopping at Hamley's ('the biggest child was Pa, who would dearly have liked to have treated himself to a train set, or Meccano, if he had had a son'). Sailing in the teeth of yet another wind, he drove around the West End in his Beardmore, shamelessly haggling over the crackers, the fruit, pork pies, tongues, the very turkey itself, until, honour satisfied, he returned to Aunt Nona with something for all, at the gross expenditure of slightly under five pounds.

Valerie Hobson – and, indeed, Valerie Profumo – was always thrifty and scrupulous about money. Despite later years when her lifestyle was passingly grand, she never forgot those lessons of pitching and bargaining, the necessary ploys by which the gentlefolk of that period camouflaged their indigence.

On 4 January 1928 there was an entrance test in Gower Street, with some sixty candidates for child-student places at RADA – a scheme then being phased out. In deliberately understated grey clothes, Babette delivered an excerpt from J. M. Barrie's *Quality Street*, boldly concluding with the stage instruction, 'Exits left', which she accordingly followed. They accepted her for two terms only, as she was not yet eleven.

Mason, the Otters' groom, would drive her in the pony-trap down the lanes every morning to a bus stop opposite the lunatic asylum in Southall. With a change at Acton, she and her nanny could reach Tottenham Court Road, and, while the student learned the arts of fencing and dancing – from Madame Bertrand and Phyllis Bedells, respectively – the faithful Nanny Bridgeland (Nanny B, as I knew her in my own childhood years) would while away the time with a nice cup of tea at Shoolbred's, or a visit to the British Museum. 'There's a reading room there,' she vouchsafed, 'but you have to get a ticket. Just to sit down and read a knitting pattern. No wonder the place is half empty.'

The aspiring actress learned the importance of having good hands – a valuable lesson in life. She gave up biting her nails, and often pointed out to me when her fellow performers were self-conscious about the way they dealt with their hands. Alec Guinness was one, who always tried to conceal them, on screen and off. 'I learned to walk tall, and how to remain on stage to the last moment as the character you were playing. How to stay still when another actor was speaking, and *never* to upstage, except when so directed.'

She was told to return to RADA after some more regular schooling, having done well enough as Arthur in *King John*, and the Gaoler's Daughter in *The Two Noble Kinsmen*, who has that lovely line, 'I am very cold, and all the stars are out too.'

Had my grandfather been a smarter speculator – though I suspect that would have made him a less engaging person – the family finances at this stage could have taken a noticeable upswing. For a mere few hundred pounds, he might have bought into an invention called the Zip-Fastener, but he explained to his wife that the whole idea sounded uncomfortable. There was also a clear wrapping 'useful for bread' by the name of Cellophane, which the Commander was convinced would not catch on. These decisions were, by any yardstick, spectacular.

As it was, he concentrated on his maritime paintings, rubbing the canvases with olive oil, and became a jobbing dealer in *objets de vertue*, skulking around the antique shops of Home Counties villages on the lookout for watches, porcelain, silk rugs, ivories. Much of my mother's childhood was involved with fine ornament, therefore, but nothing ever stayed with them for long. 'Pa could do no wrong', in her eyes, though there were frequent splenetic outbursts, and his frustration was evident to all. The moving and impermanence continued. 'We left Greenford,' she wrote, 'before they tired of us.'

Nanny Maud Bridgeland, a lovely simpleton of twenty-two with soft brown hair, was one of the few features of continuity in this nomadic life; when they moved to Ealing, and acquired their first radio set, she asked the girls to adjust the news so that the words came out slower.

Though not a Catholic, my mother was sent to school at St Augustine's Priory – 'I fell in love with everything, even the regulations'. The religious fervour appealed to her sense of the dramatic, too, and that stayed with her – as a boy I would be mortified by the elaborate way she curtseyed and crossed herself in the aisle in our parish church, the stridency with which she enunciated the prayers. She was perplexed by the fact that some of the more beautiful nuns would shave their heads and choose such a life – 'Perhaps being married to One who can and will never let you down is sufficient comfort' (a wistful enough remark to have made in middle age).

She was undistinguished at games, and never a team player. V was not one of the popular girls, though she longed to be part of the camaraderie. I think that the slightly imperious detachment she developed as an adult came from this early need to appear independent while others around her were interacting more easily. The team spirit of show business, which she always claimed was one of the things she most liked about the profession, never came naturally to her, either, despite much lip service to the contrary.

At the age of eleven, Babette began to train as a ballet dancer, taking lessons from the fearsome Mr Espinosa, a tartar with long yellow hair and a waspish disposition. He beat time on the wooden floor with a heavy cane, which was also used to indicate mistakes of posture; one afternoon, he smartly tapped her wrist when she was making a poor 'line' and cracked the bone.

Patricia and Babette both contracted scarlet fever in 1930, and were confined to a room with a blanket soaked in Jeyes Fluid nailed around the door to isolate them. Straw was laid down on the road outside, to hush the horse-drawn traffic. One morning, Babette awoke to see an angel sitting on her sister's bed – 'the apparition had been both diaphanous and solid, with a radiance which melted away but left a distinct glow in the memory.' She called out to Nanny, who was sleeping on a camp bed in the corridor – 'Ooh, I say, dear, how nice', came the reply. Pat recovered shortly thereafter, but my mother remained feverish for weeks, her body sloughing off ribbons of skin. She never resumed her ballet lessons.

The calling-in of a sizeable Hobson family loan meant yet another move – V calculated that she had lived in seventeen different places by the age of sixteen – this time to a small flat in Palace Gate, Kensington. Pat had attended secretarial college and was being squired by a dashing young man named Dennis Watney; she was still the easy-going, pretty one, but the young actress, who was now going to RADA again, was beginning to develop good long legs and a useful bosom. Her mother felt it was time they had a little talk, and lay down on the bed to explain how painful 'the whole business' would be if 'Love was not present'. Her fourteen-year-old daughter cried with horror and sympathy, imagining the worst for her dear mama – and for herself, when the time came.

Determined to graduate and become rich as soon as she could, so her father 'could order bespoke shoes from Lobb's, and her sister wear lynx collars on her coats', Babette enjoyed a strong imaginative life, and her expectations were high. Still a schoolgirl, she embarked on a round of theatrical and film agents, signing on for 'extra work' (if you were a 'dress' extra, providing your own clothes, the pay was thirty shillings a day); she started with crowd parts at Elstree, catching the workmen's train at five-thirty in the morning. She was paid a guinea for her first part, and kept the pound note as a lucky token: I have it here on my desk, as I write.

A lifelong devotion to shopping and clothes now developed in a way commensurate with the modest income, and some photographic modelling work meant Babette was able to learn about make-up and presentation. Her first job in the theatre, in 1932, was as understudy to Adele Dixon in *Orders are Orders*, also starring Basil Foster. She pretended Nanny was her dresser, which must have appeared a little implausible for a teenage understudy, but she needed a chaperone. One day, the star had flu, and my mother had her first bout of stage fright. The first line she ever delivered on stage was indeed, 'Who's for tennis?' – she played for just six performances, but that was enough to give her some publicity in the papers ('Leading lady of 15 plays opposite Basil Foster, 46'), and she was offered a week's filming at Shepperton Studios.

Eyes of Fate (1933) was shot in one week, for a few thousand pounds, under the quota system, whereby a certain number of feet of film had to be made entirely in Britain to counterbalance the welter of footage from American distributors – a godsend to the industry. In her memoir, V described this film as 'a miniature extravaganza', featuring an elderly actor named O. B. Clarence as a bearded mystic; she played 'a sad-eyed dreary drip, misused by someone or other', for which she received an emolument of twenty pounds, and was allowed to sleep in the dressing-room, to save on fares.

That spring, when the Commander was in Scott's restaurant, celebrating a successful antiques transaction and signing a contract on her behalf (Chippie the *maître d'hôtel* used to act as witness), she told him she wanted to change her name to Valerie, as it would sound better when she became famous. Babette had been chosen because it was the heroine's name in a romantic novel Bob had been reading when she was born. The newly emergent Valerie Hobson now began work on *Badger's Green*, a cricketing comedy adapted from R. C. Sherriff's novel, and bought her first furniture from Barkers, paying in cash.

There was an American-style coffee bar, the Honeydew, that had opened in Coventry Street, Piccadilly. V used to kill time there with other young 'artistes', and one morning a lumbering great American with a pockmarked face sent a note to her table asking if he might come over. He said he was completing auditions at the Drury Lane theatre for *Ball at the Savoy* and invited her to attend at ten the next day. His card read: *Oscar Hammerstein* II, with a New York address. This was more like it.

There was one part for an English wife to play opposite Oscar Denish, as part of his supposed harem. The Hammerstein brothers instructed her to be 'a little bit more English' after her first attempt, so she essayed brash Cockney and then Lancastrian; she landed the role, and soon joined fifteen other 'showgirls' in the chorus dressing-room, at four pounds a week. The male romantic lead was a young Maurice Evans, who was about to work on *The Path of Glory* (a Ruritanian satire, with Dallas Bower directing), and V was also signed up; to the envy of the rest of the chorus, she filmed during the day before being driven from studio to theatre by the star himself. The film appeared in February 1934, and John Betjeman – then the *Evening Standard*'s critic – wrote, 'I should think Valerie Hobson is our youngest star-to-be . . . able to look at sixteen as sophisticated as last year's debutante. She can't actually be so sophisticated because she told me that next to playing in pictures she liked being at school best and that her favourite game was rounders. This goes to show that she is a pretty good actress.' For someone who also detested ball games, it shows she was already a canny interviewee, to boot.

At Elstree, she had her first experience of the 'casting couch' system, when the chief casting director pursued her round the room before crushing her briefly against a wall. That such sexual blackmail was endemic remained 'the dread of my life in those early days'; in America, one especially rebarbative character finally gave up, saying, with no hint of circumlocution, 'Well, Miss Hobson, I don't think we have a spot for a goddam cold bitch.'

Fortunately, nothing like that was involved when the producer 'Cocky' (now Sir Charles) Cochran was auditioning for a new musical – *Conversation Piece* – which Noël Coward had written especially to feature himself and Yvonne Printemps, in her English debut. This was a Regency piece, and V was a walk-on background London belle (with a brace of Dalmatians on a leash, in one scene). She also managed to become second understudy to the leading lady, which meant being able to rehearse for the first time with an orchestra. Printemps was the first real star she had observed up close, and V was readily impressed by the glamour – she was petite and exquisite, and would arrive at His Majesty's in a limousine, with a full panoply of furs, veils, and diamonds. 'She had a mannerism of keeping her hands in an upright position, like a doll warding off the blow of a feather.' It was her earliest meeting with Noël Coward – people who worked for him revered him as 'Master' for his strictness and perfectionism, but those in his circle of intimates (he was to be godfather to V's first child) called him 'Father'. He was certainly always paternalistic towards her.

Back home, the Commander had taken up with a card-gambling set, and was shortly to be out of his depth. He had formed a plan to open up a bridge club at Number 3 Cromwell Road – a glowering Victorian building opposite the Natural History Museum. He acquired the lease to it, and declared it was 'a great chance for the future', and they moved in 'over the shop'. This latest translation of the itinerant Hobsons filled the womenfolk with foreboding.

Den Watney had by now transferred his affections from Patricia to Valerie; they were never lovers (which must have been frustrating for

him) but he was a handsome and dutiful 'walker', safe in taxis, and with the manners of a genuine gentleman. He had been training as a policeman at Hendon College, but had to withdraw because he passed out during post-mortems. At this stage, he was considering an alternative career as a bookie; undecided about his professional future, he suggested to V that they visit a fortune-teller who lived in a council flat in Shepherd's Bush, a venerable gypsy who greeted them from her bed. She clasped their hands in turn, and exclaimed, 'Oh, such excitement I feel,' turning to V, 'so much about to happen. Soon, in a few weeks, I see you going away across the ocean.'

A week later, Universal Pictures offered her an immediate Hollywood contract.

It was not quite as simple as that, naturally. After congratulating her, Noël Coward pointed out that V was still under obligation to Cochran, and that she was only sixteen. In the event, Cocky agreed to release her if she worked in his show for a further three months, and she signed her own contract with Universal on 16 March 1934, just before she turned seventeen. The deal included provision for an accompanying chaperone, and options 'on their side, not ours' for another six years.

The proprietor of the new bridge club gave his support to the idea that Vi should accompany their daughter, and he thought he might come over to America later on, once things were running smoothly with his business. The teenager went to Fortnum's and, quite judiciously, spent most of her money on a travelling outfit – 'a white woollen skirt and dashing cape, with a black fedora hat which I wore at an angle, to give me confidence.' Aboard the *Berengaria*, mother and daughter set sail from Southampton for New York.

Valerie Hobson won the ship's sweepstake *en route*; each day, bets were placed on the mileage the liner would complete on the morrow, and the absurdly low numbers went for just a few pounds at the auction. Engine trouble developed, and she won enough money to buy her first car. They arrived on Friday 27 July and the smile came easily as she posed for the news photographers.

This unworldly duo took a train to Chicago, where the *Daily News* reported that she didn't know the difference between a hot dog and a hamburger. They went to view the gangster John Dillinger's corpse, lying in an open coffin at City Hall, his sutured face crawling with bluebottles, then headed out West on a three-day railroad journey of great luxury (the American food seems to have impressed them as much as the scenery: hot corn rolls, fresh mountain trout, blueberries). In Los Angeles, they were taken to an apartment in the Chateau Elysée and introduced to the agent David Todd. It was a far cry from Ealing.

Universal City was the largest lot in Hollywood – hundreds of acres of sets half an hour's drive through the canyons and out into the desert. In Britain, you would often see stills of a camera crew 'waiting for the sun', but out here there was nearly perpetual sunshine. This was good for filming, but the pale-skinned Hobson ladies disliked the heat and, even when on the coast, 'the disappointingly un-blue, rather hostile ocean'.

The first role V was expecting to take was that of Estella in *Great Expectations*; however, during her transit time the part had been re-assigned to Jane Wyatt, so the new arrival had to be content with a small appearance as Biddie. When the picture became overlong, this was the only part they could delete without having to reshoot, so her earliest Hollywood effort was swept off the proverbial cutting-room floor. It was a salutary beginning and a dashed expectation, but one perhaps greatened a decade later when she acted grown-up Estella with such glacial aplomb, in the superior English version.

There was no time for licking wounds, not least because the contract meant, in practical terms, she would only be paid for the weeks that she worked. Several pictures followed – a smallish part in *Strange Wives*, and her first lead, opposite heartthrob Ralph Bellamy, in the modestly successful *Rendezvous at Midnight*. Her first proper break came when the English director James Whale cast her to play the Baroness in *Bride of Frankenstein*, now something of a cult movie and a family favourite. Boris Karloff was 'the monster', and the first time V saw him he was already in full make-up (pretty impressive, even by today's animatronics standards) and he came swinging through a doorway, so they could record her unrehearsed reaction (the Hobson scream was to become quite bankable). 'I think we deserve a cup of tea, don't you?' was his towering rejoinder. He had 'the kindest eyes', and a lisping, gentle voice, but he was seldom assigned much dialogue in those days. V was introduced to Colin Clive (the eponymous Baron) when she was delivered on set attired merely in a scant night-dress, and directed to climb into a four-poster with the bored actor – 'Oh, Mr Clive, Miss Hobson,' said James Whale briskly; 'now, let's get on with the rehearsal.'

Always a fan, even when becoming a starlet, V avidly watched other actors working – Leslie Howard in *Romeo and Juliet*, Claudette Colbert ('so small') – and while on the set of *The Mystery of Edwin Drood* (with Claude Rains) she spent too long gazing up at the gantry lights and went down with an alarming case of 'Klieg eye', a blinding inflammation that lasted for several days. The 'village atmosphere' on set appealed to her, though. She had her own, modest bungalow, and a dresser – Hermy – a willowy, 'fourth-generation Negress' with notably long arms, that she used to flap slowly by her sides. Hermy preferred to be called V's maid. She was the granddaughter of a former slave, said to be one hundred and nine years old, then living in San Francisco. When V visited her, she still wore on her left ankle an iron bracelet, the remains of a leg cuff from the cotton plantations, yet she referred to her years of bondage as 'that Happy Time', when she had been treated with kindness, and after which she had only known poverty, loneliness and dismay.

One looks back with what Nietzsche termed 'a retrospective shudder' at the innocence of the female Hobsons abroad: much of the time they seemed to proceed through a cloud of unknowing. V was billed as 'the Irish Girl' by her publicity department, and, with her buxom, faintly horsy looks, was presumed to be much older than she was – copies of her birth certificate were circulated, to prove she was only eighteen. In the evenings, she had to be 'ready for collection' by a studio chauffeur, to attend parties with the real stars. The Hispanic villas, elaborate security, universal sycophancy and occasional de-bauchery were never remotely to her taste. Under strict instructions from the Commander (who had researched the matter sufficiently enough to know) she avoided alcohol, and toyed with water-on-the-rocks as if it were vodka, and at private screenings she learned to avoid the sofas, where 'necking' was inescapable. 'When the lights went up, I was amazed at the shrewd criticism of the film, since it had appeared to me that nobody had been watching the screen at all.'

Although she was busy with ancillary diversions – opening an oil pipeline, attending photo sessions, participating in charity galas, singing 'Mad Dogs and Englishmen' with Bing Crosby on his radio show – the significant career break had not yet happened. She enjoyed playing in another 'monsterpiece' (*The Werewolf of London*), where she was the puzzled but adoring wife of the lycanthrope, who considerately kept away from the marital bed when having one of his turns. Henry Hull was the star, famous for his long run touring the US in the play *Tobacco Road*, so there was extensive publicity, and V was being spoken of as 'the new Fay Wray'. She herself felt there had not yet been a chance to do much in the way of quality acting.

Apparently on a whim, the Commander now wrote announcing that he and Den Watney were coming to visit. They arrived in a silver-blue Rolls-Royce, a present from the adoring Den, which they had had shipped over. The real cause for this sudden reunion was the news that Patricia was engaged to Harry Beasley, a widower of thirty-six, a jockey. Two days later a telegram arrived, saying they had in fact already wed; Vi was heartbroken that her girl was marrying a much older man, and that she had missed the ceremony.

With his little-boy enthusiasm for novelty, Bob loved it in California. He announced that he was staying. He had sold up his interest in the bridge club, and left Nanny in charge of their possessions – in typical buccaneering fashion, he had managed to let go the only proper home his family ever had.

On a visit to the State Fair, they saw an exhibition called 'The Growth of a Baby', which showed human embryos, in glass containers, representing the progressive stages of gestation. Bob and Den fainted away at around the six-month foetus stage (this was almost as traumatic as those police post-mortems) and had to join a number of other stricken men in a sitting-out area with cold drinks and reviving fans. The women continued their tour, and entered a marquee where an Indian squaw, swathed in tribal blankets, would – for a dollar – answer any question silently put into her thoughts. Vi paid, and framed the query in her mind; the creaky reply came, 'She is carrying a son at this moment.' When they returned to their lodgings, there was a letter from Patricia, saying she was expecting a baby.

On a last drive through the San Fernando Valley, before he left for home, the increasingly heroic Den proposed to V, but she knew she did not love him 'like that'. 'Well, never mind, never mind,' he said apologetically. He never asked her again, but remained a close friend and admirer for another forty years.

Another second-rate film followed – *Chinatown Squad*, with Lyle Talbot – where the Irish Girl wore an embroidered cheongsam and a straight black wig. Universal Pictures began to reorganize itself, and a small item in Hollywood *Variety* magazine announced, 'Hobson Dropped'. The dream was starting to unravel, and V even took a Max Factor course in case she needed to work as a make-up girl.

They decided to quit. Bob was packed off back to London. But the terms of V's contract, since she had now been in Hollywood more than a year, no longer underwrote the cost of two return tickets – and there was a problem to be resolved with the American tax authorities, before she could leave the country. In urgent need of funds, V accepted the lead in a picture being made in British Columbia; she had to play a strident female tugboat captain in *Tugboat Princess*. She and Vi travelled to Seattle by rail, and settled into a dreary hotel in Victoria on Vancouver Island – 'it reminded one, for gaiety, of Elgin on a Sunday in Lent.'

One day, after filming around the docks, they had a dubious message from the porter that a man was in the lobby who claimed to be a relation. There appeared a shabby old shambler with sea-blue eyes. 'It's Freddie,' he said.

Now a semi-vagrant, who cleared the streets of snow for a living, the oldest Hobson brother had of course never struck his gold. They refurnished his single room, took him to a ranch with them for Christmas, introduced him to the film crew, who were charmed by his old-world manners. He was proud, and wanted nothing to do with the rest of his 'old family' back home. A few months after they left North America, a contact at City Hall wrote to say that Freddie had died, and had bequeathed his new belongings to an even older man, in the room next door.

———•◆•———

Valerie Hobson's precocious American experience had not been a fiasco, but it was a considerable disappointment. She was eighteen, had appeared in a total of ten films, and was no longer entirely an *ingénue*. To save money, mother and daughter went to New York on a Greyhound bus, and then sailed on the *Oceanic*, decidedly not a *grande luxe* liner. It was imperative that she did not return from the world's greatest film-factory broke, or 'showing a loser's face'. There would be an immediate need to promote herself to the British film industry, to camouflage those dented expectations – the girl who had been billed as 'one of the most promising actresses in Hollywood' had to appear buoyant, even though effectively starting from scratch. Certainly, she had panache. Needing a 'good address', V checked into the Hyde Park Hotel, and held court (her mummy reckoned there was enough in the kitty to stay five days). A new agent – Bill O'Bryen – offered to represent her, and advised her to tell the press that she 'had been brought over to star in a new film, which would be announced shortly'. This afforded them a little time to find something.

Patricia was now living in some prosperity with her husband and baby son in Newmarket, and had the means to accommodate her father for a while. For years, the younger sister would envy the way Pat was loved and protected, though, after domestic complications that perhaps only the Irish can engineer, she fetched up (quite contentedly) in later life running a confectionery shop in Bognor Regis.

Meanwhile, Valerie was low in funds, and took on all the work that the ingenious Bill could supply. There was a minor film with pianist Billy Milton – to be honest, I had never heard of him – entitled *No Escape*, and she was tested for the first screen adaptation of a Dennis Wheatley novel, *The Eunuch of Stamboul*. This was all thin gruel, but when you are a freelance you must on occasion sup with a long spoon, or else forget all thoughts of changing for dinner.

The two V's found a small flat at 247 Knightsbridge, and moved in together. The overall rudderlessness of Bob in his campaign to discover a new home for the family was therefore both obviated and condoned. Whenever my grandmother discussed a *modus vivendi* with Valerie in those years, and there were abrupt decisions to be made, she resorted to using her childhood pet name of Jimmie – as if the masculine adjustment would somehow make things more manageable. Theirs had become an uncertain world of packing-cases, and possessions gone adrift, and a debris field of broken promises.

Something mysterious had happened to Nanny Bridgeland. The Cromwell Road club claimed that she had gone to live with her parents (retired in Sudbury Hill), but they had in fact not seen her. Reluctantly – since she had always abhorred the place – Vi went to the club; 'she eventually found that Nanny was in a small basement room, and so far pregnant that she was almost unable to move.' She had been raped by a barman, and was so ashamed and ignorant that she told no one, even when a toxic complication virtually immobilized her.

A boy was born, in St George's Hospital, and the initial reaction of her parents was to shun the event. With patience, and the sort of imagination which was by no means common in those days, my grandmother persuaded them that life had begun, rather than ended. Bob Hobson discovered the rapist, and beat him up so severely that the new owners of the club threatened to call the police. None of the family ever went there again.

While filming *Eunuch* at Shepperton in August 1936 – which involved a number of scenes where she peered over a chiffon yashmak at the saturnine young James Mason – Valerie fell 'instantly' in love with a producer called Anthony Havelock-Allan. They started dating seriously the following month, after the inaugural opening of the new Pinewood Studios at Iver Heath in Buckinghamshire; Tony made sure he was seated next to her, at the same table as Arthur Rank and George Bernard Shaw. They went dancing at the Savoy, and later, he had a bunch of orchids delivered to her in a wastepaper basket 'so you can throw them and me away without any trouble'. I was never a great fan of Tony Havelock-Allan's code of conduct, but he certainly had style.

It was one of the more exasperating elements of my mother's autobiographical manuscript that, even scribbling away at it in her sixties, she could not bring herself to criticize Tony for anything that caused her subsequent heartache, though it is apparent to me that he was a selfish husband and a peculiar, indifferent father. Fourteen years her senior, he was from a North Country family, descendants of Sir Henry Havelock, the hero of Lucknow (whose statue still stands in Trafalgar Square, generally garlanded with pigeon guano). The second son of parents who divorced when he was a boy, he was 'an Englishman of education and lineage, but no fortune', in my mother's words, meaning, I think, that he went to Charterhouse but not university, was eventually heir to a baronetcy, and was perceived practically as a *nouveau pauvre*. His career began with the jewellers Garrard's; he spent some time in Berlin, then back in England was in charge of hiring cabaret acts for the chic Ciro's nightclub, before joining his friend Richard Norton in the film industry as a casting director.

He was offered a job at Paramount, producing 'quota quickies' – 'of exactly one hour fifteen minutes running time at exactly one pound per foot' – and between 1935 and 1937 he produced more than twenty of them (he and Norton formed the Pinebrook Company for this purpose, and by the time he popped his head round V's dressing-room door Tony had a residential office suite at the new Pinewood Club). Norton was a monocled wit, a gentleman-entrepreneur whose wife Jean was in love with Max Beaverbrook. Their daughter Sally was later to become the first of Bill Astor's wives.

Agent Bill O'Bryen now iced a good deal, signing V to star opposite Douglas Fairbanks Jr. in a Raoul Walsh film called *Jump for Glory*, to be made at the Worton Hall Studios in Isleworth. There was a sizeable budget for the picture, and V was to play a rich society girl who falls in love with a burglar. The chief attraction of the part was that her clothes were designed by Elsa Schiaparelli, the first time such a celebrated couturier had ever been engaged to work on an English film wardrobe. She also didn't have to deliver any of her famous screams. Everyone on the crew loved Doug, apparently, who was possessed of athletic good looks, and a gleaming charm.

All his life, Tony Havelock-Allan was attractive to women (he later enjoyed a dalliance with Grace Kelly, whisking her from beneath

Clark Gable's nose). He was elegant-minded, immaculate in his dress, and had the aerodynamic appearance of a buzzard. There can be no doubt that the couple adored one another, and my mother maintained she loved him for the rest of her life. He certainly had a practised way of persuading girls to care for him, and it seems Valerie was especially attracted to his ears. It is to Tony's credit that he agreed to his latest girlfriend's idealistic belief in retaining her virginity until some later date (she was that *rara avis*, a pin-up who was also *intacta*). This arrangement lasted two and a half years, and must at times have seemed most unsatisfactory, to such an accomplished *beau sabreur*. But he appeared to be just what she imagined she was hoping for in a man.

There's no doubt he was most influential on her tastes – introducing her to opera, for instance. She also acquired a rich patroness. Sir Adrian Baillie (a director of Technicolor) lived at Leeds Castle in Kent, with his shy, aesthetic wife Olive (nicknamed 'Coonie'). Theirs was then one of the grander private houses, and the chateleine surrounded herself with exquisite things and sophisticated house guests. Here for the first time the young actress had the chance to mingle with politicians, lawyers, diplomats; if in later years her screen persona was said – perhaps detrimentally – to be 'ladylike', it must be partly the Leeds coterie that helped shape it.

One of the Baillie *habitués* was David Margesson, the powerful Government Chief Whip, who was there almost every weekend. In October of that year (1938) he stayed with the Profumos at the family home in Warwickshire, and was instrumental in sponsoring the emergent political career of their son, John.

My nautical grandfather was not quite so enchanted by this acquisition of an older boyfriend. He turned up at V's flat and informed her that his card-playing pals at Crockford's said Tony had been living with a married woman. His indignation was explosive, and doubtless horsewhips were mentioned. The lovely daughter he knew as 'Chilo' reassured him she knew about that, it was long ago over (this particular paramour was called Babe Bosdari), but Bob remained blazingly convinced of this suave bounder's unsuitability; nor did the loss of face that his sources of intelligence had been so out-of-date exactly help his *amour propre*. He had – perhaps literally, I can't say – burned many boats in his life, and this confrontation he took hard. When the time came, he could not bring himself to attend their wedding.

A welcome call came from Bill O'Bryen in April 1937: 'Alex Korda wants to see you.' This, of course, was the man most revered in the industry, but V felt an unprecedented sense of dread as she entered his house in Denham. She was convinced she was walking into the web system of a human spider – 'the passages seemed to lead further than they should, the windows needed cleaning, there were vines that almost met across the panes'. The analogy was not a careless one; like me, V was an arachnophobe of such alarming sensitivity that she often woke up if a spider even entered the bedroom. In Hollywood, she had slid into the driving seat one morning and there on the steering wheel was a tarantula-sized specimen so fearsome that the corner store later kept its corpse on display in a jar on their counter. Alex Korda was hunched in the office window when she arrived, 'and as he put his arm around me I all but backed out and fled'.

Despite the air of menace, a screen test was agreed. This was for A. E. W. Mason's production of *The Drum*, the first British film to be made in Technicolor. On the day, V went to pray in the Brompton Oratory, and refresh her forehead with a stoup from the font. Just as expeditiously, perhaps, she had also persuaded the manager of Bruton Motors to lend her a dark blue, soft-top Hudson in which to stage her arrival at Denham. The wipers failed, and she presented herself to the gatekeeper looking like Ophelia after her drowning. The whole business of make-up for colour was then experimental. The story had an Asian setting, and the only artiste who was not being swabbed with various tones was Sabu, the boy star. Throughout the day, they rubbed on to V's face green powder, plum-dark lipsticks, pancake pales. The technicians viewed the results through quizzing glasses, shaking their heads.

The rushes were not auspicious. They could not understand why her porcelain complexion appeared so wrong. 'Brick-coloured sludge was applied, and my heart sank. Even if one believed in the miracle at Cana, milk and roses from an adobe concoction was surely too much to expect.' At lunch break on the third day, she nervously lit a cigarette. There was a cry like a peacock mating – this was it! She smoked black Balkan Sobranies, the only prop in her test, and they had been using that as a benchmark, presuming it was white. 'My final make-up was practically non-existent, and I became the alabaster, English-complexioned rose which Mr Mason required. Even the North-Western Frontier failed to bring a flush to my cheek.'

This proved to be one of her happiest films, with Raymond Massey heading a contented cast. None of the main stars went to India, and principal photography instead occurred in Wales. The result was a stirring tale of Imperial soldiery, replete with elephants. It was a big success at the box office. V was impressed with the young Sabu's female attendant, who claimed to manage without sleep by releasing the spirit from her body. There was also the Hungarian trio of Korda brothers to contend with – Zoltan (director), Vincent, the youngest (set designer), and Alex himself, then enamoured of Merle Oberon. But the love affair that, in the actress's idealistic mind, overswayed all conceivable manifestations in the entire British film industry right then was the courtship of Tony and Valerie – that convergence of the twain. On her twenty-first birthday, he presented her with a square aquamarine ring.

When it opened the following April *The Drum* was a formidable success, its nostalgic view of the Raj appealing to the patriotic instincts of a nation looking nervously at events on the Continent. You could say it struck the right note. Colour was still a novelty, and the picture looked well on screen. 'Clever Korda snaps up Hollywood star' perhaps summed up the publicity Valerie received; 'career-wise it was a champagne cocktail,' she reckoned. Work began at once on a newspaper comedy – *This Man is News* – which Tony had bought for Paramount. Korda agreed to loan her to play opposite Barry K. Barnes, as a husband-and-wife team of reporters, Alastair Sim being their exasperated editor (his first screen appearance). Valerie found this the most enjoyable film she ever worked on – the pacy high comedy suited her, and it meant she could legitimately spend a lot of time at Pinewood with the producer. The film cost twenty-one thousand pounds, and took three weeks to complete; it was generally well received, though in the view of Cinema News V made 'a colourless Pat'.

By the end of that year (partly to do with some fashion shoots Cecil

Beaton did with her for *Vogue*), Valerie Hobson was being described as 'Britain's best dressed star'. She had become what today is sometimes called a 'celebrity': opening fêtes, crowning beauty queens, attending premières where police had to restrain the crowds. She appeared in a revue on television, still effectively an unfledged medium. A profile of her in *Film Pictorial* presented her as speaking four languages (she had evidently forgotten three of them by the time I was born), having an operatic voice, being an expert horsewoman (she liked horses only marginally more than spiders), and possessing 'the perfect mannequin figure, height 5' 7", waist 24", bust 34", hips 33",' adding, 'She drives an open-topped sports car, and has been nicknamed the best-dressed woman in British films.'

She was not really happy, though. Tony's work kept them apart much of this time, and there is something wistful in her recollection, 'I saw practically no people of my own age.' The Leeds Castle group were middle-aged, and her other escorts were mature men like Conrad Veidt, or H. G. Wells, 'who ate such enormous suppers, and took so much time over them, that I would have nodded off if he had not been so intriguing.' She had come of age without ever having properly been carefree, and that was not to be a trait she readily tolerated in others.

She also felt she should have had the courage to do more stage work, and to have improved her acting, perhaps because by now she was working alongside some serious talents. In *Q Planes*, directed by Tim Whelan, she played a reporter, whose boyfriend (Laurence Olivier) was a daring test-pilot, and whose eccentric brother was portrayed by Ralph Richardson. There were frequent rewrites on set, and V felt the two friends 'were a bit contemptuous of acting with someone not of their own kind. They sort of acted over me.' She found Richardson 'a dear, gentle man' but 'Larry was someone quite other. He not only gave one the impression of being bored, he *was* bored . . . it astonished me he gave so little – had, indeed, so little to give . . . he was off-hand and cold in those days. The famous voice held no warmth or humour, and off-screen lines were grudgingly given, if at all, if no one else could be pressed into service. It was my first taste of an un-generous performer.'

Olivier was made restless by the constant attendance on set of Vivien Leigh – with whom he was 'madly, though not happily in love'. During one especially complicated shot, in which the great matinee idol held his screen lover while she dealt with some expository dialogue, Valerie fluffed several attempts, and when at length all was proceeding smoothly, Miss Leigh – just out of eyeline – produced a hankie and blew her nose with a flourish, spoiling the take. With a little sigh of regret, she rose from her chair and told the director she had better go, as she was clearly putting off the leading lady. 'When I heard Viv had captured the part of Scarlett O'Hara I was one of the few people who wasn't surprised. I could still hear that pussy-cat voice leaving the set.' (The following year, they were to be next-door neighbours. This allowed her to 'get to know Viv and Larry really well, to love them both and delight in their company'. Ah, that show-business camaraderie.)

The star of her next picture – *The Spy in Black* – was the astonishingly handsome Conrad Veidt, tall, sleek, enigmatic, but at heart a big baby whose favourite card game was Snap, and whose idea of fun was to administer the 'hot shoe' trick on set, and to steal lumps of sugar from the tea trolley to see if he would be caught. He played a U-boat captain, and on the eve of another possible war there was a pronounced sense of *déjà vu* among the cast and crew. The director was Micky Powell, whom V later considered her greatest favourite but initially found temperamental and sarcastic – 'the thing that stultifies emotion in me quicker than anything'. (Oddly, sarcasm was a trait she developed herself.) She particularly remembered his 'impertinent sex appeal', but, despite her voluptuous looks, it seems this was never something to which she responded much, throughout her early life.

Tony and Valerie were married at St George's, Hanover Square, on 12 April 1939. The bride wore a plain angel-skin satin dress, cut like a sheath, a Juliet cap of tulle, and a cross of orange blossom round her neck. She was given away by her mother, but as they were signing the register a phone call came to the church office from the Commander – 'Beloved Chilo – God bless you both.' He was crying. At the reception held in the Dorchester, the new Mrs Havelock-Allan drank her first ever glass of champagne.

Upstairs in the bridal suite, the night was an excruciating fiasco. After all the waiting (talk about great expectations) 'it proved impossible to finally make love'; the attempts were dreadfully painful, and the hymen could not be ruptured. 'I felt a sex-fraud,' wrote my mother. She blamed herself for not having been to visit a gynaecologist. It was indeed an inauspicious beginning. The honeymoon was increasingly tense, the atmosphere not helped by the choice of venue being the Ardennes, complete with creamy Belgian food and a boat ride through caves inhabited by blind fish and a myriad of bats. It culminated in a visit to Paris, where they squeezed in a meeting with Harry Cohn, owner of Columbia Pictures. As his managing director stooped to tie up his shoelace for him, the charming mogul offered V a second Hollywood contract, adding airily, 'Don't worry about your husband – we'll find something for him to do.' They left.

The price of this newly-married loyalty was that they began life with the princely sum of £34 8s 3d in their joint account (Tony was always good at finding work, but never very successful at making much money). They had rented an Elizabethan cottage near Gerrard's Cross, and rather grandiosely engaged a married couple to act as butler and cook. This would be handy when Larry and Viv called round.

The day before war was declared, Tony was still directing his first film, *Epitaph for a Spy*, in the South of France. It starred Anton Walbrook, who was German. Alerted that hostilities were imminent by Beaverbrook, who had a villa nearby, they decided to drive north, along with Richard Norton, who was recovering from a motoring accident. Anton began by masquerading as their chauffeur, and was eventually consigned to the boot. At Dieppe, there was a vast queue for ferries, but they managed to edge ahead on foot behind Richard's nurse, and made it safely aboard, the big Packard left abandoned on the quayside along with hundreds of other vehicles.

Back home, the studios and cinemas closed down, and Tony joined the Officers' Reserve as he was already thirty-five (their butler, Mr Pearson, joined up straight away). V bought two bicycles. She then missed her period.

With the outbreak of war, and neither parent in gainful employ-
ment, a child being brought into their world just then seemed ill-
advised. Without telling anyone, V resorted to various housewife's
remedies, jumping off chairs and pummelling herself to no effect. She
then ran a very hot bath and – never even having tasted it before –
drank the greater part of a bottle of Booth's gin. Tony rescued her in
time, semiconscious, but she had begun to bleed. In a nearby nursing
home they 'tidied her up', but guilt and moodiness soon set in and for
months she would – in typically extravagant fashion – go out into the
coppice beyond their field, throw herself to the ground, and 'pray to
the very earth for forgiveness'. Fortunately, her parents – who had
been in Ireland, where Patricia was now living – came to look after
her.

As soon as the studios reopened, Tony went back to work, being
pro tem in a reserved occupation. Throughout the war, V felt ambiva-
lent about continuing to provide entertainment – and trying to look
glamorous, despite the nation's privations – and worried whether
they should be driving ambulances, or working in the Air Raid
Precautions service. Producing films and supporting ENSA may not
now look like a very heroic way to spend five years, but there was
only a limited number of people who could manage such work, and
it certainly maintained morale. Although she was always inclined to
feel guilty about not doing enough for other people, V did good
work for the Ministry of Information, and toured the country
holding sing-songs in factories. One morning, Tony cycled off to his
ARP shift at Denham, and she was in the kitchen when she heard
his voice call, 'Louise' (his pet name for her). He'd been knocked
over by a truck, and she saw the ambulance coming up the hill as
she set off for the hospital, surprising them by turning up before she
had even been contacted. She said such intuitive experiences were
quite common for her, and I think this vague belief in the paranor-
mal probably did her more harm than good. Tony's face was badly
cut, and he grew a beard that gave him the mien of 'an elegant cava-
lier'.

In 1940, V was directed again by Micky Powell in *Contraband*,
reuniting her with Conrad Veidt in one of the first entertainment

films to be made during the war. The cameraman was the incomparable Freddie Young, who was later celebrated for *Lawrence of Arabia* and other pictures with David Lean. There was also a 1941 flop, *Atlantic Ferry*, a saga about Victorian shipping magnates, where V was the leading lady to Michael Redgrave. The dialogue was so embarrassingly arch at times that they could not look at each other, and forty-five years later he was still upset at the laughter they heard, during one of the tensest scenes, at the première.

Although I do not think married life for this young idealist was ever really idyllic, she always protested that Tony was supportive of her throughout this early period, despite what were emotionally complex times. 'I was still young enough to want my male figures to be heroic,' she admitted, and since – despite the actual heroism being enacted abroad – this was precisely how many of the men in the entertainment industry saw themselves, there was still a sufficient level of illusion informing her world.

The Denham social life sounds vigorous enough, though was probably even more rarefied than in peacetime. In Black Jack's Cottage nearby lived Leslie and Phyl Mitchell, both of whom became enduring friends – not just the product of being thrown together *force majeure*. Leslie was an erstwhile actor, but by then the voice of Movietone News in the cinemas, and he had been the first ever presenter on British television when the studios at Alexandra Palace opened in 1936. He always retained his beautiful, dark chocolate tones, and was a gentle, humorous man who loved children, though with none of his own. His petite and arresting wife was the daughter of theatrical impresario Firth Shepherd. Leslie was probably the first Englishman to become a 'household face' from television, and he told me how, in those early years, strangers would recognize him in the street and be quite bemused that *he* did not know *them*.

I was very fond of Leslie, who became almost an unofficial godfather to me during my teens. In the 1970s he helped my mother house-hunt, double-checking properties by viewing them on her behalf, so the agents wouldn't think she was too keen. He visited one London mews house where the resident was lolling in front of a soccer match on the box; in his superlative announcer's voice, he said, 'I started all that off, you know,' leaving the youth incredulous at the old guy who claimed to have invented football.

My mother also formed an abiding friendship with the lustrous Lilli Palmer, a Jewish refugee actress from Germany who was later to prove an unimpeachable ally to both my parents (she was the first movie star I ever met, and everything about her, from her delicious perfume to the tiny, ant-like blemish in her eye, remains a Standard Candle for me as regards glamour in that industry). At this time, she was the inamorata of Rex Harrison – he was then extricating himself from his first marriage, and became her husband in 1943. They had a son, Carey, but there was subsequently much anguish in her life. V at once admired her 'guts, common sense, and humour' – one can't help thinking heroines might have furnished apter role-models than the men for my mother-to-be, then casting around for helpmeets. 'Sexy Rexy' she also *quite* liked, but he was becoming too much the professional charmer; 'the freshness of youth already foreshadowed future pomposity, and almost complete self-indulgence.'

To reduce expenses, the Havelock-Allans moved to share a cottage with the Nortons at Hedgerley. The *genius loci* here was a small, orange-haired valet named Rosslyn, who was content to iron his 'master's' shoelaces, but loathed all forms of cooking. This task accordingly fell to V, and since (to my knowledge) she could scarcely scramble – and certainly not boil – eggs, let alone dish up meals to delight such fastidious appetites (and within the rations system), the arrangement at Penny Royal was not to last, and she found a more manageable place to rent, with a name from Central Casting: Rose Cottage, in Ampney St Mary.

Tony began work with David Lean and Noël Coward on *In Which We Serve* – they teamed up with Freddie Young to form Cineguild, and Tony went on to great success with *This Happy Breed*, *Blithe Spirit* and *Brief Encounter*. Valerie Hobson appeared in none of them. She was not, I think, considered to be a 'proper' actress, with the subtlety of expression that was needed. She never said so, but the disappointment must have been keen. Another overture from Hollywood did arrive – David Selznick sent a contract, which V signed, though the starting date was left blank. 'I couldn't and wouldn't, with the future so unknown.' My suspicion is that not committing to this third approach was more to do with domestic worries than patriotic concerns.

Instead, Valerie Hobson persisted with riding carnival floats, posing for her English fanzine, singing on the *Forces' Programme*, appearing in advertisements for Lux soap. It was an admirable act of solidarity that effectively pollarded her international career. She never did work in America again.

A bomb exploded next to the basement flat in Queens Gate, Kensington, where her parents were staying. During the raid, they were crouched under the stairway and, as the walls collapsed, the Commander hurled himself over Vi to protect her. A grandfather clock fell across his back; she broke an arm, his chest had been deeply bruised but he seemed otherwise unharmed. Five of their neighbours were killed. V drove them out of town, along with Nanny and her baby. They were installed 'safely' at Rose Cottage, and seemed to be recuperating. A week later, my grandfather was rushed to Cirencester Cottage Hospital with acute respiratory problems – a nurse phoned V: 'He is very bad, please come.'

He lay on a white enamelled bed, already unconscious, breathing badly through his crushed lungs – 'it was the sound of a chain being dragged through water.' His last mooring to this world was being pulled, and the grandfather I never even met was alone with his younger daughter, as the tide of his life – well, it rushed out. 'I held one of his beautiful, masculine hands, the skin blue-white, his signet ring a tiny, worn mountain of gold. The green-painted room echoed to the dreadful rhythm of his hauling and sighing. He was already far away from us all. His great chest rose and fell, sucking in the air like a bellows. But it was just a mechanical remembrance of the brain. He was already on quite another tack.'

His Chilo held his hand. There was one dreadful sound from his lungs, one haul up from the deep, and then the breathing stopped. Her original hero, his flaws maybe defining him, had gone.

To lessen the shock for her mother, V rearranged his posture in death so that it appeared he had fallen asleep reading, with his spectacles upon the bridge of his nose.

———•———

There was so much death and dereliction during these years that the context for mourning had in some cases been altered, and there was less of an option to be demonstrably tethered by grief. It was the distant Patricia, now safely in Eire, and protesting her guilt at being so, who had the longer and more complicated discomfiture. Back home, with one man fewer to care for, but a renewed impulse towards the strengthening of family, Valerie was again on the move.

In the autumn of 1942, she and Tony entered into an uneasy ménage with the vainglorious actor Leslie Howard and his lover Vee Cunnington, an exquisite Frenchwoman. They rented an uncomfortable house outside Stoke Poges, with a single bathroom and heavy décor suitable for 'a battalion of angry Scottish schoolmasters'. Valerie did not greatly relish this proximity to the star, whom she had last encountered in Hollywood – 'I was to see Leslie at very close quarters, and was truly glad they never got any closer. Seemingly so relaxed, blond, charming and vague, he was nothing of the sort. He had his own methods of getting his way, and the quiet assumption was that he was devastating.' Vee was chic and adorable, and devoted to him; during one air raid she threw her small body over the great man, to shield him. (Next year, they were both dead: Vee collapsed suddenly when a boil in her nose caused a haemorrhage, and her lover disappeared aboard a plane returning from Lisbon, thought to have been shot down in the belief that it was bringing Churchill home from the Casablanca Conference.)

Fortunately, there was a new agent (Harry Hamm), and a new job – the lead opposite Robert Donat in *The Adventures of Tartu*, to be shot in Islington. This involved living for eight weeks in Claridge's, and being dressed up as a *femme fatale* who is in the clutches of the Nazis. The teenaged Glynis Johns played V's little sister, a waif who stole all her scenes. Donat himself was then a world star, but his stamina was hobbled by chronic asthma; his acting was meticulous – 'a treasured, fleeting thing' – and she thought 'he was probably the most truly attractive of all the actors I worked with.' Harold Bucquet – a small, unusually *simpatico* director – had come over from MGM in Hollywood, and gamely completed the picture despite the perils of London during the Blitz.

With her periodic, restless instinct that stage work was her real *métier*, V worked happily for a few months at the Dundee repertory company, and early the next year the Havelock-Allans moved into Hartlands, near Gerrard's Cross – the first (and last) home they were ever to own together. V was now feeling broody, but it was proving difficult to conceive, and she prayed unrelentingly to God to forgive her 'for aborting His first gift' three years before, and dreaded that He was punishing her and had made her barren.

They decided to take a romantic holiday, and lit upon Portmeirion (that Italianate folly in Wales which surely no visitor has left feeling undisturbed). On the first evening, a local fortune-teller – that recurrent figure in my mother's earlier life – came to ply her trade among the visitors: 'When she saw my palm, she folded up my fingers without a word, and kissed the knuckle. She cried, and cupped my cheeks. "God bless you," she said. Knowing He would, I smiled back.'

When they were going to bed on their last night, a bat got into the room. Tony was horrified by them – Denham Studios often had bats trapped in the concrete corridors – but he went in manful pursuit until he had felled it with a broom, bundled it into a towel, and thrown it by hand into the darkness. The little shock had discomposed them, and perhaps had skewed their metabolisms. It was that night, V always believed, that she again became pregnant.

For almost nine months she was sick, and seriously anaemic; Tony had to give her his blood. Her doctor, Roy Saunders, was intending to deliver her at home, unless there were further complications. Three weeks before term, she entertained him to lunch – roast chicken, followed by oranges in caramel sauce, using the precious demerara – but didn't think to trouble him with the back pains she had been having, and he never even examined her. Shortly after he left for the hospital in Windsor, she went into labour. Her waters broke in the bathroom, but the pain in her back became so acute that she could not make it to the window to alert her mother, who was gardening. The air-raid siren sounded, Tony came in, and managed to take her down to the Anderson shelter that had been constructed below their kitchen table. After an hour of labour in the half-dark, knowing something was wrong, she saw a pair of black shoes, then someone giving her chloroform, and so her first son was born.

He weighed over ten pounds, had slightly slanted eyes, and was yellowish with jaundice – a mandarin's face. They called him their Eastern potentate, and chose the name Simon (after Simon Drake, the hero of their first picture together). An Irish nanny was engaged, who covered the walls of the new nursery with crucifixes and pictures of her previous charges; *Vogue* and other magazines came to photograph; Noël Coward (entertaining the troops in the Far East) was sent a telegram inviting him to be a godfather – 'Chang Kai-shek has arrived. All three of us wildly happy and well' – but the message was censored for its political content. From the start, however, Simon fed poorly and made no baby sounds. 'He was as old as time, as old as knowledge,' she wrote, 'I knew it, and I felt Tony knew it too.'

Euphoria gave way to concern. After a few weeks, a paediatrician, Dr Nathan, arrived to inspect the baby, then went out on to the lawn to talk to Tony. They made her sit down, but already she felt the world receding into some new kind of vacuum, everything seemed to be slowly wrapped in a thin film, it sounded when they spoke as if their voices were singing.

'Dear lady, I wish I didn't have to tell you this. You have a baby you will have to forget. He is irreparably handicapped. He is what is called a "mongol". He has all the signs – tongue typically too large, creases on the hands, the unfinished palate and prepuce. There are further indications of a hole in the heart. It's no one's fault, Mrs Havelock-Allan. But you must simply forget him, and start again.'

'The bubble closed,' wrote Valerie Profumo, in a different lifetime. 'I was entirely alone. The vacuum was sealed – Tony put out his arm, but I was inside. A long time afterwards – probably weeks – Tony says I gave one huge, piercing animal cry. But I heard nothing.'

From that day for the rest of his life, Simon's very existence caused her profound distress and ambivalence; she blamed herself for his handicap, and she was never sure how best to look after him. The

Catholic nanny packed up in horror ('Look after a baby like that?') and all at once it seemed there was nobody who could offer help. The nursery was soundless, but V discerned 'there was a singing hollow in the house'. She longed for her boy to cry.

Children born with what we now call Down's syndrome were in 1943 still categorized as idiots, and at the very least were a source of embarrassment. There were no special homes, or support groups, or parents' associations. If they survived, they were often confined to institutions, under a statute of lunacy. Roy, their doctor friend and counsellor, said he felt responsible: he had been so intent on saving her life from loss of blood that he had not spotted the baby's abnormality at the time, but he did have a suggestion now. He was prepared to give the boy a shot of meningococcal meningitis, which would cause a swift death – 'My dear, I don't want you to suffer this baby – you love him now, of course you do, but he'll never amount to anything, and will cause you great sadness, and indeed he may suffer, too.'

The doctor was in tears, the mother was revolted by his suggestion. Later, she learned from others that this type of discreet assistance was not uncommon: 'Best leave him in our care'. . . . 'We understand such tragic beings'. . . . 'It might be kinder to reduce nourishment, gradually.' A progressive lady doctor merely advised, 'Just love him.' (Simon, the boy with no future, died in January 1991.)

It seemed, though, that the father could never accommodate this child into his scheme of things, and Valerie quickly spotted that she and Simon were effectively on their own. She grew increasingly nervous and volatile – 'hysterical' would have been the routine diagnosis. And it was in a doctor's waiting-room that a chance meeting turned her away from the routine medical advice (forget it, and try again) for there, as V was numbly re-dressing her son after another unhelpful examination, she saw an old woman, a nanny who had earlier that day been paid off on the spot by the distraught parents of a baby who had died of a convulsion in the doctor's surgery. Her name was Agnes Moth, and she had remained in her seat there, quietly waiting for something to happen.

She became their Nanny Moth. V always regarded her as a godsend, possibly some fairy godmother. Now there was some tenderness and physical help in the home, it seemed less sealed in with ignorance and horror. 'I was in many ways half dead to the world,' wrote V, 'but knowing everything possible was now being done for my baby, I realized that I should return to work.'

Although not exactly desperate, her circumstances were insecure. There was a widowed mother in the city, a tenuous nursery arrangement, and a busy husband who, with glacial imperceptibility, was sliding away, the beginnings of a moraine forming between him and his small family. When David Selznick called her agent to remind them he had a long-standing contract with her, Valerie used Simon's incapacity to extricate herself from it – 'I never wanted to go back to Hollywood, ever.' She had become socially withdrawn, in an industry where gregariousness was essential. That 'bubble' (the second caul) might have gone, but she still felt removed from the milieu in which she lived. For six months, she developed a hideous case of *acne rosacea* and, knowing her face was literally her fortune, was certain this was a divine retribution for her supposed vanity and ambition. The condition responded to none of the known treatments, and she feared she would be irredeemably scarred.

At a party she was reluctantly attending, she met the dangerously graceful but imaginative David Lean. He saw she was in trouble, fed her with brandy, and persuaded her to discuss some of her anxiety. He suggested she might visit an analyst friend, Dr Hilde Maas; after six sessions, Valerie was told she no longer needed her mask of spots and pustules, and during the next week her skin was restored to its former, unblemished pallor.

Now able to put a brave new face on things, Valerie Hobson was offered the part of the grown-up Estella in Cineguild's version of *Great Expectations*. Tony was producing, and David Lean directing, so her first reaction was that this was a case of nepotism, a charitable gesture to help her back into the limelight. She made the mistake of saying so to Lean. 'No,' he assured her, 'you are exactly right for the part. Estella is a woman without a heart, dead, unable to feel.' This response did little to buck her sense of well-being, but she proceeded anyway – the truth can be a sharp instrument, but she refused to be deflated. It was also Lean's idea that she should play Molly (Estella's mother), so she was uniquely to have acted three parts in that same story, though her Hollywood cameo never made it to the screens.

It was probably the only real masterpiece in which my mother ever acted, but she remembered it as the unhappiest film she made. Although it won two Oscars, and was effectively the first time Alec Guinness achieved screen prominence, her experience was defined by the obsessive presence of its director. Lean was married to the actress Kay Walsh, who had been in two of the films he previously made with Noël Coward; it was she who wrote the final scene to *Great Expectations* (the one set in Miss Havisham's house, which catches out students who have not read the book closely enough), and was to write the opening scene to *Oliver Twist* (1948) where she memorably portrayed Nancy. Their marriage was unhappy. Lean was manipulative and adulterous – it is said that on returning from their honeymoon he made her wear a pair of silk pyjamas, destined for a mistress, to avoid detection at customs. In her fragile state of self-esteem, this was perhaps not the ideal person for V to work for.

She found Lean disconcertingly cold, and poor with the actors. His genius at that time was as an editor, and he was intolerant of anything which impeded the realization of the perfect picture he held in his mind – not so rare among directors now, one might think, but the manner in which he strove to achieve it seemed overly demanding to her, then. In one scene, Estella had to sit with her crochet at Miss Havisham's feet (Martita Hunt played the scary old lady) and deliver a line of dialogue to Pip; Lean called for forty-two takes, before deciding to print one of the earliest. This working habit threatened to destroy V's confidence and leached out any remaining spontaneity from her performance. It was a most impressive film, but her part was restricted by the director's view of its ruling passion. It was Jean Simmons, as the young Estella, who caught the eye for her warmer, more fulsome portrayal, and this, too, was clear to V at the time. I think this film suggests why she was admired and even desired by the public for her screen appearances, but never widely loved.

(My mother may not have held it in much affection, for personal reasons, but *Great Expectations* remains my favourite of her films, and the one I have watched most often, even though I first saw it at my prep school, when, during one of Estella's scenes, a ten-year-old, double-barrelled Irish *confrère* of especially loutish disposition, bored and doubtless bemused by the plot which contained no diversionary scenes of horseback racing or woodcock shooting – dug me in the side and hissed, 'God, she's ugly.' Naturally – he was fully a year my senior, and my consanguinity was unsuspected – I freely concurred.)

Simon was two when the war ended – still a year away from being able to walk, and he had not yet once cried. The household now included V's mother-in-law, Anne, who had been fire-bombed out of her flat in Bath; she roundly declared that any disability that her grandson suffered was entirely in the minds of his parents, which at least exonerated her from any need to pay much attention to him. Tony himself went off to Hollywood to report on the wider situation in the movie world for the Rank Organization, and on his return he announced that he had fallen for a starlet but had just restrained himself from swerving into bed with her out of loyalty to his wife. It seems he expected grateful congratulations. Relatively naïve and idealistic as Valerie still was, she was horrified that he would even contemplate such a move – 'I started for the first time that sad thing which every woman does at such time, feigning ecstasy in bed.' Not yet was she going to acknowledge properly the steaming auguries of betrayal.

More ominous still was Tony's withdrawal from his son. He evidently felt distaste at the boy's physical appearance (despite his faintly exaggerated physiognomy, Simon always bore a distinct facial resemblance to his father), and concocted the excuse that he had such an unbearable empathy for V's unhappiness that it was surely better he stay at arm's length, for fear of compounding the dismay. I'm sure his masculine pride was offended at having sired such an inadequate creature, and his egocentric nature rejected both the practical and the emotional implications. V wanted to make the home circumstances as agreeable as possible for her 'man', but the floppy boy was unavoidably becoming emblematic of their own, seriously disabled relationship.

One of the first intense friendships she made away from the film world was with the artist Matthew Smith, whose work she had keenly admired since buying one of his nudes during the war. Her enthusiasm for painting was genuine and instinctive – V later developed some talent of her own, with a boldly impasto style – and she responded at once to the humour and impulsiveness of this stooped, uncertain figure with his baggy tweed coats, pebble spectacles, and faded sandy hair. 'Matthew was probably the gentlest man I ever met,' she wrote. Just at that time, nothing could have been more welcome. He painted her eight times, and was fiercely attracted by her physical appearance, especially the pallor of her skin (they shared the same coloration). She was fascinated to watch him myopically at work, to feel the deep sensuality with which his attitude to the physical world was suffused. He was a magpie, with a delight in curious *objets*, and such small gifts of flowers and wine and fruit that she brought to his studio. Although they were never actually lovers, the relationship was intimate and emotional – he was smitten with the theatrical world, and in turn introduced her to some of his artistic friends, such as the Epsteins. She responded to his shyness, modesty and generous spirit (traits that were in notably short supply back home), and he desired her companionship. One morning, when she was staying in his house at Tickerage in East Sussex, V was awoken at six to find him standing with a painting of peonies, the canvas still wet, to present to her; she cried when she saw him.

In what was no doubt a loving gesture, Tony then cast his wife in a Cineguild picture despite the fact that his partner David Lean was not interested in directing it (being consumed by preparing his next Dickens classic). She was to play the title role in *Blanche Fury* – an adaptation of *Fury's Ape* by Joseph Shearing, a period family saga – with Stewart Granger as the leading man; his arrogant persona made him exceedingly unpopular with the crew. It was to prove the film of which she was most fond, but it attracted mixed notices at best; the picture looked good, and the casting was adequate, but somehow the story never resolved its own contours. To his credit, Tony took a considerable risk with this venture, and almost jeopardized his collaboration with Lean: although they went on to work together elsewhere, he gave up his executive-producership, and finally resigned from Cineguild. 'In many ways it changed the course of Tony's whole career,' V wrote of this sacrifice.

The director of *Blanche Fury* was a cautious, educated, sombre Frenchman named Marc Allégret, and it is clear that V was most taken with him. 'He had particularly good hair,' she noted, 'lightly sprinkled with hazy silver and unbecomingly cut, and his walk was slightly forward-leaning, as if he had been born in the mountains.' His 'ravishingly beautiful' wife, Nadine, was the daughter of the French editor of *Vogue* and had been a ballerina before the war; fighting with the Maquis, she had sustained a leg-wound that turned septic. The Germans intercepted the cache of the newly discovered penicillin that was covertly air-dropped for her cure and the leg was rendered useless. After the war, she took her little daughter, 'Poussin', and left Marc for the theatrical agent André Bernheim. When V met him, her Gallic director was therefore sad and meditative. Allégret's apparently bohemian lifestyle appealed sharply to her romantic side, too, and she revelled in the Left Bank milieu to which he introduced her during script discussions in Paris. There were meals with André Gide, Jean Cocteau and the long-legged Zizi Jean-Maire. Marc's flatmate was the French film director Roger Vadim. For an attractive British woman who felt deprived of attention – 'half-anaesthetized', emotionally – this was an ideal situation for some sort of reawakening.

She surprised herself by the openness with which she discussed personal things with her director, and realized this would never have happened with her husband. The level of sympathy was new and exciting for her, and 'it bred a kind of love'. I cannot tell how far this was allowed to go: I doubt V was physically unfaithful at this stage (perhaps it would have been better for her if she had been) but his letter of farewell to her as he waited for the final boat at Dover was still in a small cache of her papers when I found them in her bureau drawer. Her involvement with Allégret marked the beginning of a more independent phase of her life.

Blanche Fury was not the success at the box office that Tony needed, but it still shows well on television today. Much of the location work was done at Wootton Lodge, in Staffordshire, which lent the breathless, star-crossed action a certain splendour (more than one critic reckoned it stole the show). The house was unoccupied, but V had to arrive there very early in the day for make-up and often heard children laughing and running down the passages. When she asked the caretaker if he would like to let them into the dressing-room to say hello, the reply came that there had not been a child in the house for over fifty years.

On holiday, in a seaside boarding-house, Nanny Moth died in her sleep.

Although she had managed to buy herself some precious, restorative time, V realized that her mainstay was now gone, and she had to admit that the long-term arrangements for Simon could no longer be ignored. The dilemma was acute, because it would be impossible for her to earn a living and look after him without special help – but there was virtually no expert advice to be had. Simon was slow to respond to attention, and, by not manifestly returning her love, he seemed to his mother to be, indeed, 'not completely human'. His existence unavoidably acted like a sheet-anchor to her career, and she detested herself for those moments when she wondered, in her isolation, what might have happened had he never been born. 'Now, all I see is an adorable, stumbling, inarticulate little boy with sun-gold hair and angel's skin,' she wrote, after his death, but one should not judge too harshly a single mother trying to cope with such a handicapped child at that time. She once told me it would just have been worse, had he been a girl.

Quite bravely, she was the first 'show-business' mother to speak publicly about mongolism. It was regarded as a taboo subject, like cancer, and learned opinions about its cause ranged from VD to carelessness. When she addressed a meeting in Oxford town hall, one woman stood up and screamed that 'the Nazis had got it right – they shouldn't be allowed to live, before they can pollute anyone else.' Later, V was instrumental in founding the Three Roses, this country's first-ever charity to support those with this form of mental handicap.

When she arrived back at Hartlands one afternoon and discovered Simon – unnoticed by the new nanny – fallen on the stone terrace, in a puddle of blood, having almost bitten through his tongue (but unable to cry out) the anguish so welled up once more within her that she could not think of working again until some drastically new arrangement was arrived at and it was agreed they would try to find a residential home to care for their son. The elusive Tony suggested they acquire a *pied-à-terre* in Hay Hill, Mayfair, to maintain a profile in town. In her distress, Valerie took to the Bible, and retreated frequently to pray in the Brompton Oratory. A period of soul-scarification ensued – it was not to be the last – and this certainly would not have made the marriage any sweeter. V's conviction of her worthlessness caused violently graphic dreams, from which I think she was seldom again free. One night, she imagined she was a bird winging Simon and her mother away to freedom and when Tony finally woke her and asked why she had her arms outstretched, she was crying so vehemently that she could not even answer him.

Following an incident at one institution, where she arrived unannounced to find Simon strapped with cloths, immobilized, in a chair, Valerie eventually took him to a Rudolf Steiner home in Worcestershire, where at last he began to be happy. Her own doctor recommended she go to Lucerne, for a rest cure – 'I was iller than I knew.' Here she wandered the mountain slopes, read, and slept, but one day climbed too high, was overcome with vertigo, and had to be rescued, splayed motionless against a rock-face, several hours later. They put her directly on to a small charter plane back from Zurich, which she shared with a coffin and the mother of a girl who had just died in a sanatorium. By the time she reached Croydon Airport, she felt she had regained enough perspective to face her own domestic problems.

On the last day of 1947, at the Royal Albert Hall, she encountered the dancing policeman.

Tony had formed a production company called Constellation Films, and early in the new year he cast her in a project opposite an unavoidably thrilling young star: Howard (then known as 'Harold') Keel, the centrepiece of London's stage version of *Oklahoma!* at the Drury Lane theatre. Valerie was, I think, greatly attracted to him; she recalled how 'his physical well-being, good temper, and the wood-brown of his rich voice conveyed the best of America.' He stood six foot three, and had scintillating teeth. 'Tony and I both fell in love with him.' *The Small Voice* was to be his first movie, 'a romantic gang-ster melodrama', and shooting began at the Riverside Studios that April. The story concerned a couple detained in their farmhouse by three convicts on the run (its title alludes to the voice of conscience) and was quite well received. The co-stars were seen out on the town together for a while – to the chagrin of Jack Profumo, among several other hopeful swains – and then Harry Keel went back to the States on the boat train. (Later he finally achieved global recognition as the husband of Miss Ellie, in the series *Dallas*.)

At this stage, though married, she openly entertained a number of beaux. When Jack sent her a postcard from Monte Carlo commiser-ating over a minor operation, and suggesting they might see one another again, she considered adding him to her string of admirers. In the event, it was Valerie who asked Jack out on their first date. She invited him to a piano recital by her friend Fred Elizalde, and spotted at once, backstage, that her escort for the evening was no fan of clas-sical music, and was conspicuously relieved that the ordeal was over. Attracted by his *joie de vivre*, his subversive charm, and refreshing lack of artistic pretension, she claims she resolved to beware him. 'I knew I was vulnerable, and this was a special man.' If my father voluntarily endured another concert, I would be very much surprised.

Probably the most enduring picture in which Valerie Hobson starred was the Ealing Comedy *Kind Hearts and Coronets* (1949), in which she played Edith D'Ascoyne ('a cold aristocrat') opposite Dennis Price, Joanie Greenwood (as the aptly named Sibella), and a cavalcade of incarnations by Alec Guinness – the *tour de force* for which this Edwardian extravaganza is still rightly fêted. It was an agreeably blackish script by director Robert Hamer, a talented but exceedingly unpre-dictable man, a drinker; after a long discussion of the Kinsey Report one evening at the Moulin d'Or restaurant in Romilly Street, he leaned over the corner table, pressed a steak knife (wrapped in a napkin) to V's chest, and said, 'I may finish you off.' Fortunately George, one of the brothers who ran the place, intervened before she became the savoury course, and announced, 'Your taxi is here, Miss Hobson.'

The kind of straight-faced, absurdist performance required by *Kind*

Hearts probably suited V's acting style more than any other, and she acquitted herself well. This was a happy cast and crew, several remaining friends long after she left the profession – but there was one new companion who was to become a permanent feature of her life. Ethel Salisbury was assigned as her dresser. The wardrobe mistress told V she was in a shaky state, having recently suffered a nervous breakdown (partly due, I believe, to the fact that her husband Jim had fathered an illegitimate son on a wartime evacuee billeted with them). Here were two wronged, but resilient, women who had much to offer one another, and they fitted together like allelomorphs – 'Ethel, only ten years my senior, was to be my surrogate mother.' At this stage, V still needed some versions of parental support.

When I was young – she continued to come and look after my mother's clothes for some forty years – Ethel's name had proved beyond the pronunciation ability of children, so she had become 'Essie'. She was petite, with a pointed profile and glittering eyes, but the mousy appearance belied a tough, fierce, sharp personality, though furred over with a practised display of general benevolence. V adored her, and they remained loyal to one another through every personal crisis, united no doubt by their agreement concerning the unsatisfactory nature of men. As an outsider, Ethel brought some fresh understanding to the constricted complications of V's home life; she could see how bad the marriage had become, and helped her friend to be newly resolute, establish an independent financial footing, and to make some drastic decisions about Simon.

' "But I must discuss everything with Tony," I prevaricated, "I'm not alone in this."

'Very quietly: "Yes, dear, you are." '

Tony was busy filming in Venice, and had begun an affair with the flighty and lustrous actress Kay Kendall – 'a highly vulnerable girl, a prerequisite for him, whose nature it is to be needed.' He breezed back from Italy for a few days to check some production details, and let his wife in on his exciting new secret. Her reaction was typical: 'I hope I behaved well. I wanted Tony to be happy, because I loved him . . . He was very gentle as he told me all about it, how guilty he felt, and yet how he was enjoying every moment. It's the truth when I say I understood.' He was certainly a fortunate husband in this respect, but V's lack of wrath is not as saintly as it might first appear, and I do not seek to depict her as some martyr resolutely singing hymns from her bed of white-hot coals. She was well aware of her own sexual charms, and at least one married man was hotly in pursuit (former air ace and celebrated socialite Whitney Straight), as well as that enthusiastic *amateur*, the erstwhile Tory Member for Kettering.

John Profumo was at this stage 'grooming' the constituency of Stratford-on-Avon, and took the initiative to invite his new friend the film star down to open a charity function (they habitually alluded to these as 'a fête worse than death'). She appeared in the latest New Look tweeds, driving her own 2-litre Riley – my father never missed a photo-opportunity when there was a pretty girl around, and he introduced her to his sister, who lived nearby. They had to be discreet, of course: 'I was an actress, and a married one at that. Parliament didn't take kindly to its representatives dallying with married ladies in 1948.' In short, the prospective candidate had to be careful to avoid any hint of scandal.

They had met just five times, but it seems she had fallen in love with J, though still leery of him, and his rather overbearing, gynarchic, Warwickshire county family. 'This man was supremely energetic, free in spirit, unburdened by family problems, and his world and interests were different from those I knew: politics (above all), girls, horses, parties, holidays in the sun, practical jokes, society gossip, aeroplanes (which he flew himself) and, above all, fun.' I believe this last is the key. Valerie Hobson had in fact experienced precious little fun, for all the apparent ritziness of her image. Although she was adamant that he was not a mere playboy – the commitment to politics was already his abiding passion – V saw in J the type of man she had really never been with before, someone with insouciance, to whom her familiar sensations of angst and guilt were virtually unknown. She described him as 'a boyish man', impulsive and irreverent, and that could never have been said of her husband, whose strain of irresponsibility was of a more calculated sort.

Back from his Venetian shoot, Tony breezily agreed to V's plan (suggested by her new agent at MCA, David Henly, an accountant) that they sell Hartlands and move to London – she to the flat in Hay Hill, and he ('my husband in name only') to a service apartment around the corner. Here he could nestle down with his paramour, and indeed by now he assumed that the arrangement was accepted. On one occasion, when the excitable Miss Kendall had hurled all her clothes out of the window in a fit of pique, it was Ethel Salisbury who was dispatched to retrieve them. It was, as my father later described it, 'a theatrical marriage'.

Tony's comfortable attitude towards infidelity was not matched by equanimity on V's part, however. Her account of this year is unpicked and rewoven so incessantly, like the work of Penelope's loom, that her vacillation and idealism prove exasperating. She professed still to love her 'Anthony' with all her heart, and desired his happiness as a consequence; yet there was undeniably an impulse to indulge her own desires, although she could not persuade herself to take the final step towards physical infidelity. This is a dilemma one must respect, but it was the cause of much unhappiness. It is not often in this story that I would consider typing the phrase 'poor Jack Profumo', but I think, with his carefree ways and libertine lifestyle, he had little idea of the turmoil churning within the exquisite object of his affections.

In certain tribes, a bride's virginity is taken before her wedding night by someone other than her husband, so she should never need to feel resentful towards him (that is the pretext, at least); Valerie seems to have decided to commit adultery first with another man – rather than J – as she did not want him to be 'the first one to make me "do wrong" in the most old-fashioned of meanings'. She accordingly gave in to a married Lothario – it may well have been the dashing Mr Whitney Straight – who had been trying for some while to seduce her. The experience was truly liberating, though he was 'too professionally lascivious, delicious but it smacked of masturbation.' Mission accomplished, however, she felt free to indulge herself with the ever-eager J. In 1949, they decided to go to Paris together for Easter – and there, on the cusp of their first, urgent *liaison*, I shall leave them, with my mother's words, written almost forty years later, remarkably free of regret.

Love like that, any woman! If you get the chance, even if it may be a passing thing; even if the void seems all-encompassing when it comes; even if the heart bleeds almost to death, passionate love is worth it, it is worth it, it is worth all of it.

III

This Man is News

THERE IS NO record of any tempests or torpedoes attending the birth of John Dennis Profumo, when he arrived at the family home in 28 Basil Street, Knightsbridge, on 30 January 1915.

He was the fourth child of Baron Albert Profumo, a modest, thoughtful barrister of severe mien and quiet manner, and Martha Thom Walker, an Edinburgh girl he had married in 1906. She was an actress and dancer, and they were introduced by his younger brother Charlie, the chancer, black sheep, and stage-door Johnny of the family. The union was a happy one, combining opposites; whereas Albert was pensive and anxious, 'Mattie' was demonstrative in her affections, outgoing, gregarious and artistic.

Their elder son, Peter, had died as an infant, but there were two sisters for baby Jack – Elizabeth ('Betsy'), and Mary (always known as 'Maina'), and later a brother, Philip.

Our family origins are Sardinian, and the distinctive name was an occupational one, a metonym, for a maker of perfume – the connotations were generally favourable, since this was in medieval times a precious commodity, but on occasions it was applied as a pejorative nickname for an ill-smelling person.

My great-great-great-grandfather, Antonio (the 'begat' factor here will be kept to a bareish minimum), was a Sardinian subject living in Genoa, a shipping magnate and a lawyer of some renown. He became President of the Commercial Court, a senator, and was created Baron in 1843 by King Carlo of Sardinia. He adopted the family motto *Virtute et labore* – 'By strength and hard work'. His son Pietro made, and lost, a fortune in maritime insurance, and was also an advocate. He became Principal Private Secretary to Cavour (as Prime Minister to Victor Emmanuel II), and was instrumental in organizing the Italian consular system, for which he was widely decorated. His home was Castel Guelfo, a sizeable, if unlovely, castle in the township of that name. He had a swarthy, aquiline appearance, which has passed strongly through the male line. Pietro died in 1867, having been misled by various friends into banking ventures that proved unsound. At one stage he had been worth two million francs, but 'was afterwards dependent on charity, and died a broken-hearted man'.

His only son, Joseph Alexander, was born in Turin in 1849, and was educated in England. He married a London girl, Annie Mills, in 1875, and they had four children – Emilia, Alberti, Carlo and Irene. In September 1885, though, the Profumo family became naturalized British subjects. The 3rd Baron was a tough businessman, intent on learning from the mistakes of his forebears. Otherwise relatively impecunious, he had inherited one splendid necklace of significant diamonds, each of which he sold off to finance various ventures until, in 1877, he founded a company called the Provident Life Association. He had been down to his last stone, which became his family heirloom.

The basic premise of this business was to link house purchase to endowment assurance policies. It meant that the average worker, for whom an outright deposit on a house was out of the question, could take out a policy, pay a weekly premium (initially half a crown) and, after five years, had the right to borrow, against that, the entire cost of a house (£250), which in turn would be completely purchased after another twenty-five years. The movement prospered, and the Provident expanded from its offices in Lombard Street (chosen because its founder could cut expenses by working at night from the gaslight in the street outside his window) to premises in Bishopsgate. Before long, the total value of loans was many millions, and the Baron acquired a country home – The Mole House, in Hersham, Surrey – complete with coachman, chauffeur and indoor staff.

His portrait shows a rather fierce, moustachioed face, not exactly the picture of benevolence. He was certainly a strict father, and was determined the family fortunes would slide back no longer (the Provident was finally sold when I was in my twenties). His other ambition was to be elected to Parliament, and in 1892 he contested the seat of Monmouthshire South, as the Liberal and Labour candidate. His chief opponent was the popular Conservative Member of eighteen years' standing, Colonel the Hon. Frederick C. Morgan, much of whose campaign was devoted to scoffing at the 'Profumists'. As he addressed meetings in Llangibby, Llantrissant and Tredunnock, the Baron was heckled mercilessly – 'Address us in English!', and 'What price ice-cream?' being among the milder jibes on record. In his scattershot election manifesto he pledged Home Rule for Ireland, religious equality for the Welsh, increased taxation for estate owners, support for the Temperance cause, improved inspection of mines, and the abolition of the Lords as a legislative assembly. Aspersions were freely cast on the philanthropic intentions of the managing director of the Provident, and it was rudely suggested he should be turning his attentions to improving the lot of the poorer Italian peasants.

Polling Day was not a success, either. The candidate, inspecting a booth in Newport, 'sauntered round the place where the papers had to be marked, and, catching his foot in something on the floor, he stumbled and fell over flat on his back. Rising, he declared that it was a bad start, and left the booth.' There were violent scenes at Newbridge, where a crowd of Profumists hustled Michael Taylor, a colliery worker sporting their rival's blue favours, and he was thrown over a hedge into the nearby field. The constabulary was summoned, pelted with eggs and tussocks, then accordingly made a seven-strong truncheon charge. The mob was finally subdued when the Revd Stephen Jackson, vicar of Llangynwyd, improvised some rustic sports as a diversion.

Morgan was returned with 5,421 votes, although his opponent managed a creditable 4,700. Billy Nutts, poetaster on the partisan *Western Mail*, concluded his excellent verses on the election, 'Let the Baron's friends wear black, / And send old macaroni back / To sunny Italee'. It was not the family's finest hour in politics, but nor was it exactly our nadir.

My grandfather entertained similar hopes, twice unsuccessfully contesting the High Peak of Derbyshire division as a Conservative. During his 1909 campaign, there occurred the first headlines concerning 'the Profumo Case'; in those days, peers of the realm were forbidden to become involved in political elections after the issue of writ, and it was discovered that the Duke of Norfolk had sent him a letter of support, beginning 'My Dear Profumo', which caused impassioned controversy, and resulted in His Grace being referred to the Committee of Privileges. (When Norfolk later appeared in Taunton to support another candidate, one man shouted out, 'How's dear old Profumo?'.) This original Profumo Case led to that particular rule being rescinded concerning elections.

When my father was born, the 4th Baron was already a family man in comfortable circumstances. He had been educated at the City of London School, was called to the Bar at the Inner Temple in 1901 (taking silk in 1919). During the Great War, he was a captain in the United Artists' Rifles, attached to HQ Staff London District of the Honourable Artillery Company. He never took an active part in the running of the Provident, but benefited greatly from its profits. Privately, he gave substantial sums of money to fund scholarships at the Inns of Court, RADA, two Oxford colleges, the Royal Academy of Music (of which he was a director) and several ecclesiastical foundations. For his sterling patronage of the Italian Hospital in London, he received a signed photograph from Mussolini, which has – to my chagrin – now gone missing. A prominent freemason (though, curiously, this did not help him as much as expected during his election campaigns), his legal work seems to have preoccupied him, and his main relaxation was the series of musical soirées organized by Mattie in their new London home, Number 1 Princes Gate – overlooking Hyde Park – where they moved when Jack was aged four.

Their neighbours here were members of the Russian royal family, recently exiled. My father used to play with the younger Romanoffs in the communal gardens, and took riding lessons with them from the stables in the mews behind. This was run by a Mr Meades, who was very keen to flaunt his royal connections (the King also kept a horse there), and Jack rode out in Rotten Row on a pony called Princess Mary. Although at this stage the Profumos were a thoroughly urban clan, horseback riding was to become central to their lives as the children grew up.

After attending Mr Gibbs's school in Sloane Street as a day-boy, Jack was packed off to board at Wellington House, near Westgate-on-Sea, in Kent. This was handy for North Foreland Lodge nearby, where his sisters were sent. 'It was a Dickensian kind of place,' he recalled, 'and at night a senior boy would tour the dorms, crying out, "Any holes, minus-buttons, rents or tears?"' He was not an especially academic youth, but enjoyed his games; 'cricket was played relentlessly, and I tried to keep wicket. "Stand back, Profumo," the Head would shout from the boundary, when I let through too many byes.'

In 1926, my grandparents decided to move to the country, and they bought a large, dour house in Avon Dassett, a Warwickshire village listed in the Domesday Book, deeply folded into the countryside of Shakespeare's rural Albion, and then in the heartlands of fox-hunting society. Simon de Montfort had once been lord of the manor here, and the name of the settlement probably alludes to a *deorset*, or fold for deer. The battlefield of Edgehill was close by, and it was said that at times spectral armies still clashed in the skies. (On childhood visits, I would stand and watch in hope, and once, during an August storm, my aunt assured me the thunder was really hoof-beats of the Royalist cavalry.) It was a far cry from Kensington.

The house itself – Avon Carrow – was built massively in the Oxbridge collegiate style, and its name derives from *carre*, for it was originally designed as a square hunting lodge, in 1896. The owner, Captain Cecil Boyle, would stand on the balcony each morning before getting dressed, and watch his hunters being exercised, and he also had a spy-hole from his bedroom directly on to the yard, to supervise training at all hours. He did not long enjoy his creation, though, as he was killed in the Second Boer War. The next owner was a Captain Peel, who, despite having a dog called Justice, brought calumny and scandal to the place when he cheated his bookie by getting the village postmaster to send pre-timed telegrams laying bets on a horse his wife already knew had won. He was sent to prison. The Baron bought his new home from the Stapleton-Brethertons, and the four children came to adore it.

Avon Carrow had been expanded over the years, and was on a grandish scale, though the décor was in questionable taste for a proper gentleman's residence (there were a number of curiously tiled walls, and other flourishes of oddball ornamentation). The sizeable staff included Gorton the chauffeur, and his assistant Godfrey Golder (a real old countryman, who used to take me rabbit hunting), George Woodcock the groom, Ernest his sidekick, and a butler, footman, cook, and housemaid. But despite the appurtenances of wealth and style, the Profumos must have appeared to the old landed gentry of the area as *arrivistes*, a bunch of chaps with flash new money, a foreign title and a slightly vulgar taste for conspicuous consumption. This would have not worried them a jot, as neither of my grandparents was inclined to ride to hounds – the activity around which polite society seemed to turn in those parts. Indeed, the Baroness loathed the whole idea of hunting, but seems to have been an adaptable lady, and could tolerate what made all her children so wildly excited. Her chief care was for her husband, who needed to retire from the pressures of the Bar, and seems to have suffered from a strain of melancholy and poor health. She herself had diabetes – a condition that was to claim her left eye – and had needed two daily injections of insulin since adolescence. The Baron was an abstemious man, who drank little and preferred plain food, having generally frugal habits. My father describes him often 'sitting alone in his study, brooding', but whatever black dog was daunting him, it was never openly discussed.

The house became a busy, social milieu despite this, especially once the two exuberant daughters were in their teens. It was said that, after a hectic day in the field, the Misses Profumo (ever elegant, if not exactly beautiful) would enter their first-class carriage at Banbury station, still clad in mud-spattered hunting gear, pull down the blinds, and alight in the West End arrayed in evening dresses and long gloves, ready for a night on the town. They were a boisterous lot, and the Baroness had to mediate between them and their sober, though not forbidding, father. There were visits, too, from his own siblings – Uncle Charlie (the family jester, a 'poodlefaker' who lived in northern France, and was never gainfully employed), plus the so-called 'pauper aunts', Nina and Irene. Their love lives were evidently of some concern to their steadfast and anxious brother – Nina ended up having a family in Australia, and Irene settled in Rome, where she hunted with the local pack and numbered among her admirers a dashing Italian waiter and Paul, Duc de Guise (whose family, having massacred the Huguenots, gave rise to the term 'bloodbath'). She wore wire-rimmed spectacles and a wig, and loved silly adventures, and when my father once flew her over Mount Etna in his plane, and began to run out of fuel, she merely exclaimed, 'Darling, how wonderful.'

From quite an early age, then, Jack was part of a lively and varied household, and he became used to mixing with those older than himself. It was a pampered upbringing, and one feels he always 'had his toast crusts cut off for him', and came rather to expect such treatment, where possible, *in perpetuum*. He developed an especially close kinship with his sister Maina, who shared his passion for low jinks and deflationary manoeuvres (they had once attempted to poison their elderly Nanny Kispeth by putting berries in her tea): together they were subversive, gossipy and unpredictable for the rest of their lives, a formidable duo – almost incestuously strong – for anyone hoping to enter the family circle.

Academic study did not seem to trouble my father at Harrow any more than it had at Wellington House (where the Baron donated a new chapel, in gratitude, when he finally left), and educational standards at the school had anyway been declining. The new headmaster, Cyril Norwood, was about to transform its record. J initially boarded on the outskirts of the town until room was found for him at Druries, a house noted for games and the Officer Training Corps, under the tutelage of C. W. M. Moorsom, a maths beak. This was to suit the young Harrovian, who was good at rugby (eventually being awarded his school 'Lion') and left as a cadet sergeant.

His classroom reports suggest a degree of indolence and horseplay: 'slack and untidy', 'idling in form', 'the time which he wastes in gossiping to his neighbours', 'an agreeable youth who is not stupid, but has little idea of what real work is'. He was perhaps a scallywag rather than a true renegade, though he incurred baronial displeasure for one particular stunt. In J's second year, Mr Kelland was called in from retirement to act as form master; they saw he was gullible, and several boys pretended to be foreign – my father professing to speak very little

English. One morning he had a boy called Neill throw some coal and stones through the window, and screamed out, 'Ah, sir, they try assassinate me!' Moorsom discovered this prank, but kept the deception from the old teacher, to spare his feelings.

Not surprisingly, Jack Profumo showed an early aptitude for amateur dramatics, and some of his first press cuttings record considerable plaudits. In February 1933, *The Times* reported him in tartan trews, smoking a churchwarden, in *Abraham Lincoln* (Dorian Williams had the title role and Michael Denison played Mrs Otherly): he was presciently described as 'J. D. Profumo, who in the person of Edwin Stanton, brought some delightful comic relief to the grave Cabinet meeting'. Later, he won some acclaim as the Duke of Plaza-Toro (in *The Gondoliers*); depicted in the *Evening Standard* wearing top boots and a fantastical periwig, 'he rose to the greatest heights, and proved himself a past master of the humorist's art.'

A related interest – which he maintained all his life – was in cinema photography; Jack began this at school, and his father indulged the hobby by letting him build his own cinema in a converted laundry at home. With the help of the chauffeur, Gorton, he installed a dozen tip-up seats, a screen and a Bell & Howell projector. He showed rented movies at this 'Slip-In Cinema' as well as his own, shot with a Kodak cine-camera that he was still using in the 1970s. Some of these silent, black-and-white efforts were remarkably good – slapstick comedies and spoof thrillers, for the most part – and his fascination with camera work had some bearing on his later involvement with the broadcasting industry.

The schooldays were happy enough, and J looked back on Harrow with affection, often attending reunions and sessions of old boys singing 'Songs' (he eventually became a governor); there were also good friendships formed, with Bill Deedes, Jock Colville, and John Hobson, whose political lives were to become closely intertwined with his own. There was as yet no thought of such a career, of course, and just before he left the school in July 1933 he was sent for assessment to the Vocational Guidance Department of the National Institute of Industrial Psychology, where a report by the shrewd Gordon E. Whiting suggested that he was 'cheerful and fluent, but rather erratic and liable to be too easily influenced by others. The instinct of self-display appears to be very marked. Tests indicate that he is of approximately average intelligence [this seems marvellously tactful], but academic distinction should not be expected of him.' The recommendation was not for the Bar (spelling and written tests too weak – Jack was almost certainly what we would now classify as dyslexic) and 'the Army has also been suggested, but this again appears to be a doubtful choice . . . an occupation affording more scope for self-expression seems desirable [twelve years later he was a brigadier]. Interior decorating would seem to afford an outlet for many of his special interests.' Ah, the Great Ifs of history.

Jack's upbringing was hedonistic and privileged, and idyllically remembered. Once he left school, there followed several years when, as an enthusiastic socialite, he enjoyed the rarefied existence of the self-styled *jeunesse dorée*, an experience that was enhanced rather than hobbled by the somewhat surprising offer from Brasenose College, Oxford, of a place to read law. (It is just conceivable that the friendship between the Baron, who was a KC, and his legal *confrère* W. T. Stallybrass, Vice-Principal of the college, had something to do with it.)

For some time, BNC (as it was known in university parlance) had enjoyed a dubious reputation for its lack of academic rigour; of an earlier generation, John Buchan even recorded that one of his contemporaries, who actually took his degree with Honours, was summarily drenched under the college pump. Before many days had elapsed, J realized the law was not going to be his forte, and he managed to change to agriculture and political economy, a course which incidentally permitted you to keep a motor car (if you were lucky enough to afford one) for the purposes of visiting outlying farms. He quickly acquired a spiffy Vanden Plas Continental Tourer, and was fined three pounds for speeding (always one to twit authority, he asked the officer if he would have to go to prison).

This transport was also handy for accessing his equestrian pursuits. J had promised the college authorities he would try to gain a Blue, but when the rugby trials proved a little too ferocious he opted for polo and riding in point-to-points. He also checked out which other sports were undersubscribed, and realized there was an opportunity in the pole-vaulting field ('only one other chap had got his own pole, and in fact he *was* a Pole'). In the end, therefore, he was awarded three half-Blues, though there were some pitfalls: the first time he vaulted for the university, the radio announcer called him 'J. D. Protrudo'; and on another occasion a racecourse tipster was marking his card in front of a carful of girls, when he pointed to J's name and said, 'That 'oss would win the race, if the booger could stay on 'is back.' In one race, his nose was badly broken when it was nearly kicked off by his horse, Decent Fellow, but, as they used to say in the good old days of pig-sticking, it was generally a case of 'Ride straight, and ride like hell!'

Photographs of the time show a darkly suave chap, often in white tie, Bullingdon Club tails, or natty pinstripe suits (he was always fastidious over his sartorial appearance); the oiled hairline was already receding – repeated applications of melted wax, to emulate the Rudi Valentino look, had been earlier ruinous. His social life was sybaritic, involving hunt balls, London functions that resulted in pictures in 'society magazines', and undergraduate cocktail parties (he threw one himself where they served Gordon's gin tinted a pale green with culinary dye, claiming it was a new double-strength brand). His friends included the bespectacled Prince Sevelode, a debonair Valerian Wellesley (later Duke of Wellington), and the playboy 'Jai' – Man Singh II, Maharaja of Jaipur. Those were the days when men often enjoyed lap-dog nicknames – Boofy, Potter, or Fizz – and some of the girls were dubbed with *noms de guerre*, too; J certainly consorted with a Twinkle, and there was also Bubbles (whose father was superintendent of a municipal swimming-pool). They were not all debutantes. The first steady girlfriend was a lovely German blonde named Gisela Klein, who seemed to share his taste for japes: they once toured a smart girls' boarding school, pretending to be prospective parents, and on another occasion Jack introduced her to the zoologist Solly Zuckerman so that he could explain in some detail his researches into the sexual behaviour of chimpanzees.

Having learned to fly with the University Air Squadron, he and Maina kept a Gipsy Moth at the Leamington airfield. There was not much time for 'sporting his oak' – closing the door and studying – and his unctuous 'scout' explained to the visiting Baroness, when she was concerned at the restrictive size of her son's room, 'Ah, but the young Baron likes to imagine he's staying aboard his yacht.'

Despite the exhausting requirements of this social regime, Jack also found time to pursue his theatrical predilections; he had a lifelong talent for mimicry, and appeared in the OUDS 'smoker' (the dramatic society's revue) with imitations of Douglas Byng and Jack Buchanan (who was in fact a family friend), broadcast *Doctor Faustus* on radio, and played another Mephisophelean role as 'Sir Jasper Sharpe, the Prime Minister who would not die', in *Unknown Doors*, a medical satire by an Exeter undergraduate. *Isis* magazine applauded his performance, and noted 'an occasional fleeting resemblance to Conrad Veidt'. Part daredevil and part lounge lizard – with a measure of crooner admixed – he was well on the way to becoming Jack the Lad.

In the autumn of 1935, just before his last year began at Oxford, my father set out on a Grand Tour of Russia and the Far East; it was a twenty-first birthday gift from his parents. He kept a travel journal – 'Diary of a Nomad Boy' – which is one of the few extended examples of his personal writing. It is a period piece, arch in style and ingenuous in many respects (suggesting that the student sophistication was something of an act), but when it is once more dripped on to paper, here, I think it separates out to give a chromatographic impression of his personality just after coming of age. The trip – which lasted some ten weeks – sharply impressed itself on his experience of the world, for of course few young people had the opportunity to see such places first hand; and a perceptible change in his manner of self-portraiture (which is bluff and bombastic at the start) suggests that, for all the potentially spoiling advantages of his youth, there was an eager mind, receptive to wonders, keen to respond to the quirks and quiddities of human behaviour, curious about the ways of the world. In fact, I think it shows the emergence of his abiding interest in things political.

On 22 July he embarked for Holland by steamer, in the company of fellow undergraduates John Reader Harris and Jim Harmsworth. They went by train to Berlin and through Poland, and from the outset Jack saw his role as documenting their trip on film. He persisted – heroically or pig-headedly, depending on one's view – in doing this even when it was prohibited by local authorities. Confronted by plain-clothes officials for wielding his Kodak in Warsaw station, he informed them (perhaps by virtue of his pole-vaulting connections), '*Ich nicht sprichen,*' and denied having a camera. Later, when Customs sealed it up, he notes, with juvenile glee, 'but I have found a way to open it, so I can take what I want!! The fools.' In the early weeks, there is quite a bit of this playing to the gallery.

He was never happy roughing it, and there are frequent complaints about the level of hygiene of fellow travellers, disrupted sleep, and supplies running low of gardenia soap, eau-de-Cologne, and Bronco lavatory paper.

Switching to the old-style, wide-gauge railway, they arrived in Moscow. On the first day, J recorded his view of Stalin's hypocrisy – 'a man professing to be nothing more than a brother and fellow worker, living in the Kremlin off the fat of the land. The people are like children groping in the darkness.' He was impressed by the new subway system, and the claim that there is 'no unimployment' (the stridency of his nascent opinions is nicely undercut by the spelling, throughout). The three J's went for a drink in the station, realized they had no Russian money, and paid with a five-dollar bill – naturally, grasping such riches, the waiter absconded ('I shouldn't be surprised if that waiter betters himself some day'). The swaggering, late-Imperial tone was, I think, designed to bolster his own confidence; he was daunted by the vastness of Russia, the constant military presence, the peasant conditions. By the time they crossed Siberia, patronizing jokes about Ivan Foreigner are on the wane – 'All day we pass nothing but forrest, forrest, forrest, then miles of waist land . . . I wonder if the souls of the aristocrats who were murdered can be in these trees, some of them cluster together as if wispering, some droop slightly in dispair, but on the whole they stand erect keeping their silent vigil over the land that once was theirs.'

As commercial film-makers have readily established, these long railway journeys offer almost sci-fi, *Narrenschiff* opportunities for inspecting diverse folk at close quarters. Although there is remarkably – disappointingly – little lascivious behaviour on record in this journal (and he later assured me it had not been intended for anyone else to read, so it is quite likely to have been an accurate account), an exotic *femme* did catch our nomad's eye before too long. Among the polyglot 'passangers' who gestured to one another in the dining car (the Soviets travelled separately in 'hard class') was 'a real life adventuress. She has one of the loveliest faces I've set eyes on. Blue eyes, long long eyelashes a straight nose and a lovely chin. She wares a tight white silk frock embroidered in the Russian manner and has long red fingernails. We call her Shanghai Lil.' Lustfully, they watched her from afar. Less unscathed was a pretentious tobacco broker, a snob and a fantasist called Percy Clarridge, whom they decided to bait, in what J admits is childish fashion. He had Jim inform Percy that 'Jack Pistachio is the iligitimate son of the King of Italy. I told him at supper how I had received the Pope's special blessing when I kissed the holy toe on my departure for the East.'

When they reached the station in Manchuria, there was palpable relief that they could 'breathe some non-Soviet air'; they were met by a Cook's representative in a solar topee, and J was very taken by the colour of the crowds, 'picturesque in their squallor'. *En route* for Harbin and Tsingtao, there were armed guards in the corridors to repel bandit attacks, but the trio was more relaxed, and J played up once more the enterprising, accident-prone milord image, to entertain his friends. He was robbed of his trunk keys, found beetles in his chow, had to clean his teeth in lemonade. Beneath the persona is his avid enthusiasm for novelty; in Dainin he so overpaid a rickshaw wallah that the man followed him around all day, and in Port Arthur he entered a cinema and plonked the camp stool down 'between two courting natives. I appologised profusely and changed seats.'

On 7 August their ferry approached Shanghai, and no amount of posturing can disguise the youthful awe in his tone – 'Then like some magic lantern slide the mighty international settlement, one of the world's largest cities, loomed up amid the blinding waters ahead of us.' There to meet them was John Reader Harris's father, who was

Attorney-General. His black chauffeur drove them up Bubbling Spring Road to the family's villa, which was the first proper rest stop. Here, amid the country-club teas and alfresco meals, the houseboys, visiting tailors, tennis parties, dog-race meetings at the Canidrome, and the bars along the Bund, their actual lack of urbanity was gradually revealed, and partially remedied. They were 'not used to hard drinking', but did their best to keep up. 'Mr Reader Harris laid down his book, took out his eye glass and announced, "I don't feel I'm doing my duty, I must show you fellows some of the Shanghai nightlife."' So they went to the cabaret at the Paramount (where there were 'white Russian ladies'), then at five in the morning took in the Delmonte, a place the wives had always agreed they would not visit. You chose your 'filly' with whom to dance, and when it was time to leave 'like a mirical from nowhere appeared an old hag who presented us each with a bill. The dance partners worked out at fifty cents or ninepence each, a realy reasonable figure for a good figure!' He took his green-eyed Russian companion, Lena, out for dinner another night, but that seems to have been the extent of the fun.

There were more cultural matters to be explored. John's father deputed two detectives, Mr Yui and Mr Tong, to escort them around the Old City; J started to film inside a temple, and the priest stirred up a crowd of protesters so they had to retreat ('I was quite scared'). They set sail for Tienin on 29 August and thence by train for Peking. The tatty Pullman carriage was full of inconveniently loud family groups; one boy spelled out the name on J's trunk, ' "P-R-O-F-U-M-O, Mummie, what's that mean?" "I don't know", replied the mother, but made no attempt to quieten her children.'

Although he visited the Great Wall with due awe, and toured the Forbidden City (again, with cine-camera covertly in operation) and never became blasé about the Orient, it seems J enjoyed the shopping most of all. He admired the perfectionism of the Chinese – 'artists to their fingertips in everything they do' – and the workmanship in Jade Street produced several mementoes, though his major purchase was 'a marvelous caskit all carved in Imperial yellow', a cedar-wood coffin he bought for five pounds and took all the way back for his father.

The long, solo return home began on 17 September when he boarded the SS *Grant*, for Japan. The journey was enlivened by 'a party of 23 Australian girls' (I like the numerical precision), and on arrival at Kobe he bought a ticket to Kyoto, where he was bored by the profusion of temples, and on to Tokyo. He was intrigued by Japan – the chatter, the shopping districts, the clogs, the cheap cigarettes, the bloodthirsty entertainments, the new-fangled electrical tube lighting. There was a routine tour of the red-light district, and though he was too short of cash to afford the hire of a girl to film, he noted with approval their bordello licensing system: 'the country builds battleships each year with the revenue' (a decade later, he was to be in the capital with rather different views). From the train he saw the summit of Mount Fuji clear, apparently the first chance in years, and shot some footage with colour film – 'a new invention, I hope it's good.'

There now ensued a ten-day sea journey to North America. At first, he was fascinated by the onboard marvels, from his first malted milkshake to an inspection of the ice store, where he threw a frozen chicken to the floor and it shattered (not quite on a par with Sir Francis Bacon, but none the less evidence of an enquiring mind). Soon, he became fretful and bored, though he learned to play poker and mahjong; throughout this trip, he never managed to read a single book in its entirety, and literature of any sort was not to be one of his life's pleasures. One evening, he persuaded his dinner companions to pretend to be mad, so they put potatoes in the finger-bowls and 'began drinking soop through straws', rounding off the entertainment with a Mickey Mouse film. Since he was sailing second class (funds were running low), he further amused himself by 'skowling' at those on the private deck – gravitas, I'm glad to say, was never his strong suit.

On Thursday 26 September, 1935, the *Grant* crossed the meridian, and J noted, 'Today is yesterday, and yesterday is today. Tomorrow never comes. I am half the way around the world from London.' For all the excitement and novelty, he was by now looking forward to going home to his family.

On the last leg of his tour, they docked in Victoria, and he lunched at the Emperor Hotel (whether or not he glimpsed my Great-Uncle Freddie, the road sweeper, I do not know); then he caught a ferry to

Vancouver and took the train east. He was so keen to record the fall scenery that he even forswore drink so he would be awake to film the dawn colours – Banff, Calgary, Medicine Hat, all through the Rockies, then the flat farmlands, Brandon, Sidney, Winnipeg. On 5 October he arrived late at night at the Waldorf-Astoria, New York, 'And here I am, nessled down between real linen sheets in the most superb old French room in a double bed with green pyjamas on.'

Considering his later antipathy towards the country, and many things American, J was notably taken with his last port of call. In the few days he spent there, he enjoyed a visit to Radio City, saw *Top Hat*, filmed from the summit of the Empire State, had cocktails at the Rackets Club, went to the Broadway première of *Macbeth* starring Gladys Cooper, a family friend ('Gladys looks very old now' – she was all of forty-seven), danced at the El Morocco nightclub (later to be a *locus classicus* of family history), lunched on Wall Street with the chairman of the Stock Exchange, had a conducted tour of NBC, the *New York Times*, and the Police Radio Department, where he was intrigued by the way the incident room tracked its patrol cars. J had an abiding fondness for gadgets and gizmos, especially in the field of communications, so it's easy to see how the twenty-year-old regarded New York as a haven of progress, from the ticket machines on the subway to the office security systems.

Steaming back across the Atlantic, in the full luxury of the *Normandie* ('like a floating palace'), cosmopolite that he now was, he entered his verdict on the States:

> All Americans are hail fellow well met and fall over English people. Most of them are inclined to be snobby and appear brazen but I think this is because they have not much past to rely on and so won't let you forget their present prominence. A cab driver remarked to me, 'We aren't so refined as you but we sure do get there.' The Americans are great sensationalists and seem to get the relativity of the importance of things wrong.

On 14 October he arrived in Plymouth, and a number of reporters were on hand in search of anecdotes. The paternal coffin present caused consternation among customs officials; the *Evening News* quoted the Baron as saying, 'I was certainly not expecting such a gift from my son,' and J explained, 'Of course, it's not for his personal use.' Eventually, he took it by train to Banbury, and thence in the Humber home to Avon Carrow, where he was welcomed with whistles, gongs and horns. He closes his diary with a note of gratitude 'for being allowed to go on this wonderful trip. I hope I shall show how much I have benefited by the round-the-world travel of a Nomad Boy. As I said at the start, so I finish – I am indeed a lucky Boy. Thanks. Jack Profumo.'

Like a bear with its ill-formed cub, I may have licked this document into such a shape that it seems unrelentingly flippant: certainly it does not speak of high seriousness in many places, but there can be little doubt of the journey's formative influence upon my father's hitherto (understandably) insular horizons.

It does not appear that any especial efforts were undertaken to make up for time lost academically, as his Oxford Finals approached. Digs above the barber's shop in smart Beaumont Street were shared with Valerian Wellesley and Val Duncan, with most of the time spent in sporting pursuits. Midnight oil was being burnt, but not in the study of soil samples or crop-planting programmes for the colonies. By his own account, a shameful incident occurred as the practical part of the examinations impended. It was rumoured that the chief assistant in the agriculture laboratory (Benham, by name) used to lay out the question papers on the benches the night before, and that, for a small consideration, he might chance to cast his eye over the sheets while arranging them, and thus narrow down the necessary scope of revision. A fiver duly passed between hands, and a little later the anxious student received a handwritten list of topics.

J took his place quite confidently the next morning – he was seated between an immensely tall Kenyan man, and a nun – but, when he turned over the paper, none of the predicted questions was on it. Benham, of course, never did have prior access to these papers, and perpetrated this scam each year, safe in the knowledge that there was no possible forum for legitimate complaint. J. D. Profumo, of Brasenose College, was awarded a Special Pass degree – rather like one of those rosettes you get just for participating in a gymkhana, but never qualifying even as a runner-up. According to a contemporary at Christ Church, at Jack's 'going down' party there was a mini-orchestra playing calypsos, and dons performed sketches that were specially written skits on themselves: 'Nobody else in the university could have managed it,' he recalled admiringly, almost seventy years later.

When he graduated in the summer of 1936, my father had already determined that his would be a political career. Although (unlike most aspiring Oxford politicos) he did not spend much of his time there debating at the Union, during his last year as a student he had already begun to work for the Conservative Party, canvassing and campaigning in London on behalf of the Member for East Fulham, the Hon. W. W. 'Bill' Astor – 'not a very nice man, but I didn't know that at the time.' (In view of the subsequent Cliveden imbroglios, it is of some interest to learn that my father recalled Bill's 'fondness for lovely girls – he used to go in for clothes models', and on one occasion, 'when I was still almost in short trousers, he introduced me to a couple of loose ladies who lived in some flats, on the pretext of going canvassing.')

Politics was no dilettante interest; he determined to succeed where two previous generations of Profumo men had not, and there was still a lingering ethos in this pre-war period that political service was something you owed to your country if you were in a position to offer it, and had the means to do so (more a case of *tempora mutantur, et nos mutamur in illis*). By July 1937, J had spent three months at the League of Nations in Geneva, and then became chairman of the Lillie Ward Conservative Association of Astor's constituency; the MP described his protégé as 'a young man of exceptional personality and brilliance, and I am sure before long we will see him in the House of Commons, where I know he will make his mark' (that proved true enough). In December of that year he became, at twenty-two, the youngest man on the Conservative Central Office's list of prospective parliamentary candidates, and he made his first political pronouncement in public, telling the *West London and Fulham Gazette* – who quoted him as 'Mr J. D. Perofuma – that, however unpopular, the Government's policy of non-intervention regarding the Spanish Civil War was correct: 'It would have been criminal to have jeopardized the life of a single man in Britain by interfering in a war which had nothing to do with this country.' He went on to become chairman of the East Fulham Conservative Association, and ran the Warwickshire Division of the

Junior Imperial League – the party's youth wing, to whom he recommended the oath, 'What I can do, I ought to do; and what I ought to do, I will do.' He was certainly building up a head of steam.

By the time the Chief Whip, David Margesson, came to spend the weekend at Avon Carrow in the autumn of 1938, and arranged for him to have an interview with the Chairman of the party, J had already cut his political teeth. (Feelings ran high at those Fulham meetings, and when Herbert Williams, MP for South Croydon, came to speak he actually had a tooth knocked out by a heckler.) In March 1939, he was adopted as prospective candidate for Kettering, a seat held for the previous eight years by J. F. Eastwood KC, who intimated that he would not be standing at the next election. When he resigned from his Fulham post, J was praised by Mrs Fraser of the women's branch: 'There had never been a chairman of the association who had taken so much interest in the women's branch as Mr Profumo.'

In a magazine profile of the time, J described his likes as 'Beauty, Laughing, Choc Bars, Working People'; the dislikes included 'Malicious Gossip, Trousers on Women, and Whisky.' He played up to the image of having been widely travelled (fair enough), speaking on economic conditions abroad, and foreign policy ('Are the persecutors of the Jews fit rulers of native races?' he fulminated, over Hitler's demand for the return of certain former colonies). That month, he told the *Northampton Chronicle* that the world was witnessing 'the beginning of the end of the Nazi regime'. He advocated conscription and raising the old-age pension to one pound per week, but felt there was not going to be any war. (For him, there almost was not: piloting their Fairchild back from Italy with Maina, he was forced by bad weather to touch down at Lympne, where a mechanic discovered that all but one of the bolts were missing from their propeller and they would have had just minutes of flying time left. 'Phew,' he said to the *Daily Mirror*. 'That cloud certainly had a silver lining.') We have been quite fortunate with our family landings.

———•———

Jack Profumo's prediction of the collapse of the Nazi regime proved a little premature, and in June 1939 he signed up as a Territorial with

74

the 1st Northamptonshire Yeomanry, which formed part of the 20th Light Armoured Brigade. On 1 July he was gazetted as a Second Lieutenant. In August, they went under canvas at Houghton Down camp, in Hampshire, where the officers' mess included three peers and three prospective Tory MPs ('a blinking House of Commons,' reported the *Mirror*). In November, based at RAF Upwood, near Huntingdon, there was instruction in aerial navigation and recon- naissance photography, and flying lessons on Blenheims and Ansons, but J wrote that there was little equipment beyond Bren guns, and the other officers seemed very old – 'I can't make out if they wear the ribbons of the Crimea or the Peninsular.' By December he was at Bovington in Dorset, driving Mk4 Light Tanks and Cruiser A13s. It was still slightly amateurish, knockabout stuff, though this phase of military experience was to be short-lived.

One day, Brigadier Evelyn Fanshawe summoned the Second 'Leftootie' to his tent, and told him he was wanted in Downing Street. 'I thought they were pulling my leg,' he recalled, but it seemed the Prime Minister had heard that J was thinking of withdrawing from the Kettering by-election because of his new military commitments, and was keen to dissuade him. He duly presented himself for an audience with Neville Chamberlain – 'I was scared out of my wits' – and agreed to continue, on three conditions: 'I could fight the election in uniform, I could return to my regiment even if I won, and I would receive assistance from experienced agents from other seats – I knew I needed all the help I could get.' This was duly agreed. On the way back from his interview, in a state of blissful relief, he boarded a bus, heard the air-raid siren, and hurriedly donned his gas mask; the pas- sengers gave him curious looks, since it was the All Clear.

Polling Day was set for 6 March 1940. As it was wartime, the Labour Party had agreed a 'truce', whereby they would not oppose the return of the new candidate, but there was some other opposition. Fred Gould JP, who hailed from Somerset, where he had already been an MP, put himself forward for the Co-operative and Labour interest, supported by the National Union of Boot and Shoe Operatives. Mr J. A. Whitehead (a noted fruit-grower from Bedfordshire) intended to stand as an Agriculturalist. Both eventually withdrew, but at the eleventh hour Labour nominated Councillor William Ross of Corby, a Glaswegian steel dresser who stood as a Workers' and Pensioners' Anti-War candidate.

By now a lieutenant, J fought a khaki election, with an indecently flamboyant fur-collared coat over his uniform. 'I am not in the least bit frightened,' he announced, 'because I realize that I stand for national unity.' He addressed over ninety meetings, and was dubbed by the *Daily Express* 'Lieutenant John ("Speedy and Just Victory") Profumo'. 'The eyes of the world are upon the Kettering by-election,' he assured his audiences, later warming to this theme with 'A vote against me is just another bullet in a Nazi rifle. Dr Goebbels is watching us.' This rhetoric was ideal for the times, and the claim was not entirely bombastic: Lord Haw-Haw on the radio scoffed at the British being reduced to putting up a 'boy' for Parliament, and described how his two sisters sat nearby in their Warwickshire castle, wearing fur coats and eating butter (a ludicrous claim, naturally). To the policies of Bill Ross, J retorted, 'I hear some cry "Stop the War," but the war will stop of itself when right is proved stronger than might, when the right to live in security has been restored to the homeless, when the refugee can smile again, when persecution has made way for toleration and when God rules again in the hearts of men.'

This was a leap year, and the *Daily Mirror* reported that the Tory candidate received a mystifying telegram: 'Feel unable to wait another four years. Will you marry me? Love Fifi', but continued that 'He has no knowledge of any person of that name'. Quipped the *Northamptonshire Evening Telegraph*, 'Fifi may even be an old-age pensioner, who knows?' (I have been unable to establish the identity of this correspondent).

There was a small turn-out of 38 per cent, counting was completed in forty-five minutes, and the result was overwhelming: with a majority of 11,298 John Profumo became, at twenty-five, the youngest MP in the House. The *Daily Mail* observed, 'The Profumos have been trying to get into Parliament for 50 years,' and Miss Leonard in the Avon Dassett post office ran out of greetings telegrams.

On 12 March 1940, he took his seat and was sworn, with Captain Margesson and Solicitor-General Sir Terence O'Connor acting as sponsors. It was unusual for a minister to introduce a new member to the House, but O'Connor had been an Inner Temple colleague of the Baron, who – despite having been admitted recently to a nursing home – was able to witness proceedings from the Distinguished Strangers' Gallery, and to hear the applause as his son took the oath in uniform. He died on the twenty-seventh of that month, officially from 'uraemia and chronic nephritis', though the family view is that he had cancer. He was sixty-one.

So began what J called 'this curious double life', as a junior officer and an MP (with an annual salary of £600) in a House 'full of serving members past their best, some virtually carrying flywhisks'. Nobody dared hold a general election, and Chamberlain was anxious that J should not look like a mere political creature, so he was instructed to attend a certain number of debates. In the event, his first ever vote in the House – before he had even made his maiden speech – was on 8 May, when he was one of thirty-three Tory MPs who sided with the Opposition (rather than abstaining) in a vote of confidence in the Government's policy over withdrawing support for Norway. J felt this decision had 'reflected badly on the prestige of the British nation' and was proving 'terribly bad for morale'. Fellow 'rebels' who shared such views included Leo Amery, Bob Boothby, Quintin Hogg and Harold Macmillan; the result was such a small majority for the Government (eighty-one) that, although Chamberlain was not forced to resign, he took the hint, and made way for Churchill. The old guard remained faithful to him, however (he continued to lead the party), and their reaction to such betrayal was furious.

'It was not easy to walk into the Opposition lobby,' said my father, underplaying his courage. 'I remember Walter Elliot, who was a minister, spitting on my shoe as we were waiting in line. In the House.' For several months afterwards, he wrote, 'Many faces still scowl at me here. Never mind. "This above all: to thine own self be true," that's my motto.' It is reported that next day Margesson called him 'an utterly contemptible little shit', and said he would be ashamed of what he had done for the rest of his life. (In the event, J became the last surviving Tory rebel, and on 7 May 2003, Frank Field led a motion in the House that it 'publicly salutes a gallant and honourable gentleman to whom this country owes a huge debt of gratitude.')

He delivered his maiden speech on 20 August, rising from his seat at 5.21 p.m. and speaking without notes. It was a veritable, patriotic tub-thumper, that appealed to religious conviction and courage ('Decisive Elliment', as it appears in his outline notes), with the rousing culmination, 'While we breathe, we live! While we live, we fight! And when we fight, we win.' There were prolonged cheers, and the press reported it as a stirring and noteworthy début, 'quite an astonishing performance'. J was soon made Secretary of the Serving Members' Committee (which entailed regular meetings with the Prime Minister), and Hansard records him as quite active putting questions to the House during the year.

The Speaker did not recognize my father's newly inherited title – 5th Baron Profumo – so he decided, in the interests of simplicity, to renounce it entirely. The surname alone was sufficient to cause confusion, however: that November (according to the *Evening Standard*) during a luncheon at the Over-Seas League for officers of the Czech forces, an English girl spotted his place-name and complimented him, very slowly – 'You – really – speak – English – very – well – for – a – Czech.'

As well as being the 'baby of the House', the Member for Kettering was also learning the rudiments of soldiering at Upwood, Cavenham, Newmarket and Park Hatch. In 1940, particular attention was being paid to the German use of motorcycle units in invasion tactics, and as part of No. 5 Troop it was Lieutenant Profumo's duty to learn motorcycle manoeuvres along with Corporal Jackson, Lance-Corporal Rawlings and Trooper Wright. They were billeted at Brackley in Berkshire during this training period, and some of his platoon were trophy-winning stunt riders: 'They were cock-a-hoop at being under my command, constantly ragging me, as I had never even ridden a motorbike. So I wasn't entirely in control of the situation. One day, in great secrecy, a VIP was coming to watch a special exercise – other troops were brought in to make the manoeuvres more impressive, because in case Germans ever arrived in England, we were to be the main defence.' J set off at the head of his men, but soon lost his way on the map: 'I realized I had the whole British Army following me, plus the press corps, so I had to make it look like deliberate subterfuge.' There were several accidents – his lifelong friend Paddy Corbett, blithely following the leader, came off his machine when J suddenly changed direction, lost two front teeth, and wore a plate for the rest of his days. It transpired that the VIP was His Majesty the King, who actually congratulated J over lunch: 'We had to go back to barracks then, at any rate, because there was no more petrol for the bikes.'

Brackley marked the enjoyable time of the war, before he was sent overseas. It was here that one fellow officer landed himself good and proper in the mulligatawny when his young wife came down to stay for the weekend, as newly allowed under GHQ regulations; he had been carrying on a little with other women, and his batman – in civilian life a roughish coalman – was so habituated to waking previous female companions in the billet that he greeted the officer's wife with a desultory nudge on the shoulder, and the usual line, 'Come on, now, miss, it's time for you to be getting back to the village.'

Partly due to his civilian experience in flying, J emerged from all these exercises as an Air Intelligence Liaison Officer with 241 Squadron RAF, and in May 1941, having served at Henlow and Bottisham, he became a General Staff Officer, was promoted to Captain, and peeled off from his regiment. In the House, he urged further co-operation between the services, and proposed the appointment of a Supreme Commander-in-Chief for all home-based forces. A brisk and snappy presence at constituency meetings, he also answered some three thousand letters in his first year as an MP, and excited public opinion by suggesting that too many people were sheltering behind their reserved occupations. Robustly, he advised anyone capturing downed German pilots not to treat them with tea and kindness, as this raised their morale prior to interrogation. On leave that June (despite being the proud possessor of a 'Hundred Mile an Hour' Invicta car), he wanted to see how difficult it was for ordinary serving men to move around, so hitch-hiked the 120 miles home; it took twelve lifts, but he reported never having to wait more than a quarter of an hour before someone obliged.

The enchanting actress Frances Day was a girlfriend at this time, and with her he wrote and staged an entertainment in aid of the Services

Charities, a revue of sketches and songs entitled 'Night and Day'. This was performed at the Arts Theatre, Cambridge, in April 1942, to promote 'togetherness' between the two 'junior' Services; the gimmick was that for each of the four performances one-half of the cast, orchestra, and audience would be comprised of Army, and the other of RAF, personnel. Captain Profumo naturally did a turn, and indeed by June he had been promoted to Major. But these home-based jollifications soon came to an end. In November it was announced that he was 'serving overseas', and his colleague Mr Spencer Summers (MP for Northampton) was undertaking parliamentary work in his absence. The rehearsals were over, and it was time for action.

———•———

It is sometimes hard to appreciate, in today's 'shoot and tell' culture of military reminiscence, that my father's generation was notoriously reluctant to discuss openly its experiences of war; this may have been some sort of warrior's code of silence, at odds with the modern notion of military service, and there was certainly an old-fashioned idea that they were all in it together, and you should not complain if you had survived. When I was a schoolboy, I was aware that a number of dads turned up with an eyepatch, or an empty sleeve pinned across the jacket or, in at least one case, alarming facial disfigurement despite the best handiwork of pioneering surgeon Sir Archie McIndoe, injuries they had received a mere ten years before their sons were born. I knew my father had been a soldier, and – this was around the time I fell in thrall to Commando comic books – I naturally asked him for grisly details ('Did you kill anyone?' 'Were you ever wounded?' 'Did you see Hitler?'). None were forthcoming, and indeed he never really told anecdotes about that period until the questions came – at a safer distance – from grandsons.

In a series of pocket-sized Asprey's diaries, J kept a daily record of his wartime movements, from 30 October 1942 until the end of 1945. They are all inscribed in pencil, the minimal space requiring a Lilliputian script that varies according to the daily vagaries of evening light, tiredness, and alcohol consumption. While they do not offer many dramatic revelations concerning military strategy, these entries are immediate and free from artifice. The diaries were never kept with an eye to posterity, and it was only after I saw them in his desk drawer a decade ago that I was aware of their existence, and became the first person other than their author ever to read them.

These modest quotidian bulletins comprise an *olla podrida* of political drive, boredom, a concern for creature comforts, an interest in all types and estates of men from top brass to captured prisoners, a devotion to family, nostalgia for the *status quo ante*, and details of an enterprising amatory life – elements not unique to him but, taken together, nicely indicative of his states of mind. I was struck in particular by his sympathy for his fellow men (not a trait obvious from his earlier days, but something that was to surface later), and, cognately, his steadfast Christian belief. 'How many wretched men are bearing a cross today,' he writes on one Good Friday. For all his canniness, my father was not an intellectual, and his faith was of the uncomplicated, Anglican, 'Tory Party at Prayer' variety – albeit with a vehement mistrust of the Catholic Church. Throughout his life, religion was a genuine source of succour to him, and he always said his prayers each night kneeling beside his bed, like some dutiful boy, until his final infirmity prevented it.

'Greatest difficulty getting my massive luggage into cabin,' he noted, on what was to be the first day of 'Operation Torch'. Once aboard the *Strathmore* and sailing from the north of Scotland in rough, foggy weather, the initial feeling was one of adventure – 'Invasion starts at one o'clock tomorrow morning! Rule Britannia' (7 November). *En route* to the Mediterranean J suffered from orchitis (an inflamed testicle) and the lack of booze, but had somehow managed to get his own batman, Private J. W. Bryan, aboard, even though he was not properly on the fighting list (they were still exchanging Christmas cards in 2005).

Under the direction of Eisenhower – who until then had no experience of command in battle – American forces had landed at Rabat and Casablanca, on the Atlantic seaboard of French North Africa, while the British sailed via Gibraltar to land amphibiously at Oran and Algiers. J arrived at the latter, and at first it was 'just like a pre-war holiday', with exotic seaside smells and dinner in a restaurant

(Randolph Churchill – a recurrent feature of the African tranche of the diaries – was characteristically rude to the waiter).

In the battle for Tunis, which the Axis heavily reinforced with several armoured divisions, the First Army had to cross some mountainous terrain through snow and rain, and there were serious transport problems as they approached the front. Troubleshooting mechanical glitches became a familiar refrain, along with the occasionally shambolic lack of co-ordination – one convoy overshot, and almost went through, the enemy lines (18 November). Along with Major John Hare, J was in charge of quite a small unit called Army Air Support Control, which dealt with tactical reconnaissance ('Tack R's') and co-ordinated requests for air support, though at this stage they were only working with a handful of squadrons. In common with most troops, they felt under-staffed and ill-supplied, and there was a constant element of improvisation, but it was a task involving considerable variety, and my father's personal flying experience was of some help in mediating between the Services (he sported wings on his uniform, though I'm not certain he was formally entitled to them).

Before that November was out, we have his first comment that 'the USA are hopeless'. J was to spend three years working, with increasing closeness, alongside American forces, and although he admired several of their leaders ('Blood and Guts' Patton and General Mark Clark, especially, for the physical example they set) he could never tolerate what he saw as the slovenly behaviour of many of their troops, who cut corners, were under-disciplined, and showed no subtlety or style – 'not properly house-trained' was his semi-hyperbolic verdict.

On Saturday 5 December, during the advance along the Tébourba road in foul and muddy weather during a blackout, J was 'told at short notice to report to 5 Company. I went ahead on motorcycle in dark and ran into a tank transporter. Bust or cracked shoulder and squashed foot. A very close one.' His bike had skidded, and was run over by the German vehicle, which fortunately kept going; he was fired upon, but escaped into a ditch. He refused to go to hospital at that stage, and phlegmatically recorded, 'First whisky and soda since arrival. Slept on ADC bed. MO strapped me up in morning. Crushed foot cut leg and nose and cracked shoulder. Vv lucky escape' (6 December). Later, with a collar-bone and broken shoulder in plaster, he was walking on sticks for three weeks. On the 8th, they arrived at the monastery of Thibar (where the liqueur Thibarine was made), and his spiritual level was raised: 'Monks very kind and gave me lunch – pâté, vol au vent, chicken, meringues and tangerines and endless wine. Bought 24 champ. 6 red and 4 brandy.' Newly fortified, it was perhaps timely that the troops then withdrew to regroup.

According to his New Year letter to the Kettering constituents, J reported that – without disclosing his whereabouts – he was dwelling in a tent beneath a cactus bush, being dive-bombed and using his hunting horn as an air-raid siren. On Christmas Day he held a service under a haystack, and then the officers enjoyed a dinner 'in the field' that included *rhum flambée* omelettes, Lafite '05, and a rendition of 'Eskimo Nell'.

The final push for Tunis, and its aftermath, show a typical mixture of contrasting crises and shenanigans. One day he was off duck-shooting with John Hare – 'I had tommy-gun, great fun' (8 February 1943) – then he was typing a letter back to Spencer Summers to request from the Commons an airmail service for the North African troops. On the 11th, he witnessed the interrogation of '8 Wop and one Jerry POW. Fascinating method of doing it. I asked Wop if he knew Raymondo [a socialite friend of J's from Taormina] as he came from Sicily. He said he hated the Duce as he sent him out to fight.' The German was a tank commander, and they gave him an especially hard time, because his was a new type of tank. They made him dig his own grave. 'My heart bled for the German, who kept refusing to tell on his friends and was subjected to much devilry. HE won. Well done him. I admire the Germans the more for him.' (It is said the prisoner was eventually flown back to London, where a general effectively debriefed him over dinner at the Savoy.)

J's immediate liaison was with the 6th Armoured Division, and he noted that they went into Tunis 'like schit through hole' (5 May); on the 13th, with the captured city 'v disorganized and full of drunk soldiery' he saw General Von Armin, Commander of Army Group Afrika, who had just surrendered along with some 200,000 prisoners. When Churchill came to address the troops in the amphitheatre at Carthage (1 June) several papers photographed J photographing the Prime Minister; also 'Lost my hat. Talked to Anthony Eden.' He obtained the keys to the bathing pavilion of the Bey of Tunis's summer palace, and proceeded to help organize a victory dance there, which went on until three in the morning (5 June); he was granted an audience with 'the Bay', 'then we were shown all round Pallace by his three sons, including the harem, which was very odd' (though perhaps not so odd as some of the Harrovian spelling).

The first significant *amour de voyage* involved a girl named Janine Tixier Vignancour, whose husband was in the Resistance. J's first impression was that she was *soignée* and intensely desirable – 'So smart, I must say. I could eat her' (16 June). Soon they were enjoying intimate dinners – 'Boy, was the moon full' – and then spending almost all his spare time together. There were happy excursions shopping and swimming, and lazy luncheons *à deux*, but then a notorious fly came slamdunking into the exotic ointment. On 4 July Randolph Churchill returned on a flying visit, drank a bottle of J's scotch, and took an evident shine to Janine. She reported that 'he had visited her and had been very pressing'. The next evening, Jack and Randolph – two very determined characters, when it came to womankind, and both with velvet on their antlers – had an incandescent altercation (the ambient heat actually being 105 degrees could not have helped), and the Prime Minister's son appeared to back down. On 7 August he was at it again, though: 'Randolph admitted he tried another attack on Janine. I had a terrible row with him, and after he apologized abjectly. We all bathed and I lost my lovely signet ring in the sea.'

His swashbuckling comportment did not make Randolph a welcome visitor socially:

> He was great fun to be with, but I'm afraid I must say he was a poisoned chalice. He had charm and charisma, but he was very dangerous. He loved intrigue, that was his milieu. He was his own worst enemy. He used to vent his fury if people didn't agree with him. He was spoiled by his father, who followed his every move, sending messages in cipher.

Right: Commander Robert Hobson RN (Retd.), my maternal grandfather, and his pet spider monkey (*c.*1923)

Below: My mother, aged three, in her first role, as the 'Little Mother', (1920)

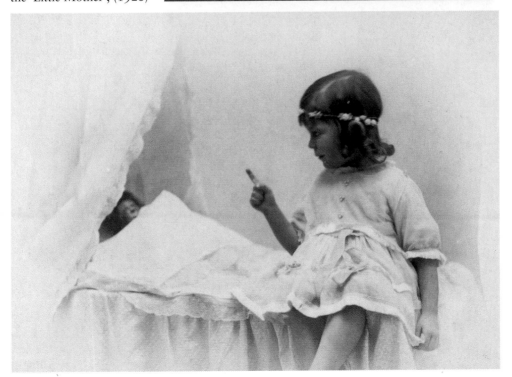

The Picturegoer Weekly
No. 207 (New Series), Vol. 4   Registered at the G.P.O. as a Newspaper   May 11, 1935

THRILLS! THRILLS!! THRILLS!!!

PICTUREGOER

2ᵈ
WEEKLY

Valerie
HOBSON

Left: Valerie Hobson's first front-cover portrait, promoting *Werewolf of London,* (11 May 1935)

Below: Boris Karloff as the Monster (*right*) and my mother as the wife of his inventor, in *Bride of Frankenstein* (1935)

Above: Laurence Olivier as the pilot Tony McVane, and Valerie as his girlfriend Kay Lawrence, in *Q Planes* (1939)

Right: John Mills (Pip) with Valerie (Estella) in a scene from *Great Expectations* (1946)

Left: One of a series of portraits of my mother taken during the Blitz (1940)

Below: As the imperious Edith D'Ascoyne, Valerie is questioned during a murder trial in the House of Lords (*Kind Hearts and Coronets*, 1949)

Top right: Tony Havelock-Allan (*left*) and Rex Harrison at a party in New York (1945)

Below right: Matthew Smith (*left*) and Augustus John discussing one of several portraits Smith painted of Valerie, in his London studio (1948)

Top left: Dinner at the Royal Command Film Show (1949). *Left to right:* Tony Havelock-Allan, Valerie, Noël Coward, Olive Bailey (chatelaine of Leeds Castle), and David Margesson MP

Below left: Valerie Hobson inspects the troops on a visit to Bromley on behalf of the Conservative candidate Harold Macmillan during an election campaign in the 1940s

Right: The first photograph taken of my parents together: dancing in fancy dress at the Chelsea Arts Club Ball, Royal Albert Hall, New Year's Eve, 1947. They were married exactly seven years later

Below: Herbert Lom and Valerie sign autographs outside the Theatre Royal, Drury Lane, after a performance of *The King and I*, (October 1953)

Left: Valerie and Jack in a nightclub (1952). I believe this is El Morocco in New York, where my mother was spotted dancing by the composer Richard Rodgers, in November of that year

Below: Jack prepares to carry his bride over the threshold of their home at Chester Terrace, London, after their wedding on New Year's Eve, 1954

It was a freakish position for Randolph – no wonder Winston was concerned for his safety, and the fear of kidnap. Although it was foolhardy, for instance, he jumped into Yugoslavia.

Randolph was a remorseless tease, and often picked on John Hare – he was my father's superior, but they were close colleagues (and remained so all through their political careers). Although the more reserved John was temperamentally different from extrovert Jack, the latter was protective of his scrupulous, diminutive friend, whom the garrulous Churchill *fils* 'taunted as Mister Hare; it was terribly painful for him'. Randolph was to show his own true colours of loyalty towards my family one day, but the general feeling in the desert was that they had a sufficiency of troubles without his breezy presence.

Years before I ever started writing this book, I was lolling on the banks of a salmon river with my father, chatting about family matters as we sipped from his hip-flask, and, in a moment of fairly unprecedented directness, I asked if he had had any children apart from me. Nothing specific had prompted this, nor, frankly, was it a question that had been festering away in the mulch heap of my imagination. It seemed theoretical, but he replied yes, he thought there might have been a wartime baby, a boy, in North Africa. I had let so much glide away between us, aired but unexamined, in the best interests of *politesse* and dignity, that for the time being I consigned that mentally to the stream, along with other, copious jetsam. There are times when you don't especially want to ponder in your heart the sex-lives of your parents, and, as far as I'm concerned, a fishing trip is one of them.

So, in 2005, I asked him about his beloved Janine. It was how our interviews often went.

'You did once tell me you thought a girlfriend of yours had had a child during the war, in North Africa.'

'Did I?'

'Yes. Was it her, I wonder?'

'It might have been.'

'That's not much help, to be honest.'

'No.'

85

'Well, could you possibly – conceivably – answer me this: did you have an illegitimate son, to your knowledge, in Tunisia?'

'I think you're right. She was the only possible girl I could have found out about. I was very fond of her. It might have been, because she was in a very difficult position. She was married to a person in the Resistance. She did have a baby, but I'm not sure it was by me. It all got muffled up, in the end.'

'Did you see her again?'

'Yes, afterwards in London. She stayed at the Connaught, so I dug her out, but it was embarrassing for her, because her husband was there too.'

After the war, he did see her little boy; in 1946 and 1948 he seems to have revisited his lady-love of those years, yet again, but then my trail goes cold – until a sympathetic letter written during 1963.

'She wasn't my usual type of girl, at all. She looked like a governess, that sort of thing. She had a little hat.'

'Operation Husky', the amphibious invasion of Sicily, began on 9 July 1943; it included the largest seaborne operation in history (covering over a hundred miles of coast) following a large-scale aerial bombardment of the Italian 6th Army and General Hube's two Panzer divisions. After his unit had refitted and moved to Tripoli, J finally flew in a parachute plane to Sicily on 14 August, just three days before the island fell. He later wrote to his constituents of 'the sullen, blazing heat, and defeated, hungry people wrapped in a mantle of war'. (Those months of unprotected exposure to the desert and Mediterranean sun caused skin cancer in later life, as it did for so many of the troops.) He collected his orders on the 25th: he was to land on the mainland with forty men and ten vehicles of the Royal Armoured Corps, as part of the 5th Army, a joint Anglo-American force under the command of General Alexander and the stylish Mark Clark. Their spot was Salerno, near the Greek ruins of Paestum, and they finally arrived on the third day of the landings, 11 September.

In Clark's words, 'Operation Avalanche' was 'a near disaster'; they had not been expecting extensive opposition, but the Germans had received advance intelligence and were ready for them with five divisions. 'Landed Amber Roger about midday after eight attempts', runs the diary, 'and a very narrow escape by self when two men by me blown up by mines.' Amidst the heaviest shelling he was ever to encounter, J threw himself into the undergrowth, and eventually made his way to the RAF assembly area and established radio contact with John Hare. 'Heavy 25-pounder shelling all night. Terrible insects. Germans V close. Situation sticky.'

From Salerno, the 5th Army pressed on for Naples, reaching it in early October; but they had suffered twelve thousand casualties, seven thousand of them British. J was promoted to Lieutenant-Colonel (he was twenty-eight), and later Mentioned in Dispatches – 'which I suppose is quite nice!' (21 October) – and was appointed to Alexander's staff as Head of Air Branch. This involved co-ordinating all air problems relating to ground forces under 'Alex' (who was Eisenhower's deputy within the 15th Army Group); they were based at Bari, where J soon acquired a caravan that he customized with carpets and lamps. Alex liked to maintain as compact and mobile an HQ as possible, which afforded J frequent opportunities of working personally with a man he came to admire almost unreservedly (he also took a number of photographs of him in the field). 'He was a real soldier, a real gentleman. He had excellent manners, and never took the credit for anything. And the greatest thing he ever did? It was to command Monty.' It was to his spirit of generosity that J responded, and to Alex's occasionally mischievous nature – neither of these traits for which Monty was renowned, and I can't imagine my father ever prospering on the staff of a non-smoking teetotaller. (Monty's relations with that other martinet, Patton, were not helped by the fact that the American was a smoker of some commitment.)

In December, Clark cracked on with the 5th Army west of the Apennines, but the advance was perilous and slow, and they were still a long way short of Rome. This was the most exhausting phase of the war for J, and he wrote repeatedly of the difficulty of the terrain and 'this bloody, bloody weather'. Kesselring was now in command of the German troops, and there was clearly going to be a prolonged campaign. On a visit to Kettering, just before Christmas, our MP (toting a Luftwaffe briefcase) stressed to his constituents that it was imperative Germany suffered a military defeat, with no soft negotiations for peace. (A year later, he was wisely to modify this stance: 'Terms must be harsh, remembering as we must do the terrible crimes Germany has committed. But we have got to give the Germans something to look forward to, other than clinging to Nazi doctrines.') By most accounts, J was a good soldier – conscientious, full of stamina, and with a keen eye for detail – but however embroiled he was in the fighting, he did not forget the importance of a political pronouncement.

The major plan during January 1944 was for 'Operation Shingle', the strike for the heart of Italy. The idea was to land behind the Gustav Line at Anzio, and then push on north to Rome. It was the start of a frenetic period of activity for J, though throughout the campaign there are diary glimpses that suggest the flip side to the harassed man of action – graphic moments (he was a competent water-colourist as well as a photographer) that serve to italicize the fears and frustration elsewhere.

> The day is crisp and sunny. I walked along the shore. So peaceful. The sea flat and calm. Little coloured fishing smacks hovering around. The clear blue water lapping against the long flat rocks that stick out to sea. Brown skinned men sitting around doing nothing. Coloured carts. Women feeding babies in the sun. White horses. So nostalgic and peaceful. I nearly cried. Then I returned to the war and found the air plan for Shingle had gone wrong. (12 January)

His task was becoming increasingly complicated, and there were some serious reversals of fortune in the air; the first onslaught on Monte Cassino had begun, and J accompanied Alex to watch the air strikes ('General Alex came to look at Air Map and asked me a question and I didn't know the answer. Big scowl!!!' (6 February) With a degree of self-discipline impressive under such circumstances, J always gave up cigarettes and alcohol for the (shortest) month of February, so he was especially 'tense and nervy'; however, the pressure was having a cumulative effect: 'Feeling depressed, no end in sight. Itching to start politics again. Also I seem to be changing a bit and becoming arrogant. Must grip.' (13 March) The gung-ho patriotism at the start

of 'Torch' had of course long since evaporated, and the newly intro-
spective tone is mirrored by the lean, tired physiognomy J shows in
photographs from this stage of the campaign.

The foul weather was hampering air efforts over Cassino, where the
third battle was about to begin. It was thought that the Germans had
occupied the monastery there, and Alex was determined to put the
safety of his men above the value of any buildings (however sacrosanct)
so he authorized their bombardment. 'I wouldn't like to be in Cassino
tomorrow,' wrote J (14 March), 'all the heavens will open up. My God!'
Then, 'A memorable day. Cassino show. Up at 0530 and went and
watched from OP with Alex, Anderson, Cannon . . . Bombing erratic.
2,000 tons dropped, some right next to us. Saw bombs come out and
shouted but even if they'd been nearer we couldn't have done anything
anyway. Anderson put on his steel hat. I hope we'll have Mont. Cassino
tomorrow. But tomorrow never comes!' In the event, there were no
Germans in the monastery, and as soon as the bombardment subsided
their paratroops had no compunction about occupying the rubble and
digging in. There was a fierce push by ground forces – including a
New Zealand division *inter alia* – and many casualties. J felt the BBC
was guilty of 'terrible exaggeration' about the ruinous extent of the
bombing, though eventually it proved decisive.

Although restless and run down (he had to have an operation to
remove an abscess from his nose) J's duties meant he flew quite regularly to visit various operational centres. In January, he had been in
Algiers training French officers in new warfare tactics (and later
revisiting Janine), and in early May he went to Cairo for meetings at
the US air base. From this trip derived his nickname of 'The
Professor', because when he arrived there was no transport to meet
him as per arrangement: they had apparently been on the lookout for
some visiting Balkan dignitary by the name of Prof. Umo. His entries
for these flying visits suggest he had not lost his appetite for parties,
though – 'Drinking kummel at a girl's house', 'they took me home,
Thank God', 'I must admit to being a shade tired' – and in Cairo there
was much merriment with at least one officer's wife, then a lady
named Sofie 'in a falouka until 2 am'. Sprawled on the futtocks, our
Professor of Forces' liaison was perhaps developing a nautical bent.

The battle for Rome began in May 1944, and the bombing was intensive ('216 tons bombs on Kesselring,' he notes on the 12th). The 5th Army was now advancing so rapidly that he thought they might have to be supplied by air. 'And so the battle progresses and the CGS smiles and Alex said looking at the map, "Well, I must say that *is* good."' The paperwork was proving onerous to J (it always was) but still he found it increasingly hard to delegate: 'Can't leave anything to my subordinates. I suppose I work them too hard and don't let them have any fun, as I do most things myself.' He was a perfectionist, but he was also tired and homesick (though perhaps not as ineluctably as the beleaguered John Hare, who had been shot in the thigh by a black American sentry on night duty, mistaken for a spy).

Rome fell to the 5th Army on 4 June ('The Americans were allowed to take Rome, it was all political'). 'So battles are won on the playing-fields of Eton [a reference to that school's sports day, the Fourth of June] but by Old Harrovians [viz. Alex]. How wonderful to think of the first City of Europe to be liberated, and how much nearer this brings us to the peace and home and all one loves. Good night yesterday and Welcome Tommorrow'.

They had to move on towards Florence, but Alex – as he had feared he might – now lost seven divisions to 'Operation Dragoon' (the invasion of southern France) and his next phase, 'Operation Anvil' was therefore even tougher to plan. J's branch was expanded, an extra major and captain being added, and they moved to a new lakeside camp. On one of his many shopping forays to the capital (he always had a knack for spotting home-style comforts) J obtained chairs, tables, a fan, and an escritoire for his caravan; he also engaged the services of a local Italian to create a rock garden, with a fig tree and a fountain, and a little cellar to prevent his precious stock of Lacryma Christi red wine from spoiling in the heat.

The studied insouciance of the entry for Wednesday 19 July should be set against his anti-Catholicism: 'I suppose today was a biggish day for me. Went for a private audience with Pope who was full of charm and gentleness. Spoke in English, French and Italian. Asked about Mama and blessed constituents and family and was pretty impressive as were the Goblin [*sic*] tapestries and the Swiss guard.' I like the impression of a polyglot *conversazione*: despite his surname, Lieutenant-Colonel Profumo's combat Italian, gleaned from the black-market night spots of his erstwhile homeland, was execrable, many sentences beginning, '*Ecco allora*'. (Mind you, it could have been worse: if W. H. Auden is to be believed, an Anglo-Italian phrasebook rushed out to assist the troops contained the handy line, '*Posso presentare il conte*', which becomes *anglice*, 'Meet the cunt.') To his constituents, J reported on 'the extreme simplicity of this great man', but privately he was suspicious that the Vatican had been amicable towards the Germans. The Pontiff knew my father was an MP, and received him as if he was some kind of spokesman for the conquering Army; J explained that he represented Northampton, and the Holy Father responded, 'Oh, I know Southampton. Very good!' There was quite a lengthy audience, and J was given a special rosary, which, rather against the grain, he kept in his desk drawer as a talisman (I keep it there, still).

Following this encounter with Pius XII, there was to be a visit by King George VI, who came to stay with Alex on the 24th. 'It was well worth the long wait. He looked straight at me as I suppose at everyone else, and he looked like England itself.' The next day, 'We had the Monarch to the War Room this morning, and I was presented and had to describe the air set up and targets etc. Later HM knighted CGS [Alex]. It must have been the first time in shorts I feel. Hottest day so far.' Later, there was a photo-call where a press flashbulb exploded and 'the King was furious and I think a little frightened – ' "It sounded like a pistol" he remarked, but didn't flinch. "Shows you what valiant nerves I have." This was a very embarrassing moment.'

So was another occasion in mid-August, near Siena. 'General Alex has a rabbit now which he adores and plays with'; it was a white specimen that Marshal Tito had given him. At the same time, J had adopted a pet of his own – a bloodhound which had strayed over from the German lines. One night it took off on a forage, but J never volunteered the reason for the disappearance of the beloved Alexandrine mascot.

With special permission to attend the debate on demobilization proposals, J managed to hitch a series of air-rides back to England in

November, arriving on the 8th, then heading straight down to Avon Carrow, where, though scarcely a Sebastian Flyte, his reaction suggests how authentically Waugh was to evoke such homecomings in the novel he was then writing. 'The cold rather dank misty air was like some priceless scent to my nostrils. I found Mama in wonderful spirits. No servants. Abbots and Eastman on their last legs, the garden full of cabbages, and Godfrey as an LAC [leading aircraftsman] on leave to greet me. Food as good as ever, cooked by my Mama and my mad aunt. My study has always been kept in readiness, and was too good to be true.' For tea, my grandmother served him 'switched egg', a boyhood favourite of his, comprising whisked egg yolk and sugar, on toast. This sudden respite, without the reek and soundtrack of war, must have been entirely delicious.

Having sent a note to the Speaker requesting permission to speak on behalf of his troops, J was informed by the Chief Whip that he was to open the whole debate – 'I nearly wet my trousers on the spot.' He had not spoken in the Commons for two years. At 12.12 on 15 November 1944 he rose, and began: 'Nothing outside Heaven could be expected to meet with the complete approval of all the thousands of men and women who are interested in this scheme.' In a speech lasting thirty-eight minutes, he played his 'long absence' card, and over the 'order of release' urged MPs to give priority to those in the Forces who had been serving overseas, and pre-1939 volunteers. His delivery was reported to be 'dramatic': he alluded to Alexander as 'the greatest General of our time' (cheers) and recommended that 'no woman should be sent to serve within possible range of the Japanese animals' (further cheers). From the Minister of Labour, Ernie Bevin, on behalf of his men, he sought assurance about the reallocation of manpower after the war – would employers feel it was a point of honour to reinstate ex-servicemen to their jobs, for instance? – to a resounding 'Hear hear'.

The reaction to this speech was positive and gratifying. J received an ovation in the lobby, there were more than eight hundred letters, plus requests to write newspaper articles (at twenty-five quid a pop, the rate was relatively better than many commissions that have come the way of his son and heir), and an invitation from Duncan

Sandys (the Prime Minister's son-in-law) to be his Parliamentary Private Secretary (declined). A couple of days later, J struck while the irony was hot and asked the Premier to ensure the shipping of 'large and regular quantities' of English beer to the troops in Italy. Churchill (who had visited Alex during the summer) replied that 'Like my Honourable and gallant friend, I returned from Italy with this earnest request and I gave immediate instructions that every effort was to be made to meet it.' If for nothing else, my father enjoyed a hero's welcome when he returned to his unit.

In a dexterous reverse fold of political origami, Alex had been made Field Marshal on 27 November. Montgomery (who had actually been one of his instructors at Staff College) had attained this rank on the field of battle that September, but Alex's promotion was backdated to the Fall of Rome, giving him effective seniority. It is said that – in contradistinction to Alex's own fulsome note – when the time came for reciprocity Monty sent a terse, 'Congratulations. Montgomery.'

The new Field Marshal invited J to dine but, once the routines of military administration resumed, he had to confess, 'It's an anticlimax after public life.' He was more interested in directing his energies at Kettering rather than Kesselring. He felt low: the narcotic thrill of Westminster and the press now seemed impossibly distant. (It was not to be the last time he would undergo such withdrawal symptoms.) His heart was not in soldiering – why should it have been? – but I think he was always aware of the rank and file. From the relative comfort of his heated quarters he reflects (9 December) on the conditions of 2 Para (2nd Battalion of the Parachute Regiment, at that stage fighting as infantry): 'those wretched troops, always wet and cold . . . I wish some sort of comfort and entertainment could be thought of for them, but they haven't even light after dark so what but to end the war quick. God help us. The men are tired, and can you wonder. Home 3 am.' (These things were not completely forgotten when, some sixteen years later, he was to have the entire Army in his care.)

News came through just before New Year that Profumo had been awarded a military OBE: 'That's nice and of course I'm very proud and have told my lads it's just as much theirs as it is mine and thanked them for their labours.' He was a punctilious, uncompromising, but –

I'm guessing, here – generous-minded taskmaster, and I'm sure there were those who were content to follow him, if only out of curiosity.

When J turned thirty at the end of January 1945 – 'How old it seems' – he was heavily committed to planning air missions for the Allied spring offensive, and was subsequently awarded the Bronze Star medal by the Americans. The citation 'for meritorious achievement in connection with military operations in Italy' describes how (in terms suggesting the very bureaucracy with which he had daily to contend), 'As Chief of the Air Liaison Subsection of the G-3 Section of Headquarters 15th Army Group, Lieutenant-Colonel Profumo, in a tactful and outstanding manner, co-ordinated the requests from two allied armies for medium and heavy air support of ground operations . . . by his untiring energy, quick grasp of tactical requirements and his willingness to short-cut routine . . .' (*virtute et labore*, perhaps). This liaison between the 5th and 8th Armies involved frequent flying, and the supervision of thousand upon thousand tons of bombs. General Clark later wrote to him that in the final Italian attack, 'over 1,000 heavy bombers were used in front of each of the . . . Armies. This represented probably the largest force of heavy bombardment planes ever used in support of ground forces.' The outcome of the campaign may no longer have been in doubt, but the business of attrition was demanding and grim.

It was my father's invariable habit to transcribe from one year's pocket diary to the next those telephone numbers he might most frequently call. Of the list that makes it into the cramped rear 'Memoranda' section of his 1945 Asprey's 'Grafton', sixteen of the twenty-four are female names, including actresses Hy Hazell and Frances Day, and other exotics such as Countess Zofi Tarnowska (Cairo), Madeleine Ballonque (Algiers) and Maya Sepgardi (Siena). There is also a number for 'D of K', whom I take to be the widowed Duchess of Kent. (A couple of decades later, when there was a deal of speculation about my father's private life, one book authoritatively declared, 'A distinguished wartime career and his political activities had left him little time for romance.')

In fact, he had developed a lifelong penchant for the nightlife, and there are intimations of heroic sessions lasting well into the early hours (on one occasion he returned to find his staff offices in flames, and all hands to the pump). On certain days, he would conscientiously pencil in the journal entries while extremely keen to lay down his head, and on others the matutinal snarl of the *Katzenjammer* still echoes down the decades. There is an impression of a candle sometimes being burned at three ends. In the New Year he was going to parties with Kitty, Baroness Moro, but she waxed possessive when he insisted on dancing with other girls ('What a pitty!') and then on 8 February, on a visit to the American dentist, 'Met a lovely girl called Donina. Most desirable but married. Must see her again soon.' This he accomplished, taking her out dancing ('She pretended to be a nurse – I ask you, with an ostrich feather hat on and the most beautiful figure in the world') and soon falling for her headlong ('I just can't get her out of my mind').

It seems they finally spent the night together on 5 March – not especially quick work by the khaki seducer, but then Donina Gnecchi did have a husband; indeed, Alberto arrived suddenly on the evening of the 29th and they ended up dining together *à trois*, though he does note she was 'very unsettled'. But she later declared 'she thought of leaving Alberto for me, so all was well'. (I suppose that would slightly depend on one's *punto di vista*.)

The German surrender in Italy was initially discussed at Caserta on 28 April 1945 and a document was signed the next day agreeing that it should take place on 2 May. At 1830 hours Alex's HQ made the announcement: he was senior to the American commanders, so was responsible for the arrangements. He duly dispatched J, along with an Allied escort, to 'a hastily prepared Alpine hideout where stood the Headquarters of the German C-in-C South West.' The first eighty miles to Verona were flown in Mark Clark's private plane, through nasty weather, then thirty miles over the mountains by Jeep and then, where the roads had been blown up, the journey continued on foot. Finally, they boarded Nazi transport, and the rendezvous took place by torchlight at 2100 hours the following night. 'It was an extraordinary thing, to enter a German camp during the war. Of course I was terrified there might be double crossing. And then I saw a man who said, "Profumo? Why, we haven't met in ages." It turned out we had known each other in Oxford. "Yes, it's true, we're giving in."' This was to be the first unconditional surrender of the war.

'It was very formal and quiet save for the clicking of Nazi boots. There was no hand-shaking. They all spoke English and had great charm. General von Senger was an old Oxford man and a cavalry officer. Gramm a tennis player. All had mutual friends.' One general recognized J's cap badge and said, 'Northamptonshire Yeomanry, I see. I used to hunt there before the war.' 'They're really un-Nazified,' the diary says. 'We ate and decided to fly tomorrow morning. Many interesting discussions before bed.'

They returned with General von Senger, the commander, a representative of General Wolff (Head of the SS in Italy) and a retinue of other plenipotentiaries. On the journey, J cast his mind back to 'that morning in September '43 when over the long flat beaches of Salerno we first set foot in Italy. The German beside me was fast asleep and breathing very heavily. I woke him up: he might be dreaming of another war.' There was a summit meeting in Mark Clark's pre-fab hut, and Von Senger was handed the instrument of surrender, which he took into his quarters for an hour to discuss with his staff, escorted by J. 'We watched the formal surrender in front of all the Generals, and I was assistant to von S.' Also in the war room were Generals Clark, McCreery, Truscott (5th Army), and Chidlaw (Mediterranean Allied Tactical Air Force). General Al Gruenther signed it for the victors, and thereby one million men surrendered. 'Too many photos and movies and broadcasts', concludes the account for 4 May. 'Nearly the end.'

'Such a lovely flight,' he wrote in his last entry, flying home, 'but my depression at leaving Donina is excessive.' He never did see her again. The diary ends: 'May the 16th. 1945 begins a new life. I must live it well.' He certainly lived it to the full.

———◆———

Back in April, J had written to *The Times*, 'I believe that to conduct a hasty General Election while the dust and smoke of battle still hover over Europe would be an injustice and an insult to the fighting forces', arguing that many serving people needed time to catch up with the political situation at home before deciding how to vote. In the event, he realized he had to fight for his political life in Kettering – furthermore, the British Council had decided to film the campaign there, as being a constituency representative of Middle England. The director was Ronald H. Riley, and the result was to be shown world-wide. This appealed to J's showmanship and fondness for *mise-en-scène*. Filming began on 22 June in the village of Lamport, where thirty folk were assembled, told not to look at the cameras, and watched as their incumbent MP drove up, 'the strains of his signature tune "Knightsbridge" from his car's loudspeaker' competing with cows and sheep on the soundtrack. A few days later, while speaking at Kettering Central Hall (Earl Spencer being in the chair), the heck-ling got out of hand, and J announced, 'If you want to talk, I will get on with my dinner,' turned away from the meeting, and opened up a packet of sandwiches.

As J feared, on 26 July the Labour candidate, G. R. Mitchison (Dick was husband of the novelist Naomi) was elected, with a majority of over six thousand; this huge swing was a nationwide trend, the general perception being that Churchill was revered personally, but people no longer had faith in the Old Guard (the average age of Tory MPs at the end of the war was fifty-three). 'Congratulations on your valiant fight', ran Winston's telegram to the unseated Profumo. The govern-ance of the country had changed hands: the beaters had taken over from the guns.

Since he was in release group 22, with no immediate prospect of being demobbed, the officer referred to as 92407 went to the War Office to see what they might have to offer him. He had no constituency, no other trade, no home of his own (there was even talk of having to sell Avon Carrow), and felt generally dispossessed. He was informed – by 'a young Major Starkey, who enjoyed cutting me down to size' – that he would have to be downgraded, and, following his leave, he could choose between the command of a camp for displaced persons at Lossiemouth, or the post of number two running Monty's mess. 'It was a bit of a comedown. I spent quite a lot of time in the Berkeley Grill.'

There arrived a telegram from Michael Crichton at Major-General Gairdner's office (23 October) calling my father to a meeting 'with view to interesting job overseas next six months'. Charles Gairdner had been appointed Head of the British Military Mission in the Far East, and was about to depart for Tokyo; he invited J to come out as his second-in-command, an offer that was accepted on the spot. 'By the way,' he added, as his newest member of staff turned for the door, 'it's a brigadier's appointment.'

They flew from London on the last day of October 1945, in Gairdner's personal Dakota (his brief encompassed such large areas of China and Australia that he had his own plane), landing *en route* at Cairo and Bahrain, where J's camera was stolen – 'the most God-awful hole you could imagine, like an outpost in a Foreign Legion film.' Just before they left home, the General had said, 'You'll take your guns with you?' (referring to shotguns for game-shooting). J admitted he only had one, not a matched pair. '*Really?*' came the incredulous reply. They enjoyed a stopover in Delhi, staying with Viceroy Wavell. Overnighting in Bangkok, their fuselage was cut open and all the baggage disappeared – including the sporting firearms and J's newly tailored Savile Row uniforms. They were left with just bush hats and shirts for their arrival in Japan, and the tunic J subsequently wore was a uniquely modified American design, with British insignia.

For eight months, he lived in the British Embassy in Tokyo, as Chief of Staff to the UK Liaison Mission. He was attended by a butler, Katto-san. Under J were departments for all three Services, plus Consular, Shipping, Education and Press, all headed by experienced staff. Since Gairdner was frequently travelling, his assistant was very often the direct link to London. He was thirty, and said to be then the youngest brigadier in the Army.

The Supreme Commander of Allied Forces in the Pacific (SCAP) was General Douglas MacArthur, a near-legendary warrior who had been decorated thirteen times in the Great War, became the youngest superintendent of West Point, and had accepted the Japanese surrender on board the *Missouri*. (He was also responsible for that unimpeachable military tenet: 'Never give an order that can't be obeyed.') His word could have been law in the subjugated Empire, but he cannily implemented his designs through the mouthpiece of the Emperor. There was a vociferous band of critics who clamoured for Hirohito to be tried as a war criminal, but MacArthur (who had first served in Japan in 1905, as an aide to his own father) realized the 'living god's' value alive was much greater than anything the drive for retribution might achieve.

Inevitably, there were those who felt the SCAP was himself imperious and *entêté*, but my father was not of their number. Here was another world-class leader with whom he was working closely, and from whose ways he felt he was always learning. Brisk and businesslike, the corncob-pipe-smoking Arkansas veteran was, in J's eyes, 'a man of great stature: he was simple, unobtrusive, dynamic and just.' When he emerged from his HQ in the Nippon Yushon Keishen shipping building at noon for lunch, he was cheered by the Japanese. 'But there is little of the conquering hero,' wrote J, 'he goes about unescorted and unguarded,' adding that 'he is the master builder, and his brain is like a knife.' He enjoyed dining with the Supremo and his wife Jeannie, whom the SCAP liked to call 'the greatest little soldier in the whole Pacific'.

Compared to the colourful country he had toured before the war, J was subdued by what he saw of Japan – 'even the blossoms on the trees seem to have lost their lustre,' he wrote, and his inspection of both the atomic bomb sites left him astonished that there was not more evidence of hatred and resentment among the defeated people. There was little sympathy for the Japanese, though, and the desire for revenge was strong in many Allied quarters. Without a commander as steadfast in his views as MacArthur, their hardship would have been even more severe; the edicts he issued through the Emperor included freedom of the press and universal suffrage (it had been almost unthinkable that women would have the vote). In a country hitherto run by secret societies and an oligarchy that controlled most commerce, such reforms would have taken years to implement constitutionally. To avoid giving positive directions to the Japanese Government, MacArthur developed 'the Raspberry technique', which (according to my father) consisted of 'a persistent refusal to indicate the right course, combined with the issue of warnings and prohibitions when the wrong course is about to be taken.'

None of this could be achieved without maintaining Anglo-American unity; the SCAP was aware that many of his men were homesick, and there were still some three million Japanese troops in the Pacific waiting to be disarmed. The Emperor – or 'Charlie', in military parlance – was the key, as his subjects held an almost infantile belief that he could do no wrong. He may have been reduced to living in a gardener's cottage in the grounds of his burnt-out palace, but Hirohito was still so revered that when he dismissed his tennis coach the sacked man committed hara-kiri, because traditionally no one who had looked upon the Emperor could live, once they left the precincts of the palace. He had largely been kept from public view, travelling in a vehicle with blinds drawn, and along his intended route all subjects were removed from the upper storeys of buildings, so that none might look down upon him.

MacArthur changed all that by making His Imperial Majesty call on him at his HQ, and then casually receiving 'Charlie' in his shirt-sleeves. As a further part of the new democratic process, he had the Emperor filmed. On 27 November 1945, he opened an extraordinary 89th session of the Diet, and J was in the gallery, next to the Russian delegate (with a Communist Party now permitted in Japan, the Allies were wary of Stalin's 'protective' intentions). He was due to arrive at eleven, but so great were the crowds that he was delayed; an official stopped the clocks until just before his arrival, as it was impossible for the Son of Heaven to be late.

Despite having lost his Purdey to the Siamese robbers, Brigadier Profumo did manage to enjoy some field sports with his boss. On one occasion they went quail-netting, which involved these little birds being driven by prisoners of war ('very sullen') towards hides where you crouched and caught them in a hand-net with a frame like a tennis racket – the birds were served up barbecued on skewers after each drive. Another *battue* which made a memorable entry in his game book occurred in Hokkaido, when pheasants were driven across the water between little islands, where the guns were placed: J bagged one spectacular bird, but at the end of the drive the beaters, rather than retrieving it, crouched in awe before my father. He had shot a *yami-doro*, a bird of paradise reserved exclusively for the Emperor himself.

In a newspaper article just before he left Tokyo in the summer of 1946, my father's valedictory verdict on the Japanese was this: 'They are mostly an inscrutable lot of untrustworthy heathens.' It was a widely shared view.

His journey home took six weeks, encompassing as it did visits to Nanking, Delhi (where he met up with brother Phil, just out of Staff College at Quetta), Karachi, Baghdad, Cairo, Malta, Trieste and Vienna. He reached London on 13 July and rented chambers in the Albany, off Piccadilly (the family home in Warwickshire was sold soon thereafter). He had a period of ninety-seven days' leave, and his last day in the Army was 28 October, though it was not until April 1964 (the year after he had resigned as Secretary of State for War) that he was officially released from any obligation on the Territorial officers' reserve list. He dropped his military title, and reverted to being plain Mister.

Having been readopted as candidate, J continued to groom Kettering, to the extent of turning down a safer prospect – Market Harborough – because he felt it would look like breaking the faith. He indulged in the usual Opposition sniping, and covered most of the bases: society under Labour was riven by class warfare ('crime and discontent are rife'); 'this Humpty-Dumpty Government is even now tottering'; 'the Conservative Party has something greater than policy, it has principles.' Central Office was keen to make use of his now considerable international experience, and his interest in the media, so in May 1947 he was appointed as the Party's first Broadcasting Liaison Officer. His brief was to monitor the BBC, which Churchill was convinced was riddled with communism, and, as he explained in a letter, 'by fair means or foul to induce the BBC to put over more of our stuff'. J placed an advertisement in the *Daily Telegraph* for volunteers who were hospital patients – inveterate listeners to the wireless – and selected six to comment each week on the political content, and possible bias, of programmes selected from the *Radio Times*. Historians of modern 'spin' might do worse than to start their investigations here.

A number of photogenic women were seen on his arm at this time: actress Glynis Johns was one, and 'Madame Kent' (as he later dubbed Princess Marina) was another. My father was passionately fond of her.

This tall, elegant, Greek aristocrat had been married to HRH the Duke of Kent – son of George V – an exquisite, Epicurean, and probably bisexual morphine addict who had perished on active service in an unexplained air crash during August of 1942. They had been one of the golden couples of London 'society', and J had for some while been associated seriously with the royal widow. She was accordingly not best pleased when he was photographed in fancy dress dancing with a well-known married actress at the Chelsea Arts Club Ball on New Year's Eve of 1947. I don't know why Jack Profumo elected to go as a policeman, but, in Shandean terms, that encounter incontrovertibly accounts for my arrested development.

In the spring of 1948, J moved to Number 3 Chester Terrace, overlooking Regent's Park, a Crown lease property once described as 'the smallest house that Nash built' (there is a bust of the architect on the westerly façade). A detached, white-stuccoed house with its own garden and lugubrious Regency interiors (introduced before the war by Lord Gerald Wellesley, later Duke of Wellington) it was smart enough for a bachelor abode, but rather too full of heavy brown furniture and not exactly welcoming. He was looked after by a cook and a maid, and engaged the services of Stanley Brisco, a former batman from the Household Cavalry, to act as butler. Mrs Havelock-Allan was entertained to dinner there for the first time at the end of August, J describing himself in the letter of invitation as 'one of your really ardent fans'.

They began to see each other frequently enough for some of J's political friends to warn him off, lest he become caught in the crossfire between husband and wife – 'some of Tony's film cronies were pretty ruthless types'. (I'm not sure what it was thought they would do: send Larry round with his poniard, perhaps.) It was especially important to avoid any taint to his moral probity because, on 11 October, he transferred his candidacy from Kettering to Stratford-on-Avon, a new constituency in Warwickshire created by redistribution under the Representation of the People Act. 'The changeover has been most distasteful, pretty worrying, and rather unpleasant,' he wrote in a letter, despite the fact that the Kettering Association knew full well he might transfer elsewhere eventually. An unwitting adumbration, the headline in the *Northamptonshire Evening Telegraph* ran: 'Profumo Resigns'.

Shortly thereafter, on a visit to Chartwell, to brief Churchill on a broadcasting matter, J was conducted to the garden pond. 'Mr [John] Strachey is very good to me, you know. He has never reduced the rations for my fish.' The party leader began sprinkling food for his pets. 'They are all named after famous veterans of the war – you know, they come when they are called, in order of seniority. Ike – watch this, there, very obedient – Alex, Monty . . .'

Seeing that the new candidate shared his sense of humour, they then spent a profitable hour discussing Opposition tactics. Later, Churchill told Jock Colville (his PPS), 'Do you know, I'm beginning to think I rather like Mr Profumo.' This approval was to be of considerable value, and when the time came Jack Profumo was also ready to rise towards the surface when his name was called.

There's no doubt that my father knew he was playing with fire as his latest desires quickened. The degree of subterfuge that was necessary for those early meetings with V was also part of the fun, and he seemed to hold that late-Edwardian view of the theatrical world that it was slightly forbidden fruit – acceptable for a risqué affair, but not to be introduced into polite society. (This was certainly his sister's opinion: Maina regarded Valerie from the start as a scarlet woman who had ensnared her younger brother.) The pursuit was proving delicious, but at this stage he had no thoughts of much permanency.

In a notebook memo she wrote much later, my mother does not recall it otherwise. 'There was instant, electric sexual attraction,' she noted, 'he's totally free sexually, and in love with sex.' She did not seem to be labouring under many misapprehensions about her ardent beau: 'It was I who persuaded him to have our affair, but he was frightened of love – certainly of commitment.' (Nothing too extraordinary there, then.) She reckoned she allowed herself to be treated with less than gallantry by him, however; he never drove her home after dinner and hardly ever introduced her to his friends and family (though I expect she understood why). The simple explanation, I suppose, is that he was a self-centred bachelor, and he was charming enough to get away with it. They had become so fascinated by one another that it did not seem to matter at the time.

For a man whose literacy levels were notably low, J sometimes managed to write love letters displaying considerable brio; how much of the emotion was flowered-up for rhetorical effect, like the patriotic burden of some of his parliamentary speeches, it is hard to tell, but I expect it was all nicely persuasive. He wrote to her on 21 January 1949, from his sister Betsy's cottage in Shotteswell (in the heart of the constituency he was now nursing). First, he described the wintry view: 'the sun has just come out and the gusty clouds are racing away for all they are worth. The clouds pass, but the sky remains.' He mentioned the new red braces he was wearing, a gift from V, and 'a somewhat drab ordinary tweed suit which I've got on has a strong nostalgic cling, and a slight suspicion of femme . . . I miss you desperately and my heart's rushing ahead skipping over the houses to next Wednesday – I can't keep up with it so get ready to catch it and keep it warm till I can catch it again and catch you close to it in my arms. Um um um um. xx.' The schoolboyish quality of his letters – bursting with urgency and apparently having no time for guile – must have appealed sufficiently for my mother to keep them all those years.

I have literally hundreds of such notes and *billets-doux*, full of the banter, flirting, baby-talk and petty jealousies with which all but the most high-minded of couples lard and bard their intimate correspondence. I had expected to find such chronicles of endearment merely embarrassing, but in fact I read them with a sense of reassurance: my parents-to-be were just as silly and serious as the rest of us. There were the usual drawings of love knots and eternity symbols, the pressed flowers and pinholes where cards had been attached to actual bouquets; in one fit of devotion, worthy of a Renaissance swain, there is a russet smudge of his blood on the paper, and the protest, 'My heart is dripping through this ink, and had I the words to match my feelings I could do justice to the stirrings of my soul.' That April he wrote from a pub bedroom in Stratford that V's film *The Small Voice* was showing at the local cinema, but he could not bring himself to watch it, knowing how fond she had been of Harry Keel, her co-star – the very thought makes him feel physically sick. He began signing himself 'Jacket', the nickname that endured between them, others including Jacaranda, Pidge (for pigeon) and John Peel. The latter – a pun on the initials he shared with another keen hunting man – was a trifle confusing in some later letters, as (Sir) John Peel was also the real name of V's gynaecologist.

Their first proper expedition together was the Parisian trip of Easter 1949, and it marked a point of no return in the Havelock-Allans' marriage – not because there was yet more adultery afoot, but because she and Tony had always vowed they would put each other first, and he wanted her to stay in London (his own paramour, Kay Kendall, being temporarily elsewhere). He therefore felt his wife had let him down, and he never forgave her: it was indeed, as my father repeated, a theatrical marriage. For four days they stayed in a rooftop suite of the Hotel Lancaster, in the rue de Berri. 'It was a heavenly Easter,' she wrote. 'Whatever came after I should always remember it as perfection.'

The lovers were necessarily apart for professional reasons, but maybe it suited the pell-mell nature of their affair. 'V stands for Venus and J stands for Jupiter,' wrote Jack excitedly, 'and between them both the world has evolved – it's a lovely lovely world just now full of fog which makes it mysteriously exciting and I never felt so enterprising so electrified so engrossed so enchanted so enamoured so elevated so *que reste-t-il?*'

Despite their domestic situation, Valerie and Tony formed a new company together – Valiant Films, its name the conjunction of their own Christian names. Their first production (*Interrupted Journey*, with Richard Todd) was in fact the story of a young couple who are experiencing matrimonial problems, and what happens when the husband pulls the communication cord on a train (it was originally entitled *The Cord*). This made little impact, but was followed by a picture which has become a minor classic, *The Rocking Horse Winner*, adapted from the chill short story by D. H. Lawrence. Playing opposite Johnny Mills as the groom, who acts as go-between for the disturbed boy (John

Howard Davies, who had recently portrayed Oliver Twist), V was cast as the relentless mother, Esther, and had her hair bleached for the first time. The director was Anthony Pelissier (son of the actress Fay Compton) who could be sharp and caustic, but endeared himself to my mother for ever by rescheduling part of the shoot because her Simon fell badly ill with pneumonia – Down's children seem highly susceptible to chest and lung complaints, although he proved more resilient than many.

After filming was completed, J suggested they take a holiday together, and they put his car on a plane to France for a tour of the chateaux; they stayed at the Hotel Hermitage in La Baule, then visited Chambertin, Fontainebleu and Chambord. An invitation to the villa of John Hare and his wife Nancy made V feel 'like Jack's girl' for the first time. Then came an event that never found its way into my mother's 'official' account of her life for the family to read, but the staccato notes concerning it were in an envelope, with quite unrelated papers, in an attic box.

> In Reims I felt sick – no period – I knew I was pregnant yet so happy –
> for both reasons, guilt and fear didn't allow itself to spoil my complete
> bodily joy – my breasts heavy as we drove. On the battlements of
> Chenonceaux I told J I was pretty sure – he was enchanting and said
> he loved me. But assumed – as he naturally would – that I have abor-
> tion. I do not blame him for this – it is usually a woman's desire to
> 'make' her man marry her. And I *was* married. It simply wasn't on –
> babies out of wedlock were *not* allowed then – and J has a brilliant
> future.

In September, Valerie went into St Mary's Nursing Home in Hendon. 'J had a note and a red rose delivered to my flat before I went. I took a taxi there. He never paid – not because of meanness, I know, but because he couldn't acknowledge to *himself* what we were about to do. I was alone. I was working all the time and so was he.' This pragmatic tone belied a distress that I suspect J never cared to guess at. In the autumn, they visited Maina and her husband (Harold Balfour) who had just had their first child; when Valerie saw the healthy baby and their comfortable, regular household, she realized that the situation with J was simply not going to work. 'He had his whole career planned out,' and was hardly in a hurry to settle down – nor was she free, anyway. If there was to be a divorce, and he were implicated, his political future would be ruined. (This had probably not occurred to Kay Kendall, when she invited J to cocktails at Claridge's, snuggled up to him, and implored him to take V off Tony's hands to clear the way for her. In fact, she ran off with Lilli Palmer's husband, Rex Harrison, instead.) For the rest of 1949, therefore, V and J agreed not to meet. She told me she used to walk down St James's Street on the off chance he might be emerging from his club; he said he would do something similar, lingering in the shadows outside her Mayfair flat. Jack and his girl (luckily for me) were not very good at their trial separations.

Meanwhile, J had been indefatigably making himself known to the voters of the new Stratford Division, where he was to run in the general election against a Labour candidate (a young law student from London named Ronald G. Brown, who had served in the Navy and studied at Cambridge) and the Liberal, Hadley Seaborne (director of a contractors' agency for quarry plant). The area was traditionally a Tory stronghold – many of the electors had previously been in Anthony Eden's neighbouring constituency – but it could not yet be regarded as a safe seat. As part of his activities for Central Office, J had been training MPs to speak on radio, had made records of conference speeches that he sold to local associations for three pounds a throw, and had even made a promotional 'talkie' of himself touring the villages of Warwickshire, many of which he had known since his schooldays. So when Seaborne proposed that no posters or loud-speakers be used during the campaign, in order to preserve the peace-able atmosphere of Stratford, there was no agreement.

There were four hundred square miles of this largely rural division to cover, and some 140 villages – so, because of the petrol shortage, J took to canvassing in a pre-First World War brougham pulled by Priscilla the pony (he called this 'vote trotting'). 'Handsome, debonair and always charming,' noted the sempiternally objective Royal Leamington Spa *Courier*, 'he makes conquests wherever he goes.' 'The choice is handcuffs or keys,' the conquering Tory explained, 'being handcuffed to a Socialist state, or getting the key to personal success and achievement.' Not everyone saw it in such simple terms; when Eden, in Shakespeare's home town, spoke out in J's support, a heckler objected to his Italian name – 'Would you like to change his name to Prospero?' came the rejoinder.

Polling Day was 23 February 1950, and J was elected with 21,492 votes – a substantial majority of 9,349 over Labour – in an 80 per cent turn-out. 'Little Clem' Attlee was still in power, but by a slender margin, and not for long. Commenting on the names of current MPs, one journalist in the *News Chronicle* observed, 'I am consoled by the thought that Mr Profumo and Mr Nabarro will be there to keep Mr Mikardo and Mr Albu in order.' It did not take him long to return to the fray in the Commons that he so relished. When Woodrow Wyatt (Labour MP for Aston) criticized the reputation of MacArthur, under whose command there were now British troops serving in Korea, J denounced it as 'the most monstrous and disgraceful speech I have ever heard', and his comments were reported everywhere from the *Cork Examiner* to the *Buenos Aires Herald*. He was vociferous in flagging up the Communist threat to the reputation of the trades unions, drew the Chancellor's attention to the 'widespread concern' at the level of purchase tax on ecclesiastical cassocks, and yet was equally assiduous over such local concerns as 'the long delay that had occurred in the reconstruction of the road connecting the villages of Bearley and Snitterfield'. As any MP will tell you, such issues are ignored at your peril.

Not really by chance, my parents met once again in Dover Street, and decided to fly down to the South of France in August to stay with the Balfours at their villa, La Lavandou. This reunion was not a success – 'the absolute joy wasn't there,' V remembered, and just prior to her journey back she forced J to agree with that (though the incorrigible swain was immediately at it again with his epistolary croonings, from Aiguebelle: 'They haven't moved me yet from our room, and it's too full of memories to be peaceful. Your soap is still in the bath and your smell on the pillow and your lipstick message on the dressing table.') At the time, this syncopated arrangement was causing more *bouleversement* for her than for the busy politico, who, it could be argued, was having his cake and eating it – a situation that was to be curtailed drastically by the evening she went to the opera with Tony, and let him stay the night.

Her estranged husband professed to be delighted at the subsequent news that she had conceived, and was especially relieved to learn that she intended to continue independently. ('It would take quite a bit of understanding on the part of his mistress,' noted V, in a last-ditch attempt at even-handedness.) She worked hard at convincing herself she had all along desired 'one last satisfactory baby', and that this was not simply to be some *garçon gratuit*, the result of what is less classically known as a *boffe de politesse*. Either way, she was committed to having this child and, if not exactly hoping to repair her fractured family, there was a strong impulse to show her estranged husband that she could bear him an unblemished offspring. Quite how she expected her lover to react, I am not sure: when she told him of her pregnancy, her account records: 'He is appalled, and says we must never see each other – perhaps not ever, certainly not until the child is quite old.' Whether it was from the fear of innuendo, or an understandable desire to be as far away from such irregular domestic arrangements as were patently in the offing, J decided it was high time to bolt – and quite right, too.

Prior to her baby's arrival, Valerie Hobson moved to a more spacious flat, in Mount Street, and started work on a series of children's programmes for television. She could count on no financial support from her husband – or anyone else – and needed to make money while she still could. On 4 April 1951, her second son (Mark) was born, and, to her immense relief and joy, the doctors assured her that he was physically fine (he is now His Honour Judge Havelock-Allan). By now she had moved Simon to the Rudolf Steiner home – Sunfield, near Clent – and felt she had to admit that this constituted 'the final negation of being his mother'. (At the age of sixteen he finally spoke, after a laying-on of hands by the Revd Tim Tiley.)

With a sudden, but not unpredictable, enthusiasm V embraced the Church, and was confirmed into the Anglican faith. She followed (non-clerical) advice, and embarked on a solo social life. In July, she was photographed dining at the Café de Paris with Orson Welles. By September, she was in a position to act once more, and took on the role of the Countess of Chell in a screen adaptation – by Eric Ambler – of *The Card*, a novel by Arnold Bennett (a writer probably now better known for his eponymous omelettes). Alec Guinness had the title role, with Petula Clark as his wife, and Glynis Johns as a snobbish dancing teacher: This 'warm-hearted comedy of character' was crisp and stylish and fun, and the location used for 'Sneyd Hall' was the Astors' home at Cliveden. It received its Royal première on 28 February 1952 at the Odeon, Leicester Square, in the presence of the Duchess of Kent, but – despite the choice of former escorts this presented him – Jack Profumo was nowhere to be seen.

With the possible exception of his immediate family, political ambition was the ruling passion of my father's life; this remained the case, even long after his parliamentary career was ended. Harbouring as I do the average Englishman's sanative distaste for all things governmental, I find this phenomenon astonishing, but the strength of its impulse should never be underestimated, nor the high-octane opportunism that fuelled it. In the general election of 25 October 1951, J held on to his seat with a majority of 9,349 over the Labour candidate Harry Hilditch, who had won an MC at the Somme. The triumphant Member toured Stratford in a tractor-drawn trailer, standing on a bale of straw (perhaps emblematic of the fact that his victory was based on the agricultural and village votes).

In the House, he was beginning to acquire a reputation as something of a phrasemaker, and the subjects on which he spoke were aviation, the military, and broadcasting. He had roundly denounced the Labour proposals to cut the BBC overseas services as 'plumb crazy' in view of the Cold War, but what kept him in the news himself was his persistent lobbying for an end to the BBC's monopoly – advocating sponsored stations for local radio, and the introduction of commercial television. His argument was that Labour had a vested interest in maintaining the monopoly, as competition was anathema to their principles, and the intellectual Left, generally dismissive of entertainment, wished to dictate the taste of the nation. Following the government White Paper on the future of the BBC, a vote was carried on 12 June 1952 to develop sponsored television. J reckoned that if the people did not want it, it would not work, as 'It will not pay to advertise' – a notion both progressive and populist – but Lord Reith spoke despairingly of 'the scorn that is poured on those who suggest that moral issues are at stake', and reminded supporters of the recommendation that it was 'the BBC and its friends who are fighting to preserve the freedom of the ether'. (In Lord Reith's time, it will be remembered, moral issues were so imperative that you could not work for the Corporation if you had been divorced.)

It was announced that during the summer recess six MPs were to visit the United States to monitor the presidential election (Eisenhower was running against the Democrat Adlai Stevenson); they were to do so separately, travelling for two months and paying their own way. On 28 August J set sail on the SS *United States*, sharing a cabin with 'a typical American, who washed his underwear in the sink'. There were also some fetching snapshots of a dark-haired, cinch-waisted fellow traveller by the name of Barbara Barb, with whom he clearly hooked up *en route*.

He went first to Philadelphia, where he joined Eisenhower's train, then on to Washington, where he had meetings with Dean Acheson (Secretary of State) and Averell Harriman (Director of Foreign Aid). With a special brief for aviation and 'wireless', he toured the Piasecki Helicopter works in Pennsylvania, went to New Orleans, San Francisco, Hollywood, and Chicago, and made his first appearance on television (he could hardly believe there was a viewing figure of five million, at seven in the morning). He was impressed by the sloganeering – the 'I Like Ike' button badge was a significant memento – and the sheer size of some of the meetings. In Milwaukee he watched Governor Stevenson address a crowd of fifteen thousand. Backstage, struggling to weigh up the arguments, J was asked by an aide, 'Bud, are you a Democrat or a foreigner?'; when he revealed that he was British, the man said, 'I thought something was wrong. Boy, you don't react to nothing.' The rabble-rousing showmanship was another useful experience when he returned to report to Churchill about the style and scale of how things were being done across the water.

★

Although they were technically apart and effectively incommunicado, J and V had been tracking each other's movements. She had decided against writing to congratulate him on the election result, but he had sent round a cuddly toy on Mark's first birthday that April. When she called to thank him, he tried suggesting another date but was refused (this did not leave him too lonely, if his photo album is anything to go by; Princess Marina and a young French girl with whom he was enamoured are both quite well represented at this stage). He was aware that she had several other men in tow (the latest being Jack Heinz, of the '57 Varieties' family), but was evidently hopeful of coaxing into flame the embers of their passion.

From several venues along his whistle-stop American schedule, he wrote schmoozingly to her of his adventures, but it became clear that his professed enthusiasm was no longer reciprocated. 'Please be careful of that soup man when he arrives,' he wrote from Washington on 3 September. 'In fact, be careful of all men. They're all the same – bloody dangerous!' ('they', and not 'we', *nota bene*). From New York, he said he was sending her a little present via friends, 'and, oh, I do hope you like it my darling', but you can sense he feels things are slipping. Puzzled that the usual box of verbal indoor fireworks does not seem to be working, he resorts to some modest rockets: *en route* for South Carolina (19 September) he begins: 'My Darling My Dearest', chiding her, 'the only thing I haven't had is a letter from my girl.' By the end of the month he was in Beverly Hills. The host of one party there, Jack Warner, asked J if there was anyone he'd like to meet, and when he mentioned Ava Gardner's name he ended up with an invitation back to her mansion. He didn't relay this to V, naturally, and when he came to write his letter dated 4 October there still seemed to be only one actress on his mind.

'My Dearest of Dear Forever Girl. Suffer this letter kindly. I'm drunk and dreadfully unhappy and lonely and I must – I just must write to you. The moment I got your cable I tried to get hold of you, but the Atlantic weather was so bad that they couldn't put in a person to person call.' It seems he had finally heard from her, and V had said she was coming to the States to promote a film, but did not feel they should meet up. 'Although you can't answer me I can tell you something of my misery . . . I don't know what happened but it's ghastly, Death like in its awfulness. You used to write me such lovely letters, full of your heart and soul.' He senses from a number of signs that,

It could only be that there's someone else with whom arrangements have been made and that they can't be broken and that can only mean that they're more important than *us*. Don't ever let me see that last sentence again. I don't know how my hand was able to write it . . . Don't leave me standing alone – I can't stand without you my sweet other half and I don't believe you should try such a thing. It's wrong. Before God it's wrong now we are one. Come to me my Pidge, come quickly. I'm weak and I want you. Oh please send a message to keep me going. XxMExx.

Such anguished pleading was, for him, unprecedented, but then the situation back in England had become more complicated than he could know. On a visit to open a bazaar in Darlington, Valerie had met Robin, the 8th Marquess of Londonderry, a tall, shy, bespectacled widower who lived at Wynyard Park. By his own admission, he fell 'instantly' in love with her, and began to woo her in a hopelessly chivalric and awkward way. His wife, Romaine, had undergone a glossectomy and died of mouth cancer the previous year, at the age of forty-seven, leaving him with three children (one daughter, Annabel, was to lend her name to London's great nightclub, and later married Jimmie Goldsmith). They became deeply fond of one another, and a source of mutual comfort. V found Robin 'endearing, gentle, vulnerable' – 'an unusually nice man, not particularly gifted, but with a steadfast heart'. Her rather mercurial temperament seemed to enthral, rather than deter him, and his careful flattery and heartfelt adoration made a welcome change from some of the flightier beaux she had been entertaining. His estate, near Stockton-on-Tees, was a place of some grandeur, and he owned an extensive part of the North-Eastern coal industry. Unlike some plutocrats, he was undoubtedly solicitous of the welfare of his miners, knowing many of them by name. (A fellow magnate, near Leeds, was evidently not a kindred spirit: his house was physically built over one of the main mines, and when a guest asked if he did not ever find that a little disturbing, he blithely replied, 'Ah, no, not at all. They make very little noise, d'ye know.')

It had also occurred to the Havelock-Allans that the time had come to 'make things tidier' and consider a divorce. With characteristic dismay, V found the finality of such a prospect suddenly disturbing. A familiar farce ensued whereby (to satisfy the grounds of adultery) Tony had to be caught officially with another woman – ordinarily not such a challenge, but on two occasions he was frustrated in his attempts blatantly to be discovered. The first night he spent in Brighton (with a lady conveniently hired for the purpose) was witnessed by a waiter, but by the time a detective had gone to collect the evidence he had returned to Spain. In an attempt to reprise this performance at Skindles Hotel (this time with a different *fille de joie*) their chambermaid tried to protect the hapless husband by refusing to identify him from the investigator's photographs.

At last, the case was satisfactorily settled, but after the decree absolute V drove herself in a distraught state down to Climping on the Sussex coast and screamed aloud to God that she was dying. She lay face down on the turf for a long while: 'The sandy earth was warm and sweet. I had expected damp dark earth like the earth into which I had seen coffins lowered. I turned over and looked at the sky, listening to sea birds and the ruffle of the wind on the sea grasses, and the sighing which came from them and from me.' (I've no doubt she was distressed enough, but her self-dramatization is slightly alarming.)

That autumn, she was invited to switch on the Blackpool Illuminations, and among the sizeable crowd by chance she saw one tall man waving to catch her eye: it was my father's butler, Stanley Brisco, who always went there for his holidays.

In early October, V took ship for New York aboard the SS *Queen Elizabeth* to promote *The Card* (in fact retitled, stateside, *The Promoter*). Largely unappraised of these convolutions, Jack sent her a cable on the 7th: 'Still sadly confused why not permitted meet you arrival haunted prospect serious involvement emplore cable denying. Deepest love. Homing Pidgeon.' The desired reply did not come. Following some screen tests for colour television, and a showing of her film, V was invited to the CBS studios for their election night party on 4 November and there, too, was J. They went on to another party at General Sarnoff's house, and then he dropped her off at the River Club where she was staying, with the promise of a luncheon date later that day. 'It was dawn,' she wrote, 'and the Hudson river flowed with promise.'

In her account, my mother – presumably to romanticize the situation in hindsight – claimed that until that evening neither had even realized the other was in New York, a harmless enough (yet typical) example of memoirist's re-embroidery. She did have to leave a message cancelling the lunch, however, as there was a last-minute summons to a photo-appearance with the New York Police Department, after which she was to go straight to Connecticut by train for the weekend, and thence home by air. 'Well, that was that . . .' On the Sunday, J called her hosts the Harrisons, having somehow tracked her down, and announced that he happened to be coming their way the next day and would be collecting their guest. ('I'm sure I glowed as if covered in fireflies,' she wrote, with novelettish precision.) They spent the night in a motel, then drove to New York, where J gave a supper party for eight people in the nightclub El Morocco – 'a good number in which to hide a special attachment from too-prying eyes'. They were still drinking toasts and dancing into the early hours, and V was getting ready to leave (she had a plane to catch that day) when the band began to play '*Que reste-t-il?*', a song they had loved since their first sojourn in Paris. As they danced, another man was observing her closely, and sent a note to their table asking if he could come over and introduce himself. It was Richard Rodgers, the composer.

He enquired whether she had seen his show *The King and I*, a long-running Broadway musical hit (Gertrude Lawrence, its star, had just died) and V admitted she had not. He invited her to do so, but she explained she had to leave for England.

Dick Rodgers looked at me more sharply. 'I'll ask you now, then, what I would have asked you tomorrow. Can you sing?'

'A bit.' This was exactly true.

'I'll have a play-script sent round in the morning. In four months from now we'll have you back here for an audition. We're putting on the show next October in London. Take singing lessons if you have to – I want you to succeed.'

On the flight home, V read the script, and felt that the role of 'Mrs Anna' – the widowed Victorian governess who comes to teach the children of the King of Siam – was surely the part for her. 'The fact that I couldn't sing, and had never played a part on stage for longer than a week, seemed not to matter.' Sworn to secrecy about the project – Essie and Lilli Palmer, her two contrasting confidantes, were the only others who knew – she set about preparing herself. There was going to be precious little distraction or support from the wayward Jack, however: 'He knew very well I wanted him to marry me, but he didn't want marriage. We separated again.'

He was soon busy elsewhere. On 25 November 1952 J was appointed Parliamentary Secretary to the Minister of Civil Aviation, taking over from Reggie Maudling. At thirty-seven he was now on the front bench, with one of the seventy-six ministerial posts in Churchill's Government. His career may not have been assisted when, flopping down with relief after answering some of his earliest questions in the House, he heard the Premier's canine growl, 'You have sat upon my hand, confound you.'

This was a good first appointment for my father, as both in war and leisure-time he had some first-hand experience of flying. His boss and mentor was Alan Lennox-Boyd, the tall, rich and cultured Minister for Transport (now including Aviation, after a merger) who became a discreet and close personal friend, and subsequently my godfather. It was an exciting time to be involved in aviation, as this was the beginning of 'the new jet age' we civilians so take for granted – the era of the Viscount and the Comet (despite some fatal disasters), and the mass discovery of holidays abroad. It was a geographically active job, and J flew around the country with notable pleasure. Following his American visit, he developed an especial interest in the civil potential for helicopters, and one of the frequently discussed projects throughout 1953 was the plan for a London 'helidrome'. At a meeting in Penistone, South Yorkshire, in his enthusiasm he referred to his department as 'The Ministry of Civilization', adding, 'I don't know what I'm doing here, when I ought to be at the Palladium.'

On several occasions, he was photographed dancing with the Duchess of Kent, and magazines liked to describe him as part of 'her circle', which also included Noël Coward, Malcolm Sargent, and the ubiquitous Douglas Fairbanks Jr. This was as smart as café society came, a thoroughly enjoyable milieu for a reasonably well-heeled, heterosexual bachelor in his thirties, who was beginning to be marked out as – the phrase is from Pepys – 'a very rising man'.

On the advice of Lilli Palmer, V contacted Elsa Schreiber, a leading Hollywood acting coach, and borrowed the necessary money to fly her over for lessons in London. For three intensive weeks, she rehearsed in a service flat off Portland Place, with the part of the King being read by a dreamy-looking, patient, modest man named Gregory Peck ('his voice was so low and rich I expected ripe fruit to issue from his beautifully shaped lips'). It was the first time V had ever had such professional coaching, and she felt it was 'the best thing that ever happened to me in my whole acting career'. It was a rigorous course in analysing the role – something for which there had never been time, in the hurly-burly of cinema – and it raised V's sense of self-esteem at a crucial juncture. First thing in the morning, and again just before supper, she also took singing lessons with Dino Borgioli, working on breath control, lung power, and the broadening of her range. Her voice was strengthening, but it was by no means certain she was going to pass muster when, in March 1953, she flew back to New York for the biggest audition of her life.

A car was sent to the Hotel Pierre, and she was driven to the St James Theater. She had chosen a simple, English dress – slightly longer than was in fashion, as a token gesture towards the huge period crinoline the part required on stage, and with a large collar to show off her neck (a good feature) plus a wide belt tightened to accentuate her waist and support the diaphragm. There was a pianist on stage, a large rehearsal light, and two men in the auditorium – Richard Rodgers and Oscar Hammerstein II. 'Mindful of all Elsa had distilled into me, I was confident and sure of simply being Mrs Anna.'

The King and I was an adaptation of *Anna and the King of Siam* (1944), a novel by Margaret Landon about the life of Mrs Anna Leonowens, the youngish widow of an army clerk (Tom) who founded a school in Singapore and then in 1862 took up the position of governess and English teacher at the court of the imperious King Mongkut of Siam. The show is long, and the female lead a taxing one, demanding unusual stamina and also the projection of a strong yet poignant character, who alone stands up to what she sees as the antiquated mores of the court, yet manages to beguile the overindulged monarch. The part had been played to great adulation by Gertrude Lawrence on Broadway (succeeded by Constance Carpenter) with Yul Brynner as the King. Valerie Hobson had scarcely been on the stage for twenty years.

They bade her sing two songs: 'Getting to Know You' and the plangent 'Hello, Young Lovers' ('You fly down the street, on a chance that you'll meet, / And you meet not really by chance'), then play the long final scene of the first act. This culminated in her lying full length on her face, and 'I had been in this position only a moment when the two great men of the American theatre were helping me up and hugging me – "Congratulations Mrs Anna!"' Finally, this was the big time. I used to marvel at this anecdote as a stage-struck teenager, and even now the exquisite thrill of that moment vicariously carries a *frisson* that brings a clot to my throat. As it was, she found that she and Oscar were crying. 'We're taking you to Sardis for lunch,' interrupted the more phlegmatic Dick, 'go blow your nose.'

Much to the subsequent horror of her agent, they drew up a contract there and then on the back of a menu (£300 per week, with her guarantee to stay for the duration of the run, due to open at Drury Lane that autumn), which she signed, and the deal was sealed with a kiss. V reminded Oscar how he had once spotted her in the Honeydew café, and Dick said, 'Well you've come a long way – this time you were spotted in El Morocco.' They introduced her to Jerry Whyte, who was to be in charge of the London production, and, to her relief, they took to one another. Then it was time to fly home – at last, returning in triumph from America.

Before rehearsals began, V made her last ever film, *Knave of Hearts* (1954), with Joan Greenwood and the French heartthrob Gerard Philipe; the wardrobe was by Balmain, which entailed some delightful fittings in Paris, and the director was René Clément. They shot the scenes twice over in immediate succession, the English version followed by the French, and perhaps inevitably the project overran, so that singing lessons and discussions about costumes for her stage role began to preoccupy her simultaneously. It was also a busy time on the social front, with Jack Heinz taking out the entire cast and crew for dinner when they were on location at Medmenham (he was now courting his future wife, Drue, who became a latter-day patroness of the arts). There was also a new admirer, the saturnine, risqué, limping artist David Rolt; and the odd cameo appearance still came from Marc Allégret, Fulke Warwick, or the Member for Stratford, but she had virtually given up on that score. Her ex-husband also remained marginal to the scene, and in September they were filmed leaving an Odeon première to have supper together – 'We adore each other,' she blithely assured the reporters, although privately Tony was advising her – 'for safety' – to marry Robin Londonderry. This very nearly happened.

Many letters survive from Wynyard Park to my mother (by now living in a Knightsbridge maisonette) and they are characterized mostly by *tendresse* for the woman he thought might offer his entire family a happy life. Robin's sense of self-worth was subject to conspicuous fluctuations, and he was prone to depression and serious drinking; but even when things were going against him there was never any nastiness, despite a rather unedifying vein of self-pity. I think he sensed from the start that it was never going to be the fairy-tale romance he craved, but he tried his best: he suggested looking after both V's children, promised to give up alcohol, and renounced any suggestion of sexual demands, if only she would agree to love him 'a little'. He courted her assiduously, and engagingly depicted himself as an unworthy, doting, foolish fellow – on 13 October he described reading the lesson at harvest festival, becoming distracted with thoughts of V, and tripping over a heap of potatoes – but, while I do not suggest she led him on, the time was now not right for any serious interruption to her professional commitment, and the challenge that imminently faced her.

Jerry Whyte was a big, white-faced man with red hair, a reputation for being as tough as they come, and a deal of experience with handling the histrionics of stage stars. With this production he clearly had an unusual task, in that both the leads were from the movies, and came with relatively few preconceptions. It was understood that they were taking a chance with Valerie Hobson, who was seen as a surprise choice (the favourite having been Evelyn Laye), and was known to have vocal limitations. The King was to be played by Herbert Lom, a talented Czech actor who later became a household face from the *Pink Panther* films. V recalled them both being strangely confident, though it seemed fitting that the first words she had to sing were, 'When shivering in my shoes / I strike a careless pose . . .'

John van Druten, the producer, made it clear from the outset that 'every move and almost every gesture was to be a faithful copy of the production still running in New York – rather like the rules set out by the D'Oyly Carte Opera Company.' The stars were allowed a smidgen more latitude, though the chief challenge of rehearsals for V was not the characterization but her exaggerated crinoline, which practically assumed a life of its own during the choreography, although it was as small deer compared with the real costumes – 'the exuberance of the wired hoop, plus three under-petticoats, frilled and laced over-petticoats, and the huge silken dresses themselves.' It was a physically demanding role: Gertie Lawrence had calculated that it required three miles of walking or dancing per show, with only seventeen minutes offstage (and there were to be eight performances a week). What gradually emerged, though, was that V was well cast despite voice worries, because this was a strongly theatrical show (most unusually for a musical, it ends with a sorrowful death scene), and as well as being enamoured of the part she seemed dedicated to everything about the production. It was the stage moment for which she had been waiting since she was in pigtails.

Valerie Hobson was the first British 'leading lady' to star at the Theatre Royal, Drury Lane, since the end of the war. On the first night (8 October 1953), in what had been Garrick's dressing-room, she received a case of Krug from Robin Londonderry, a posy of violets from her mother, a leather visitors' book from Tony (designed to be auspicious for a long run), a silver rose-bowl filled with orchids from Dick and Oscar, a glass ruler from Van Druten (an emblem transparently reminding her who was in charge?), an inscribed ivory figurine of a potentate from Herbert, and – 'the most wondrous gift of all' – a huge portrait, 'Valerie Holding a Bunch of Purple Tulips', from Matthew Smith. Larger than life, it filled the cramped ante-room, and was almost literally in the face of any backstage visitors. Pride of place – even beyond this – went to a pressed four-leaf clover sent by Nanny 'B', with a card: 'Dear Baby I expect Simon would have sent this if he could so I'm doing it and sending my love.'

Not long before she went on stage, V felt her entire vocal apparatus was seized up. She hid in the lavatory, and felt like throwing up the casement and calling out to those queuing in the alleyway behind, 'I wish I was with you!' Then, after hugging some of the children in the cast, she was in the wings: 'The word "nervous" doesn't describe what I felt,' as she put it, 'There were equal feelings of the desire to run away, and the wish to show what one can do, all one is.' She had to make a dignified entrance, grasping the hand of the boy acting her small son – at once protective, anxious, uncertain. 'I no longer cared whether I was on trial by the dim sea of pale ovals seen mistily behind the conductor. Like the character in the play, Mrs Anna had arrived, and there was no going back. "Whenever I feel afraid . . ." .' It is a matter of record that her song was greeted with a roar of applause: in the old days, such a reception was said to endanger the very fabric of a building, threatening to bring the house down on the heads of the audience, even as they revelled in the performance.

'There were about five hundred guests at the Savoy ballroom, and when Herbert and I arrived people got up and applauded; it was like events I'd sometimes been asked to,' wrote V incredulously of the reception that followed, 'only this time it was me.' Gielgud enjoyed the show, as did Sybil Thorndike, though Gilbert Harding was overtaken by sleep. Noël Coward wrote, 'Darling Valise, you were quite quite QUITE marvellous – you're a dear, darling clever girl, and Father is very proud of you!' (He really seems to have thought so, adding in his diary that she 'made a triumphant success'. Sometimes, one has to double-check with theatrical approbation.) The show ran for 900-odd performances, which may not seem much by the standards of today's global *über*-musicals, but it became incontrovertibly the toast of the town.

When it came to published judgements and criticism, the reactions were quite favourable, and it was felt the show would be a winner – 'a night of enchantment', 'brilliantly staged' – with the highest praise reserved for the seventeen 'Siamese children', and the outstanding Muriel Smith, who played the principal wife, Lady Thiang. Lom was warmly received, on the whole, but some reviewers seemed uncertain how to evoke the impression made by Mrs Anna.

'A Theatrical Mount Everest' was the front-page view of *The Stage*, but the *Daily Herald*'s Milton Shulman described her thus: 'as beautiful and passionless as a long-stemmed tulip', while – further along the floral spectrum – there was Derek Granger in the *Financial Times* commenting on her 'lavender coolness, very neat and modest in her bearing, graceful and discreet to a fault'. Not exactly a sweetheart notice, but then came Kenneth Tynan in the *Daily Sketch*, who loved the exuberance of Lom ('never were arms akimboer'), lamented the London regulations that prevented children under the age of twelve being allowed on stage (thus stealing maximum impact from a crucial scene), and then pronounced, 'Miss Hobson is entirely adequate (*not* a term of abuse: look in the dictionary); cool, capable, and sweetly piping; even, occasionally, singing and acting at one and the same time; but hers is a frill-less performance of a part which is all frills.' There may have been trenchancy in this – I never did get to see that show – but such reservations appear to have been shrugged off by the public at the box office. The chief infidel was V's formidable namesake Harold Hobson, who concluded his *Sunday Times* notice: 'The principal parts are taken by Valerie Hobson and Herbert Lom. Their performances will not get past anyone who knows what acting is.' So it goes.

Although he managed to attend one of the charity previews, and was careful to send a number of 'first night' tokens, my father was not there to assist in the celebrations. His excuse was unimpeachable, because he had been chosen to take part in the London–New Zealand Air Race, in which BEA had entered one of their V700 Viscounts. He was to be a steward to the crew of eleven, under Captain Baillie, and they were going to compete in the handicap section for a first prize of £10,000.

The publicity attaching to such a venture was considerable – this was the world's largest air race, with twelve aircraft competing, including four from the RAF – and it was a godsend for the junior minister's profile. In September, he was snapped running in Regent's Park wearing a black roll-collar sweater, and it was reported that his training regime involved the giving up of all smoke and drink, for the duration. There was a practice run to Bahrain that month (not of the type that involved roll-collar sweaters, obviously), when his responsibilities included serving up soup and steak to the crew, though on the long haul itself there were to be carefully frozen portions of gammon, and lamb cutlets, for him to present at 'designated tummy times'.

Despite the ministrations of their caterer, in his immaculate tropical uniform, the *Endeavour* came first in the transport section, taking off on 8 October and arriving in 40 hours and 40 minutes all told, at an average speed of 301 m.p.h. At Christchurch, there was a fulsome reception, and several calls from the crowd of 'We want the cook' – possibly an ironic reference to the original captain of the *Endeavour*, but taken as a photo-opportunity for our man with the in-flight trays. 'The four corners of the earth do not exist any more,' announced J and he declared the journey had been 'one of the wonders of the world'. It all went to show that Britain led the world when it came to civil aviation, of course, and the whole enterprise had been an unprecedented coup. He returned via Australia, where Charles Gairdner was now the Governor, and on his departure for London J was presented by the chief executive of Qantas with a cookery book, in case he ever wanted to fly down again. But it was the last time, to my knowledge, that he was ever responsible for preparing a meal.

On the evening of 15 December 1953, Jack Profumo collapsed in the lobby of the House of Commons and was taken to the London Clinic for an emergency operation to remove his burst appendix. He contracted pneumonia, and became so ill that he did not return to official duties until March of the following year. The pressures of his lifestyle and workload had depleted his energy, and his doctor, Sir Horace Evans, said he would only continue to look after him during the convalescent period if my father promised never again to smoke a cigarette – a vow to which he rigidly adhered. (He said he never stopped missing it, though, and just once, during an infernal attack of midges on a distant Scottish moorland in 1974, I gave him a Silk Cut which he smoked so greedily it was practically gone in one gulp.)

V sat by his bed whenever her schedule permitted, but she maintained it was just loyalty for old times' sake, and as soon as he was well enough to travel up to the Scottish Borders – where Maina and Harold now had a home – J received a letter saying she was sorry, but the reiterative off/on relationship was now making her so unhappy that she could not agree to see him for some time. He replied with what seems like genuine anguish: 'My Girl . . . I feel hopeless and helpless. I know all you do and say is to spare me, but I'm part of you, and I know you don't believe in *us* any more.' He was about to enter his fortieth year, and feels abandoned. 'Now where shall I go to hide?' He pleads with her not to be so absolute in her sanctions: 'We might just do one of those old walks and have one proper talk, oh please, please consider this so we could have a plan fixed which had *hope* as its basis.' He liked to sign off with little bursts of poetry, in this case a natty translation of Yeats: '*Marche doucement, car tu marches sur mes rêves.*'

Now Valerie was in a genuine quandary, because Robin's letters were also becoming more urgent and his propositions were not without their blandishments. A biddable millionaire with a fine title and a superb estate, and of whose children V had become fond, would indeed offer her and the infant Mark a wealth of opportunity; she even thought she could handle Robin's drinking (her own mother had coped, after all), but she felt she just did not love him. She wanted the family life so far denied her, but the man she did love had failed to respond to the implied ultimatum, and was apparently antipathetic to such a prospect. Her dilemma was partially resolved by Robin's own erratic behaviour. At the end of January 1954, he turned up at the stage door in a sarcastic mood, harangued the stage manager, and delivered a chamber-pot (apparently, he had found a wartime photograph of J with a pot on a stick, and was intending some emblematic association). Then, over supper in the Savoy Grill, he revealed that his doctors thought he ought to check into a clinic for six weeks. To keep his spirits up during that time, would V consider his proposal one final time, and lend him a keepsake to help him through the treatment for his depression? She took off an eternity ring of little rubies, and passed it over to him. During his time away, she went to discuss the situation with his eccentric mother, Edie, who advised her against the marriage for her own sake. When she told Robin at lunch in Claridge's, he handed the ring back (he had had it enlarged to fit his finger) and a waiter saw it; soon the rumour was abroad that they were secretly engaged.

It may have been this that spurred Jack on, for by the summer of 1954 he had certainly re-entered the lists. He was smart enough to recognize when the game was up, and he did nothing by halves. 'I knew I was being led along on a lead,' he told me dreamily, 'but I didn't mind, because she was this beautiful angel.' In August, he left a note for my mother at her flat:

> My love – it is a queer sensation being alone in your home with all your beautiful personal belongings around me and even the smell of you still pungent and yet so quiet and lifeless without the lifegiver – That's what you are to me, the lifegiver . . . I've been so terribly happy these last few hours. I know life could be like that – full and real with you and in return I'd try to make you happy. In the mean time I leave my heart. I love you. Jackaranda.

After collapsing on stage during her reprise of 'Hello, Young Lovers' one night, V was confined to bed with a severe bout of gastric flu (good news for her understudy, less so for the management). 'The smell of mimosa entered before Jack did, his face peering through bunches and bunches of the pungent stuff, still in its exquisite fluffy stage. He scattered the bed with its unique fragrance, bent down and kissed my clammy forehead. "Will you marry me, please?"'

Their engagement was announced on 19 October and immediately there were differing versions of the story. 'I want to be 100 per cent wife,' V was reported as saying, and J confirmed that 'Miss Hobson will abandon her acting career', adding (with a politician's hot-wired phrase), 'That is her own idea as well as mine.' A spokesman for the management, though, was adamant that 'she is too valuable a property to be spared from the show.' That arch-snob Chips Channon MP, having misread the 'King and I' reference in the papers, stopped J in the lobby and congratulated him on marrying into royalty. Seeking official permission from the Prime Minister, J was assured by Churchill, 'You are a very lucky young man. She will be able to sing you to sleep.'

The Department of Transport presented them with the number plate PXHI (Profumo times Hobson are one). Shortly thereafter, he was fined twenty shillings at North London Magistrates Court for speeding.

They were married on New Year's Eve 1954 in the chapel at St Columba's, a pale, angular edifice in Pont Street. There were just fifteen guests, and the theatrical contingent was kept deliberately low (the bride's pianist and dressers were included, the rest had a show to do). A small crowd gathered in the dreary weather – boys on skates, coppers, a couple of chimney-sweeps (one claimed his mum was the Baroness's charlady from Dolphin Square, but I suspect they were both from Central Casting). 'The Baron and I' ran one headline, the last, feeble voltage from a sub-editor's desk before closing down for another year.

They flew to Paris for their first night, with a VIP send-off from the commandant of London Airport, and champagne to speed them and all their fellow passengers on their way. They stayed at the Ritz, and Valerie's second honeymoon seems to have been more successful than her first. When, next morning, they were about to depart for Monte Carlo – a motorcycle escort from the American Chief of Staff was already gunning its engines – the duty manager of the hotel came scuttling down the steps brandishing the junior minister's pyjamas, which had lain all night, untroubled, beneath his pillow.

Ann Martin stood in as Mrs Anna during my mother's absence, but the management were keen to get V back. From the start of their married life, though, differences of opinion took root concerning her work. J assumed he had made it clear that he needed a full-time polit-ical wife, and refused to understand her commitment, not only contractually but emotionally, to the show that was proving the

apogee of her career. 'I was in love with my husband and my work –
why should I not be able to have both?' She wanted to finish playing
'her' role for the duration of the run, and the very request to be
released – which was denied – threatened to tarnish the whole experience. 'I thought nothing could cause me unhappiness at such a
time, but this certainly did.' She was shocked to have been involved
in such an altercation at such an early stage of a production, but fortunately I was able to help resolve these local difficulties.

'I became pregnant in February to my joy and dismay' (a nice
amalgam of emotions from your own mother, but I take the point).
Of course, J met the news with especial 'joy and glee that now the
theatre would have to find a replacement. But they didn't, and
appeared to make no effort to do so.' There was an ominous lack of
rumour about any recalls or auditions, either. 'It was early days in my
pregnancy, so nobody knew anything except the management – and
most carefully they kept their secret. Perhaps they were right to, for I
could have miscarried. I'm not even certain they didn't expect I would
arrange an abortion.' (I believe that idea was more than obliquely
mooted.) The proudly expectant father – one must assume that the
protection of his spouse and the well-being of his first legitimate
offspring took priority – became fiercely impatient that no announcement was forthcoming. At three months, V had to tell her dressers,
because the boned bodices were becoming too tight. Pettish at not
getting his way, J jumped the gun and told fellow MPs of his good
news, which found its way into the papers on 21 March (this baby was
news, too).

One night in April V fainted following her waltz scene, and a
doctor's certificate released her from the show. She never appeared on
the stage again.

Churchill had resigned, and there was much electioneering and
canvassing for my father in the months before I arrived. On 26
May he beat the Labour candidate with an increased majority of
13,312.

Sir John Peel had predicted I should appear on Halloween, but –
like my mother before me – I was inconveniently born a day too soon.
Jack Profumo was forty and Valerie was thirty-seven, not the youngest

of parents. 'Almost the first flowers to arrive came from Edie Londonderry. Robin had died eleven days earlier.'

At the Chelsea Arts Club Ball on New Year's Eve of 1955, my parents celebrated their first wedding anniversary dressed as a pair of dominoes – but then, they always did have a talent for being spotted.

IV

Sleeping with an Elephant

I CAN SCARCELY pretend that there was anything remotely deprived – let alone traumatic – about my early childhood, but the circumstances of my upbringing will give some idea of the sort of family we were. I may have ended up with what W. B. Yeats called a 'foul rag-and-bone shop' for a heart, but this was not the result of any juvenile neurosis: it was a happy enough time, and if anyone suggests otherwise I'll come after him with a tyre iron.

Number 3 Chester Terrace felt virtually palatial to me as soon as I was in any position to appreciate it even though it had only three upstairs bedrooms, but it was not really a house disposed towards the activities of small children. It is said that Nash – architect to the Commissioners of Woods and Forests – built the house for himself, and ensured that the stairs were particularly wide and shallow, as his wife was an invalid. Certainly, the entrance hall and staircase were impressive for a place of its size: the stone flags gave a hollow metal ring, like a percussive cough, when the leather or steel-capped soles and heels of adults struck their way across them, but with my crêpe- or rubber-based footwear I could never emulate it. The stairway was also original stone, with a rising carpet in dark green held in place by brass rods with dramatic finials shaped like arrows.

Although my mother had helped to brighten it with specially commissioned *trompe l'oeil* panels (by Martin Battersby), this vestibule made for a gloomy first glimpse of the house, with its striped grey wallpaper. The dark inner hall, off to the right (which led to the dining-room), was permanently crepuscular, having a stained-glass window 'embellished with elaborate *lambrequins*' (according to one design maven), the sense of draped and mantled solemnity making it like a side-chapel of the most unwelcoming sort. This rarely bothered me, as it was not a part of the house where I was encouraged to spend much time.

The finest space was the forty-foot drawing-room, with French windows overlooking the garden, and the park beyond. This was my mother's domain, decorated in the Regency style (the designer was Boudin) with airy walls a wash of primrose and eau-de-Nil, an Aubusson carpet, a chandelier I was convinced was constructed from diamonds, and several draped side-tables with an array of those *bibelots* and *objets de vertu* that both parents liked collecting – pagodas carved from ivory, an Epstein head, a bejewelled bulldog by Fabergé – none of which, understandably, were for sticky-fingered touching. When I was old enough to be deemed presentable (there was a great deal of formal entertaining) my treat was to hide under the green velvet of the table that was least surmounted with treasures, and to be allowed to nibble away at rice crackers from the black japanned tin, with its picture of a single pink blossom on the lid.

Room fragrance of course now enjoys its own, demented industry, but in the fifties such domestic essentials had yet to be discovered, along with electronic deoderizing plugs, patchouli joss-sticks, and the whole panoply of aerosol bliss. You might be lucky to find an acidic-smelling Airwick bottle in the lavatory, with its slightly obscene snout damply exposed, but that was the extent of it. My mother's room, however, was often sweet with the heavy pine scent of candles in glass holders; they came from Paris, but then whenever my father gave her an exotic present (which was quite often) he would claim that it 'had been specially flown in from Paris', and I had no cause to disbelieve him. None of my other friends had houses with rooms that smelled quite like this, I think, but perhaps we were just living up to our name.

I was christened on 16 January 1956 by Dr Robert Scott, in St Mary Undercroft, the crypt chapel of the House of Commons. My god-fathers were John Hare (shortly to be Minister of Labour, and then Chairman of the Tory Party) and the Colonial Secretary, Alan Lennox-Boyd; Peggy Dunne (the first chairman of the Conservative Association for Stratford, a handsome woman, with an artificial hand she always kept gloved) and Whitney Straight's wife, Daphne, were my two godmothers. The *Star* dubbed me a 'Commonwealth baby', and the *Birmingham Mail* reported that the infant David John, upon being wetted, 'gave vent to his disapproval in lusty tones'. David and John were the year's most popular names, so that part, at least, was relatively normal.

Unlike Samuel Beckett – who could recall the (disagreeable) sensation of being born – my first memory is of pushing a large wooden handcart around the grounds of a country house, which a photograph dates at July 1957 (I was therefore not quite two). The rest of it is not all perfectly linear, of course, and much of my first five or six years is more of a time-ball, a bolus of impressionistic events. At the centre of this pleasant whorl is a small woman in a double-breasted coat and a hat like a helmet of grey felt: she was called Nanny Measor, and her Christian name (Hilda) was something I did not discover until after she died.

Because they were so busy with sundry professional matters, my parents delegated the care of their child almost entirely to others. This did not seem strange in those days, in their walk of life, as the vogue for being 'hands-on' was still more than a decade away, and it was generally acknowledged that children could prove extraordinarily inconvenient during those formative first seven years of their lives. Even by the prevailing standards of the times, however, I guess that neither of them was instinctively disposed towards the company of children; my father, I think, had almost minimal interest in the practicalities of parenthood (the pseudo-Mafioso notion of 'the family' may have registered in his imagination, but that was like some Socratic ideal). In his case, married life had not just introduced a baby, but also a stepson aged five: Mark, though never formally adopted by J, was brought up as my older brother, and over the years my mother tried (for her own emotional reasons) to convince my father that he was effectively their mutual child. Her previous visions of a happy family had so often proved leaky that she was determined this one would be watertight. (Simon, of course, was away in the Rudolf Steiner home, and I was not taken to visit him until I was sixteen.) She ensured we were largely kept out from under J's feet – irritating my fastidious father with too much circumambient infantilism was not a risk she was going to run.

The house accordingly operated on a strict basis of 'divide and rule', which I expect suited all parties, although the system could only be maintained by certain necessary tensions. Nanny's terrain – which I rather presumed was my personal fiefdom – began upstairs in what was called the 'night nursery', a bedroom I shared with Mark. There was not much concession to childish décor, but as we were five years apart it was probably hard to strike a balance. Where now, perhaps, there would be jolly posters and a pile of cuddlesome facsimiles of the latest cartoon characters, we had prints of *The Light of the World* (Holman Hunt at his most saccharine), Dürer's somnolent rabbit, and a pastel of a juvenile shepherd – probably some nascent saint – praying at dawn with his improbably pristine flock. The bathroom we shared with my father, an invasion of bachelor privacy he silently resented, so here, too, the paraphernalia of bath-time was kept to a happy minimum. I was forbidden to touch his enticing bottle of 'Coral Skin Food', the initialled shaving-brushes with wood-and-ivory handles, or any of the slim tortoiseshell combs, and was instructed never to press the bell, set in its glass splash-back, that the previous tenant had installed to summon servants in the case of apoplexy during the master's ablutions. The heated towel rail would, if so much as approached, fuse the skin of my fingertips to it for ever.

Except to the analyst or oneiromancer, people's dreams are usually tedious in the relating, but there must be some reason why for years – until I became a father myself, in fact – I used to dream of that bathroom, its ribbony wallpaper, the pink linoleum floor with a pearl-coloured star inset, the high, tiny window. I enter the room at night, the light inside is a kind of dandelion yellow; I do not want to look in the mirror above the basin – but know I must, and what I will see. The face is not (yet?) mine, but that of an old man with a curiously long neck, and trim white hair, who is nodding at me, and passing the palm of his hand repeatedly across his forehead. At that stage I always felt as if the skin on my face were tightening uncontrollably, and then I would fall through the floor into the foundations of the house.

When I was five, a magazine ran a feature about our daytime nursery, which my mother had selected as her favourite room – 'And in it we become what we like most: the Family.' The accompanying

Castel Guelfo, the Profumo family home near Parma, Italy

Baron Joseph Alexander Profumo, my great-grandfather, founder of the Provident Assurance Company, photographed in Italy (*c.*1880)

My grandmother's favourite picture of my father, aged four (1919)

Top left: The Profumo family, outside their home at Avon Carrow in Warwickshire (1936) *From left to right, standing*: my uncle Phil, my grandfather, my aunt Betsy, my grandmother, my aunt Maina. My father is kneeling, with his camera

Bottom left: At a polo match in the West Country, September 1933. *From left to right*: Captain Phil Magor, the Maharaja of Jaipur, my father (plus camera), his sisters Betsy and Maina, and June Harrison Broadly

Right: Still clutching his camera, my father poses with Stan Laurel (*right*) and Oliver Hardy, Hollywood (1935)

Below: Returning from his tour of the Far East (autumn 1935), my father displays the cedar-wood coffin he bought in Peking as a present for my grandfather

Above: My father in uniform fighting the Kettering by-Election (February 1940)

Left: Second Lieutenant Profumo training with the Northamptonshire Yeomanry at Bovington in Dorset (autumn 1939)

Top right: The official Christmas card from 16 Air Liaison Section, 1941: Captain Profumo shoots a line

Below right: My father (*left*) escorts German officers to the surrender in northern Italy, 4 May 1945

My parents in a relaxed moment during the campaign for the general election, Stratford-on-Avon (spring 1955)

My father, as Parliamentary Under-Secretary of State at the Colonial Office, officially greets HRH Princess Margaret as she arrives in Trinidad for the inauguration of the Legislature of the Federation of the West Indies (April 1958)

Nursery tea at Chester Terrace, 1958. *From left, clockwise*: my brother Mark, our mother, her mother, my paternal grandmother, myself, and Nanny Measor

The author, aged four, pretending to take a photo of his parents and Mark (*left*) in the drawing room of 3 Chester Terrace (1959)

VOTE PROFUMO

MAJORITY
14,129

With warmest gratitude for your great assistance and valuable support.

John Profumo

Left: The Conservative Party Election Victory calendar, Stratford-on-Avon, 1960

Below: Selwyn Lloyd (*left*) and my parents leaving a lunch to commemorate Shakespeare's birthday, Stratford-on-Avon (1961). They are carrying rosemary 'for remembrance' (*Hamlet*, Act 4, Sc.5)

photograph shows a shipshape space with a high skylight, a rocking-horse, a toy 'shop' in a state of preternatural tidiness, a blackboard, and a boy with slicked hair squatting on his tricycle. Although I remember it as being a place of fun, it strikes me now as lugubriously appointed, with barred windows and more of the same uplifting line in framed pictures: the Angel of Mons, a Victorian devotional sampler, a photograph of Drury Lane. I was not encouraged to make much of a mess, and the impression of orderliness was not just for the benefit of the cameras. My parents did not wish a ragamuffin for a son, and, even on excursions to Regent's Park, Nanny would distract me from any activity that might involve conspicuous dirt. There were some private gardens nearby, to which we held a key, and here was garaged my red pedal-car, which I could drive sedately around the gravel paths without fear of mud appearing on my sandals. I was cosseted and spoiled, and was, I suppose, a regular little Caspar Milquetoast. There was plenty of formal attire (often from Rowe's in Bond Street, a fabulously expensive shop that had in its *vitrine* the life-sized model of a horse), and even the concept of mufti involved dungarees with ironed creases, and knitwear that buttoned along the shoulder.

I was teasingly known as Little Lord Fauntleroy; when I played Donald Duck years later in a student production, I was pleased to discover Fauntleroy was his middle name.

It was not an unhappy regime. Nanny Measor, despite her somewhat masculine demeanour, was a lovely, gentle person, and I now see there's nothing wrong with an insistence on cleanliness, frugality (sweets were strictly rationed, and anyway could cause mess) and good table manners. In history, the most supernal instance of the latter was when the author Truman Capote, having overindulged and vomited, exclaimed, 'Well, at least I brought up the white wine with the fish.'

The downstairs nursery was actually an annexe that had been converted from a floor of the adjoining mews building (I have heard tell it was once an MI5 'safe house') but Nanny was not a part of the downstairs staff proper and took her meals quite separately, alone. The door leading off the hall led you down to the nether regions of the house – steep stone steps, uncarpeted, where once a parlour-maid named Beatrice was said to have fallen (or perhaps hurled herself) to an unspecified fate.

The presiding genius of this basement zone was the butler, Stanley Brisco, (whom I always called 'Bustie'), one of the kindliest men I ever met, a doughty Myrmidon in the service of our family and the source of much of my childhood fun. A Lancashire man, he had been under-footman and then valet to the Duke of Beaufort before the war, and he retained a lingering regional accent torpedoed by occasional attempts at gentility ('low-ry' for lorry was one). He had served as a corporal in the Household Cavalry, where (though a batman) he claimed to have seen vigorous action against the 'Nazzis' (whom in stories he often dispatched with 'karachi chops') and once presented Mark with a German submariner's compass, torn from the unfortu-nate enemy's own wrist, no doubt during one of those frequent hand-to-hand tussles between U-boats and the Life Guards.

Bustie inhabited a single room 'below stairs', the untanked walls so damp that I actually saw slugs browsing upon them, but he seemed proud of his cramped quarters and the collection of daggers displayed above the bed. His room – and the pantry where he cleaned the silver in his white apron – were redolent of the dark St Bruno mixture he smoked in his briar, a reassuring reek that suffused the first two decades of my life. Now portly, with a black waistcoat and stretched watch-chain, Bustie's side-whiskers tended to unruliness and his collar sported a furfuration of fine dandruff, but he remained a stickler for routine. He also had a penchant for grotesque impersonations. Whenever I heard his heavy tread on the wooden stairs to the nursery, I knew he might enter pulling a face, or clacking his false teeth, or tunelessly rendering some music-hall song ('K-k-k-Katie, swallowed an a'penny . . .'). He would drill me with my rocking-horse like a trooper, barking out, 'Stand t'yer 'osses. Prepare to mount!' On my birthdays – almost the only time I ate in the dining-room – he always put on fancy dress to bring in the cake. One year he was a cowboy, another it was Mother Goose with full *maquillage*. I don't know if he was any good at buttling as well: I expect he was.

One of his favourite turns was to mimic Quasimodo, but here he had to be furtive as, for a while, we had a cook named Mrs Bivar, a lizard-skinned Anglo-Indian lady with a hairnet, who was so bent from poliomyelitis that she could not look an adult in the eye, and moved, left shoulder first, with a coleopteral hunch. Although he was not overly fond of women, Bustie would never have hurt anyone's feelings deliberately. He was an old soldier, a bit of a bully and full of bluster, but with a sense of decency – 'This is my religion, in here,' he would tell me, thumping his heart. When I was little, he called me 'Master David', then I was 'Mister David' in my teens, but in time I became just 'luv'.

At the age of four I started to attend Garden House School, off Sloane Square, the fashionable establishment run by a Miss de Brissac (its turquoise-blue uniform alone was smart enough to sway parental choice). Here, on my first day I met James Chatto – son of the actor, Tom, and the theatrical agent, Ros – and was entrusted to his care. I spent the morning pushing some Lego around the perimeter of my black-and-red metal desk until the bell sounded for break, and I was appointed deputy to his milk monitorship. Jamie remains my oldest friend, and now, as a distinguished food writer in Toronto, he monitors more than mere milk.

For some years, my two 'best' subjects at school were scripture (a larval form of divinity) and geography (at that stage mostly colouring); I was adept at the former, as I had been going to Sunday school virtually since I was a foetus, and studied the Bible as soon as I could read – while my familiarity with maps came from the fact that my father's work involved what was then considered a remarkable amount of overseas travel. On the nursery wall there was a sizeable map, much of it still comfortably tinted pink, and a number of flag-pins with which I could track the global progress of the Minister – destinations that, over this period, ranged from Antigua to Zanzibar.

Jack Profumo's career may not have been exactly meteoric, but he was rising steadily through the Tory ranks. In January 1957, he had been made Parliamentary Under-Secretary of State at the Colonial Office in Macmillan's Government; he had asked to follow Alan Lennox-Boyd when he became Secretary of State for the Colonies because he did not want to become typecast in Transport. The scope was certainly broader for his political talents, as now he had to deliberate the constitutional future of Singapore as well as the sewerage schemes for Sutton-under-Brailes. There was also violent dissension in Cyprus over the proposed union with Greece, and convicted EOKA terrorists faced the death penalty. In March of that year, J – deputizing for Alan – had to sign the warrant for the execution of Evagoras Pallikarides, and in return received death threats to his own family, so that for a while my stately pram was tailed by a bodyguard in plain clothes.

My mother had a real fear of flying, but accompanied J on several overseas visits, where she created welcome photo-opportunities, and dutifully expressed an interest in what were presumed to be the feminine aspects of the deliquescent Empire. That she loathed both heat and the direct rays of the sun rendered such activities less pleasurable than she made it seem; J, by comparison, was always in his element, but then he did not have her porcelain complexion. One of the most gruelling was a tour of the West Indies that began on 14 April 1958 (her birthday), during which J was to represent the Government in Trinidad at Princess Margaret's inauguration of the Legislature of the Federation of the West Indies. V was almost enervated by the heat as she toted her collapsible parasol around sugar plantations, inspected hospitals and gave interviews to Radio Demerara. She rose to the occasion, however, and was described by the *Evening Standard* as 'a film goddess with Grecian-styled auburn hair, modest tiara and immense soft chiffon crinoline in blue', seated at the banquet next to a Roman Catholic archbishop in full magenta. They tucked into turtle soup, lobster and Dominican grouse, rounded off with pineapple. There was a display of fireworks, followed by dancing (though it was not on this occasion that HRH, surrounded by local officials beseeching her for a calypso, began, 'Eeny meeny . . .').

During a stay on Grenada, where Sir Colville Deverell was the personable Governor, a thief entered Government House on the night of 2 May and stole J's signet ring, gold watch and money from their bedroom while they were asleep. Worse, his Private Secretary (Michael Cahill) lost some official documents which had been unsecured. According to Jamaica's *Daily Gleaner*, 'an orderly, off duty, grazing a cow some distance away, reported that he saw a man running from the house and chased the man, but the prowler escaped in the dark, wooded area.' The matter was played down, to save face, and shortly thereafter V (understandably alarmed) flew home, although J had to continue his tour.

In November, a telegram from the Windward Islands confirmed that Festus Lewis, aka 'The Spider', an escapee convict 'wanted for the murder of his paramour', had been chased by gendarmes on Martinique for failing to produce a passport while registering at an hotel, and, cornered in a cul-de-sac, had 'shot himself through the heart' (which was mighty convenient for the police paperwork). In his lodgings were discovered J's watch and twenty pounds sterling, which were duly returned. No sign was ever found of what had been the old Baron's ring.

The most exotic assignment fell to J that October, when he was sent via Malindi to the Seychelles aboard the frigate *Loch Fyne*, to assess the tourist potential of those blissfully underdeveloped islands, and to report on whether they merited a possible air link. He spent a busy week inspecting the coconut plantations, the carpentry shop, the prison, and the leper colony on Curieuse. His report noted the huge disparity in income between the *grands blancs* (the prosperous planters) and their workers, who earned three pounds per month, and pointed out that 'Many of the Colony's leading personalities are bastards' (the illegitimacy rate was indeed running at 60 per cent). Gonorrhoea was a serious problem, and there were inklings of political unrest from an ex-serviceman named Harry Paget. The Under-Secretary recommended diversification into the perfumery market (naturally enough) and noted that, in the absence of her husband, the Archdeacon's wife was partial to rock-and-roll. This very thorough report concluded that the Seychelles were often thought to be the original Garden of Eden: 'The only thing which is lacking in atmosphere and which would make the tourist sceptical is the serpent' – there were no snakes. 'Even Archbishop Makarios isn't there any more!' (In 1956–7 he had been exiled on the islands for his suspected EOKA sympathies.)

Whether it was for his cheeky style of reportage, or for services more generally rendered, J was moved sideways to become Joint Parliamentary Under-Secretary for Foreign Affairs – a more senior department, making him effectively number four at the Foreign Office. Selwyn Lloyd was the Foreign Secretary: this shy, gloomy, quirky man became one of my parents' closest friends, and a stalwart in times of strife (my godfather Alan Lennox-Boyd was, too, but his covert homosexuality almost landed him in the profoundest trouble of his own). Not long afterwards, in January 1959, following a speech he gave to the First Session of the UN Economic Commission for Africa in Addis Ababa (and the first of his private audiences with Emperor Haile Selassie), J was promoted to Minister of State for Foreign Affairs after the resignation of Commander Sir Allan Noble. This was a significant fillip to his career – plus a pay rise to £4,500 per annum – but the *Daily Telegraph* reckoned it was an 'unenviable role' which involved frequent absence from family and homeland, both Anthony Nutting and Selwyn himself having found it onerous: 'It is a lonely, exhausting and rather unhealthy post.' My father was simply delighted.

It was from this stage that my parents began to be treated like VIPs, as they embarked on a heady, if heavy-duty, round of official entertaining (meeting the heads of all the overseas missions being one pressing obligation). Dinners were hosted at Lancaster House for the Spanish Ambassador and the Prime Minister of Jordan, there was a State Banquet in honour of the Shah of Iran, and dinner with Her Majesty at Buckingham Palace. They were now out more nights than they were at home, maintaining a suitably high profile at charity functions, enjoying the limelight. During a single weekend they went to shows at the Coliseum, Covent Garden, and the Palladium, and my mother's diaries show a hectic round of clothes fittings (her dressmaker was named Martelli), hair appointments, and lunch at places like Scott's. Their dinner parties (all minutely recorded in a book, so that menus and *placements* should not be repeated) list their friends as the Hopes, Perths, de Lazlos, d'Erlangers, Thorneycrofts, Beamishes and Amerys. In one October week V's diary includes lunch with the King of Nepal, tea with the Queen Mother, lunch at the Palace, and then the wrong date for my birthday. Their passport numbers were issued as 3 and 4, which was classy, but caused problems of disbelief with *enregistrement* abroad. Some in the Tory Party regarded my father as a jumped-up opportunist, though, and apparently his nickname in such circles was 'the Head Waiter'.

There were not many theatrical friends among their group, and I think at this stage V's social life was quite busy enough for her not to miss her former vocation too much. In later years, my father liked to intimate that she had never been entirely popular in show-business circles, and that she had a reputation for being prim, aloof, a little difficult and unapproachable. I think it suited him to believe this (mollifying any guilt at having uprooted her career as it was fully blossoming), but there is some truth in the suggestion that hers was not the warmest persona in that particular world. In private, her cold eyes belied a volatile temperament – she was an Irish redhead, after all – but for her newly public role she appeared ideally suited, and newspaper captions often added, after J's job description, 'husband of Valerie Hobson'. My mother had become a glamorous asset, with a fulsome figure, a gracious style, and something of a reputation for her hats. 'I wear my clothes, and never let them wear me,' she assured one interviewer, 'and they must never, never be cute. I like to feel I can go and dig for snails or play in the nursery.' She favoured English clothes, going to Worth or Victor Stiebel, but she reckoned native shoes were too stiff so she preferred Italian. One of her outfits included a fitted skirt made from genuine python skin, and she possessed an exquisite range of stilettos (I sometimes slipped them on, with Oedipal pleasure). Their schedule was so busy that often I only saw my parents in their evening clothes, and some of V's dresses were sufficiently impressive that she could scarcely squeeze down the corridor to my night nursery: there, veiled in Ma Griffe, her hair up, pearls and *diamantes* quivering from her lobes, she would say good-night prayers with me, or read antiquated tales from the old 'Brown Book' she had kept since childhood – Balder the Beautiful, Baba Yaga the Witch, the Crab and the Monkey.

So habituated did I become to the spectacle, just before sleep, of my parents coming along the landing resplendent in finery which seemed to owe something to my Ladybird picture books that I began to edit them into my somnolent montages of figures from folk- and fairy-tales. One persistent vignette – which was to prove what science-fiction writers call a promesia, or memory of the future – involved a procession of bishops closing in on my room, in full cope and cassock, wielding thurifers. This particular pageant must have been prompted by my Illustrated Bible, and the pictures of the Magi, who hailed – as the carol reminded us – from somewhere called 'Orien Tar', which was presumably why one of them was always black. Well, I was only four.

My mother left me a number of envelopes to be opened after her death, and one contained a letter (written in 1965) about her attempts to have more children, her miscarriages, and my 'unborn sister', the daughter she never had (I think, perhaps, lost). She suggests one day I might glimpse this girl in a dream, beautiful as she would have been, 'free from decay'. 'She will have your eyes and hair. Your sweet smile, and something of your heart. Warm her with your laughter, because I shall not be with you. And in your way – the way only you will have – make her know, I loved her.' (Perhaps it was for this reason, when I came to have a daughter of my own, that my mother could hardly bear to lavish affection upon her.)

In the absence of either grandfather, the senior family figure for many years was Harold Balfour, my uncle, who had moved from the Scottish Borders to Kensington when I was still quite small, and whose home, End House, became a frequent place for the Profumo clan to fore-gather, as my paternal grandmother also lived upstairs.

Uncle Harold was easy for a boy to hero-worship. Physically, he was an impressive older man (my Aunt Maina was his second wife), with thin white hair, a large face and shoulders, and an expression like a bulldog that had just bitten into a nest of hornets. His sense of humour, though, could be adolescent, unimpaired by his partial deaf-ness caused by flying in open-cockpit aircraft during the Great War (followed by five decades of pheasant-shooting without any ear pro-tection). He was already retired, and a Tory peer, by the time I was aware of him, having been elected MP for the Isle of Thanet back in 1929: on his first day, in the lobby of the House, he had met a bearded old Member who declared, 'I haven't been here since Gladstone's last parliament.' This sense of his belonging to an even remoter generation than my parents was one I savoured increasingly as I grew up. He served as Under-Secretary for Air to both Chamberlain and Churchill, then became Resident Minister in West Africa in 1944, where his 'parish' encompassed the Gold Coast, Gambia, Nigeria and the Belgian Congo (he had a fully equipped DC-3 to cover this territory). His cartridge bags – often hanging at the ready in the End House hall when I visited – were fashioned from the skin of a rogue lion he had been obliged to shoot out of gubernatorial duty. He was also a champion angler.

It was Uncle Harold's adventures as an early aviator that astonished me. He began flying at Hendon in 1915, his first lesson costing two pounds, and he received Royal Aero Club certificate number 1399. After two months in the trenches, he had joined the Royal Flying Corps, though in those days the role of aircraft in warfare was still undetermined. In 1914 the Secretary of State for War (Jack Seely) had informed Parliament, just before he resigned over the Curragh Incident, that his office doubted whether planes would have much of a part to play in any coming conflict. My uncle also recalled Seely explaining that whenever he personally was in financial straits his policy was to surround himself 'with a smokescreen of new yachts'. Flying pupils were dubbed 'Huns' because of the regularity with which they killed their instructors. In May 1916, Harold Balfour joined No. 60 Squadron as a Flying Officer and went to France, being promoted to Captain on his nineteenth birthday. In one month, they suffered more than a hundred per cent casualties. The aviators wore sidearms, and covered their exposed skin with whale-oil to fend off frostbite. He told me about the Montrose Ghost, and how he saw Von Richthofen performing acrobatics, and the way fellow airmen fell from their machines – there were no parachutes – and their bodies disappeared a foot deep into the mud when they landed. He would make me model gliders from paper, their noses balanced with a paperclip.

In 1917 my uncle, now serving with 43 Squadron, was brought down by ground fire over Vimy Ridge, but, having decided to fly with the safety harness unstrapped, was catapulted through the wing-struts into the mud, unscathed. He went on to fly more than fifty types of aircraft, and was a genuine ace – eleven confirmed kills, MC and bar, a major at twenty. He later joined the *Daily Mail* as a journalist, on a salary of two pounds ten shillings a week.

He adored Maina, his younger wife, and their daughter (Mary Ann), and was admiring and supportive of my father's increasingly successful career in politics. End House was a late-Victorian folly, with a notably large garden, and two upstairs flats – one occupied by Betty Walker (an elderly cousin and *femme sole*), the other by my grandmother, whom I called 'Granny Boom-Boom', having for a while been unable to pronounce our own surname. The Baroness always received me to tea wearing a hat and veil, the left lens of her glasses blacked out (a source of abiding fascination), and would serve switched egg on toast. Her modest apartment seemed like the *fons et origo* of the family, and my father visited his mama with religious frequency, as did my Uncle Phil (an elegant, bisexual Master of Fox Hounds, who spent much of his time overseas) and my Aunt Betsy (a flamboyant owner of dressage horses, who was madly enamoured of the married Lord Willoughby de Broke). There was always a deal of adult gossip, not least from Maina: she was stylish, waspish, and an incorrigible maker of small-scale trouble, particularly when J was around. She had been but thinly educated, yet possessed such a degree of native cunning that she could read a weakness quite rapidly. Largely because of this subversive trait – which I had not much experienced elsewhere – I was devoted to her.

End House was run by their butler, George Herbert White, a dapper and benevolent homosexual, immaculate, witty and as mischievous as the rest of them. When Valerie Hobson was first introduced to the Balfours, and his lordship had asked her what she would care to drink, 'Whitey' had sidled forward in his striped trousers and announced chidingly, 'M'Lord, Miss Hobson only drinks champagne.'

I made my 'first public appearance' (according to the *Stratford-upon-Avon Herald*) on 17 June 1959 at the Snitterfield Church Fête, the princely sum of £240 being raised. The paper reported that mine was 'a new, but nonetheless welcome, name' on the political scene, though apparently, during my mother's opening address, I piped up, 'But I thought it was Daddy who made the speeches.' (So likely.) In September, I was toted around the constituency in my short trousers to canvass prior to the general election – J was re-elected this time with a majority of 14,129. In the New Year it was announced that Macmillan had recommended he be sworn of the Privy Council.

They celebrated their wedding anniversary in the French Cameroons, where my father was HM Special Ambassador at the Independence celebrations (the royal letter refers to 'Our Trusty and Well-beloved John Dennis Profumo'): President Tubman was to be inaugurated in Monrovia, but just before the international delegates arrived there was a gun-battle at the airport, and they had to make their way to the official car park through a mass of bloodstained glass. At the subsequent banquet – the country became Liberia on 3 January 1960 – there was roast Smithfield ham, Bombe Antoinette, and a '43 Sauternes.

When my maternal grandmother died in April, V took the loss badly. 'Gee', as we called her, had not featured much in my life, being at best a passive figure on the fringes of family gatherings, but I was able to respond to my mother's deep sorrow, and its immediacy. After the funeral, J took her and Mark on a holiday to Rome, but on 10 May V underwent an appendectomy at University College Hospital following which it was announced that she was 'suffering from exhaustion' and had had a 'breakdown'. She was in hospital for seventeen days, and did not appear again in public until the end of that summer.

My first direct intimation of mortality came that same month, among the flowering cherry trees that lined the avenue leading to the park. I had been given a furry leopard with a zippered compartment in the lining designed, I think, for storing one's pyjamas. As we walked towards Queen Mary's Rose Garden, I scooped up as many as I could of the delicious pink blossoms and stuffed them for safekeeping into the belly of my new pet, intending back in the nursery to recreate a fragrant orchard of my own. Some other diversion must have prevented this doomed and vaguely paradisiacal plan, however, and the cuddly cat was forgotten until some days later when I opened it up and was assailed by the sour mash of the fermented petals. How could those crisp, coral-coloured flowers have betrayed me and become this mess of clenched and bruised tissue? (Conveniently, I overlooked my neglect of them.) That smell – both juicy yet somehow lethal – lingered in the toy, which was cast aside and never again was allowed to come near my pillow.

When my father flew off to the Somalian Independence celebrations in Mogadishu, then, owing to my mother's indisposition he went alone. She may have experienced some kind of nervous collapse, but still he was in prancing form – at least, he sounds that way in his letter to her just after departure (27 June), though perhaps the tone was deliberately injected with jauntiness to buoy her spirits:

> My Love, Lippety Pop pops. Off I go to the Turnbull and Asser of the world!! But for only a short short time in our wonderful lovely long life together. One of the fabulous things you have taught me is to be able to revel in the part – cherish the moment and long for the future – and so now I long to be home again and then to try to be more than I am to you and through you . . .
> Jackerandablossom.

There can be no doubt but that he had learned to revel in the part (what politician does not?), but soon there was to be some recasting: in Macmillan's reshuffle of 28 July 1960, Jack Profumo was made Secretary of State for War. It was to be his final appointment, and there were those who later criticized the Prime Minister for ever having promoted my father above the level of his competence; but it suited him because of his wartime experience of rank and file in the Services, and, despite the *terribilita* of its title, in truth it was not that senior a post (he never was in the Cabinet, *pace* some accounts). There was an annual salary attaching of £5,750. At a speech in Shrewsbury he later explained, 'Working in the War Office is like sleeping with an elephant – you get overlaid, and whatever you do nothing will happen for two years.' This proved to be about right.

There was another family appointment that year, which was not a cause for celebration. Nanny Measor gave in her notice, as the strain of looking after us during the holiday periods had become too much for her. From new lodgings in Acton, she wrote my mother a letter (dated 2 May) that I discovered a few years ago; she fondly records how 'I came to you for a month and stayed three and a half years' and has just returned from communion: 'I think I wept for most of the service, David was in my thoughts all the time, *no one* knows how much I miss him, it's just like being parted from my own child.' I was feeling something of the same, for her replacement (who had arrived on 29 April with a capacious carpet-bag and a dark velvet hat) was a Frenchwoman named Veve. She wore her hair in a netted black bun, had a jaundiced countenance, and was emphatically moustachioed, with a no-man's-land wire-field of nostril hair; the mouth was disagreeably thin, like the frontal view of a herring gull in flight, and her green eyes ranged along a permanent fifty-yard stare. She was styled not as our nanny, but a governess. The idea, I imagine, was that she would teach us all French, perhaps by an amalgam of alchemy and mesmerism. Our first holiday was not a success.

My parents often left London for the weekend together, but there were really just two places where we went regularly *en famille*. Rather surprisingly, one of our rural retreats belonged to my godfather John Hare (later Lord Blakenham), who owned Cottage Farm, in Suffolk. Here was my first real experience of the countryside, and its details imprinted my imagination for years – the delicious freedom of the strawberry fields, the malty tang of Jersey milk taken straight from the sinister, clicking machines operated by the cowman, the little green pond where I trailed my butterfly net for newts and tadpoles. Every visit seemed a treat, because on the farm I was allowed – in between mealtimes – to look less than presentable.

Having served for so long together in uniform, John and Jack were unusually relaxed together; my godfather was a shy, shrewd, friendly man, his voice mellow from cigar smoke, often chuckling drily at his younger friend's more exuberant behaviour. He was shortish and dark, with a close-cropped moustache, and beautiful manners. His wife Nancy was a slender, animated woman with a high laugh that threw her head back; she was a Pearson – the daughter of Lord Cowdray – and Cottage Farm, though too comfortable to be grand, was a slight misnomer. Perhaps because they had three older children of their own, and had not started their family so late in life, the Hares were always welcoming to me; for someone of his background and generation John paid an exceptional degree of attention to his visiting godson (I even frequently ate meals with the grown-ups).

As her lady's maid and *coiffeuse*, Nancy employed a severe-looking woman called Pike – a servant's name worthy of J. P. Donleavy: had Mr White hailed from the Antilles, Regency-style, then his moniker would have been perfect, too.

In the summer, it was traditional for busy parents to dispatch their children and nannies to somewhere nice and safe by the sea, joining them for little spells between other commitments. Since 1956, our chosen place had been Bembridge, on the Isle of Wight, where we stayed for a fortnight at the Royal Spithead Hotel (now no longer). I have never liked beaches, with their necropolitan tang of rotting weed, and the general ubiquity of snapping crustacea, but the experience of the hotel itself was always exciting – though I can now see that there was something of *Death in Venice* about it. Having the run of a spacious bedroom, however barely appointed, was part of the fun, with plenty of floor for laying out, over the sand-gritty carpet, Swoppet Knights in armour, metal train track, and other *desiderata* of the time. Again because of its looming size, the dining-room was a thrill, with its menu full of novelties like melon-ball cocktail, or haddock and chips. The proprietor, Mr Selwyn, was tall with distinguished silver hair, but indulged in minimal chit-chat when it was clear he was merely dealing with nannies; an altogether more fulsome *maître d'* manner was conjured for parents, in whose presence he waxed almost unrecognizably genial.

The path up and down a hill to the beach wended between the front gardens of smart weekend dwellings, gaudy with red-hot pokers and fuchsias. The beach itself was sandy enough and gently sloping, with safe shallows for paddling, a line of duckboards and a parade of wooden beach huts which could be rented for the duration. The place enjoyed the atmosphere of a club, and many of the families knew one another. There were red-and-white rowing boats for hire, and when the tide went out you could pursue razor clams by pouring Cerebos salt down their blow-holes and waiting for them to slide phallically up through the thick, wet sand. My chief fear was of crabs, which in my imagination I espied semi-concealed beneath every scrap and tress of weed – a disadvantage for any seaside holiday. Another disconcerting presence was Mrs Black, who ran the cafeteria; her dislike of children was plain from the gruff irritation with which any indecisiveness was greeted – should one order the strawberry Mivvi (ice-cream being rationed in our family to one unit per day) or the bottle of green Hubbly-Bubbly (entirely forbidden as 'bad for your teeth', unless my mother was there, and feeling indulgent)? For the adults, Mrs Black toted a kettle of fearsome size, with handles fore and aft, and as the tea was made I was assured that if she ever dropped it the water would splash and scald us all – thus making the proprietress the model of an evil witch. (My mother, as was her way, so repeatedly stressed that 'Mrs Black is really a very kind woman' that even my infant suspicions were confirmed.)

But in 1960, Nanny had gone, and there was a change of summer routine: for the first time, we were all going up to Scotland together. Along with the Balfours, my father had rented Braemar Castle, a modest Jacobean stronghold on the banks of the Aberdeenshire Dee (several papers reported that my parents were 'teaching their sons to fish', the *Daily Worker* making some subtle play about profitable fishing in the family's insurance firm). I did indeed make my first catch there – a bootlace eel yanked on worm tackle from the Sluggan Burn – and thus began a lifelong passion which is another story. But the sojourn at Braemar was notable for two other reasons.

When it came to eating, I was a cussed and pernickety child and there were frequent visits to the nutritionists of Harley Street to see why I looked so 'peaky' (anaemia was suspected, but in fact I was just a fussy feeder, and for a while my meals had even to be dished up purified). The new regimen of Veve – admirable enough in principle – permitted no resistance to whatever was on the plate, but one morning, when I cavilled at my serving of porridge, she put her hand on the back of my head and buried my face in the bowl. It was hot enough to have won the scalding Mrs Black's approval, and my caterwauls – which were never slow in coming, even with lesser stimulus – brought my mother down from where she had been enjoying breakfast in bed, and our governess was dismissed on the spot.

The castle had eighteen rooms, but they were mostly small, with thick stone walls and a massy, circular staircase running up the centre. The Hanoverians had refortified the place following the Jacobean uprisings, and the stairs ran up to the battlements in a left-handed circle, so that the troops could have their sword arms free. At three o'clock one August morning, all the bedrooms were suddenly filled with thick bluish smoke, wafted on an updraught through the staircase from the pantry downstairs, where a student working in the kitchen for his summer job had, before retiring, cleared some still live coals out from the fireplace into an ancient bucket made of leather. I was wrapped in a towel and hurried downstairs, past firemen lugging a hose – 'Haul-away, haul-away' – and I could see the kitchen area robed in flickering orange. Outside there was a mêlée, because the Ballater volunteer brigade had first bogged themselves down executing a short cut across the driveway, and then their pumps could muster insufficient pressure for such a tall building, and the fireflow only reached the first floor. A human chain was formed with buckets, but not before the combustible parts of the building had been destroyed. There was only one casualty: my aunt's elderly Pekinese (Chinky-Poo) refused to be coaxed out from beneath their double bed, and was asphyxiated. Once the blaze had been doused, an impromptu ceilidh was staged on the lawn, with sandwiches and drams for the firemen who had converged from several stations. The incident was widely reported, from the *Barbados Advocate* to the *Middlesbrough Evening Gazette*.

As today's 'celebrities' might attest, there can be unwelcome consequences of being in the public eye: in the early hours of 27 October – when it must have been known that my parents were in the constituency – burglars entered my bedroom window in London and made off with my mother's collection of furs (then still a necessary adjunct for stylish ladies-about-town). Two policemen and a detective were posted outside the door, and Scotland Yard suspected it was the work of a specialist gang, 'which has robbed film and theatrical stars of more than £250,000 in three years'. It was thought that someone in the acting world was directing their operations. 'I am not worried so much about the loss of valuables,' said my father stoically, 'but more concerned with what would have happened if David had woken up.' Had I done so, I might never have got to interpret the role of chief cherub in Miss de Brissac's Nativity play that Christmas, when the Stanislavskian donkey deposited dung the whole way up the aisle, thus festively adorning rather a curious year.

In January 1961, J flew off on an inspection tour of the Army in the Far East, involving Singapore, Malaya, Penang, Borneo, Hong Kong and Nepal. At a press conference with General Sir Richard Hull (Commander-in-Chief Far East Land Forces) he said that during a recent meeting with the Russian Ambassador in London he had explained that his position was a misnomer, and that really he was 'Secretary of State for the Prevention of War'. The post now no longer exists, but when one looks at the sorry political representatives of our vestigial military forces there can be little doubt but that Jack – and Valerie who joined him mid-January – were in every sense smarter than average ambassadors for our nation. Successive photographs show them immaculately turned out, despite the rigours of the heat and the real pressures of speech-making and incessant travelling; my mother often wore white gloves to go with her trademark parasol, and the Minister had a natty line in tropical suits, and dark Polaroid glasses (it would have been unthinkable for him to have appeared without a hat). V protested in retrospect that she disliked the protocol, the servants, the evident poverty and its contrast to the pomp and circumstance of their own treatment, but at the time I believe she (understandably) basked in the attention and the occasional theatricality of it all. Guards of honour, and multiple-gun salutes can appear quite flattering, after all.

Subsequent detractors of J's record in this post tended to overlook the fact that he was, to begin with at least, generally popular in military circles – it was not just that he had had some experience of high command, but he was unusually receptive to the daily conditions of living that concerned the mass of ordinary troops. He was also an early master of the photo-opportunity; throughout this period, the archive shows a plethora of examples from regional newspapers of the Minister chatting to other ranks, and he was careful to have copies made and sent with his compliments to their families back home. At that time, recruitment was flagging: the ambitious target was to have an all-volunteer regular army force of 165,000 by 1963, one (not wholly successful) initiative being to persuade National Servicemen to sign on for three years. J was almost as busy maintaining morale on the ground as he was discussing defence policy in the House.

On 28 January 1961 I went to London Airport to welcome them home off their RAF Transport Command Comet. Dressed in my velvet-collared herringbone coat from Rowe's, with a peculiar matching cap, I presented my mother with a bouquet and was pictured being hoisted gleefully over a puddle on the tarmac – 'Happy to be alive,' ran one caption, 'five-year-old David Profumo is lifted clear off his feet.' It wasn't just my parents who enjoyed the limelight.

There was a magazine profile of V by Herbert Kretzmer the next month, which gives some idea of the sorts of publicity they were getting while J's star was still in its ascendant. After recapping on her stage performance, and describing my father as 'a dead ringer for the Siamese monarch' (I assume he meant they had similarly glabrous pates), the interview notes, 'Today he is Secretary of State for War. Tomorrow – who knows?' V lit up a Gauloise – a very occasional prop – and explained her view of modern show business, which she thought was moving too quickly, without people serving their apprenticeship: 'You're a counter-hand one day, a guitar star the next . . . We are becoming a *Reader's Digest* nation.' At that stage, apparently, I was introduced – 'calm and well-mannered' – and presented her with a seashell I had painted as an ashtray (it was a scallop I had bedaubed artlessly with blues). Like a lap-dog, I was given two biscuits – ' "That's enough. You'll blow up with a bang." "Bang!" shouted David.' Herbie concludes, 'David shook my hand solemnly and retired' – dutifully off to say my prayers. The Fauntleroy phase was not yet over, evidently.

In May, J boarded the Royal Yacht *Britannia* in Venice and they set sail for Athens, where there was to be an official unveiling of a memorial to Commonwealth soldiers by Field Marshal HRH the Duke of Gloucester. Protocol was strictly prescribed, and in his cabin (number 9) was a copy of the booklet 'Information for Members of the Royal Household', which included, 'On discovering a fire, the following procedure is recommended – (1) Shout "FIRE".'

At Aintree that spring, my cousin Bobby Beasley had ridden Nicolaus Silver to win the Grand National by five lengths from Merryman II. Just when it looked as if the family could not put a foot wrong, however, my father began riding for a fall.

On Friday, 7 July, Jack and Valerie watched tennis at Wimbledon from the Royal Box, and then drove down to Cliveden for the weekend.

It has been suggested (though never by either of my parents) that around this time their marriage was entering a period of slack tide. Despite the harmonious image naturally presented to interviewers and the public, they were an excitable couple with strong opinions on both sides. One young doctor who came to examine my tonsils then went down to the drawing-room and found V poised and ready to hurl a piece of china at J, who smoothly ushered the GP away with murmured assurances that this was just a little spat, and it was not the first time it had happened. When feelings run high it may enliven a relationship, of course, but it cannot always be counted on as a recipe for success.

I have said that my mother enjoyed much of the attention afforded by a busy political life, but the novelty was beginning to wear off; the continual round of entertaining was becoming tedious, had badly exhausted her once already, and meant they spent precious little time together à deux. He was frequently 'working late at the House' (which history suggests may cover a multitude of sins). I do not believe my father was ever seriously considered as a future prime minister (he was a pragmatist, but did not have the intellectual gravitas), and it was not something for which he was ambitious: in fact, there was some talk between them of J quitting in a year or so while he was ahead, going to the Lords with the peerage to which he would have been entitled (Alan Lennox-Boyd had been made a viscount the previous year), and buying a house in the country.

Whatever the precise reasons, something about their lifestyle was making my mother uneasy, and I have often thought that it might have been that my father had already been conducting an affair. The circles in which they moved were conducive to vertiginous social coquettishness – 'rubbing shoulders' is a handy phrase – and there was a constant, risqué undercurrent to 'high society'. This brinkmanship was certainly agreeable to J, and while I don't say my mother actively encouraged it, she knew what an incorrigible flirt she had taken on, and life was perhaps easier when he was kept happy.

Pukka as he preferred to be in many things, J also had a penchant for its flip side – *kutcha* – when it came to women. He was not often drawn to intelligent, assertive females, preferring decorative, fun-loving, 'available' girls, and there was a certain fascination with the painted and, if not exactly the semi-professional, then the obviously enthusiastic *amateur*. (This does not put him in a rare category of men, of course.) Unlike my mother, he loved parties – even in old age, he tended to be the last chap to leave – and he was famously good company; I gave up counting the number of times a lady has asked me, 'Oh, are you Jack's son? He used to be *such* fun' (the implication being, when he was still allowed out to play). He had scrupulously good manners, knew exactly how to give the impression that someone – male or female – had his undivided attention, and he was a natural charmer, but was not, as Rosamond Lehmann so pungently remarked of Ian Fleming, 'someone who got off with women because he couldn't get on with them'.

It was speculation on my part (having heard tell, maybe from not wholly reliable sources, that he had been seeing a girl who worked in the Swedish Embassy) but I felt that one reason why J later so brazenly denied any misbehaviour with Miss Keeler was that he was on some kind of final warning from my mother, and he could not bear the thought of losing her. When I put this suggestion directly to him, he blinked at me like some rabbit caught in the gamekeeper's lamplight, and denied it as if it were an outlandish insinuation. Certain habits die hard.

Another possibility – the two are by no means mutually exclusive – is that it was my mother who was playing with fire. One of her intimates at that time told me that V was the subject of close admiration by one particular (married) man, and, though I don't believe there was a physical affair, something seems to have been in the air; having another man (or two) definitely in thrall would not have done her reputation any harm in itself, and of course there are certain husbands who would even find such a situation titillating (though I think my father, like many philanderers, was also possessive – even, at times, prudish). Asking a widower who is pushing ninety whether his wife had enjoyed a dalliance was not perhaps the easiest question to raise, but I did so with affected breeziness during an interview. He replied stonily, 'Well, I never had any knowledge of it, no. I never heard of that. I can't answer better than that.' (Coming from the maestro of denials, this did not sound super-convincing.)

There is something else that indicates all was not well between them. Among V's papers relating to this period – they are undated, but I place their composition around 1961 – was a series of lists, headed 'Things I adore about you', 'Things that irritate', and 'Things about me I think irritate you'. I have long been dubious about the process of tabulating thoughts in this way, though I gather it can seem quite therapeutic; what prompted V to draw them up with such a sense of reckoning, I do not know, but I don't suppose she was ever intending to show them to my father. Boldly handwritten – fair copies, probably – they have the outspoken nature of a confessional exercise, and I am inclined to think the contents were honestly meant, though we can all be adept at deceiving ourselves once we start writing things down.

In the first category are various adulatory lover's traits, such as 'your physical courage', 'your boyishness', and 'your smell'. The second – and much longer – list becomes progressively more specific as V warms to her theme. The gamut of things that irritate includes, calling her 'baby', winning arguments by recourse to 'a little-boy face', branding any discussion of 'the children' as 'mawkish or molly-coddling', a reluctance to listen to anyone's problems 'outside the family', and (at odds with his later life) 'your intolerance of anything spiritual or sympathetic or do-gooding'. These are quite serious charges, and there was perhaps a pause here to light up a Gitanes before proceeding to 'Your reluctance to discuss – or even mention – sex. Not "ours", but any erotic or interesting sexy things'; this rather belies the image of the raffish *italiano* and his ladylike spouse, but we're soon on more familiar territory with 'The seemingly natural assumption that any pretty woman (or preferably: girl) is fair game if you can interest her. You will stretch any manners, at any time, to do this – not quietly and discreetly, but laughing and showing off and behaving like an adolescent.' Tsk. The inventory continues with: 'The way you kiss women you hardly know "goodbye" – I do *not* do this with men', and his neglect in complimenting her on her clothes (surely a top-five item on any woman's list when a relationship is having to heave a deep breath and take stock).

Many a partner in life could rustle up a similar farrago of grievances in a fit of pique one evening over a vodka-on-the-rocks when her man is late home from the office, but this rap-sheet is both comprehensive and impassioned, embracing the way he treats servants as 'slaves', his lack of dignity and manners, his lavatorial habits. He complains that she has cut him off from his old friends; she objects to his teasing their small son ('I am firmly convinced it makes David hysterical'), the cut of his trousers ('surely there must be *some* way of concealing your penis'), and the spot-on, sockdolager blow – 'Your "put your head in the sand" attitude about *any important* subject.' This was to be a factor in the years to come, for sure.

There were many more, but I found one complaint quite poignant: 'I love dancing, and yet not for a long while have you done anything except dance with me while casing the dance floor – yet (oh dear!) with someone you're flirting with you dance as if it's the only thing in the world you love'. If anything in her sorry batch of sheets suggests to me that their marriage might have been in a friable state, it must be this: betrayal is ingenious, and can assume Protean forms, but gallantry was always supposed to disguise it.

As I have come to expect, the balance sheet is rounded off with a flurry of self-criticism that smacks to me of V blaming herself for J's flighty behaviour. She upbraids herself for bossiness, flouncing out of rooms after an argument ('maddening, I agree'), a reluctance to wear shabby country clothes and get her hands dirty, 'keeping my eagle eye on you at parties', her liking for clergymen and the crucifix on her bed-head, 'my day-dreaming and introspection', 'my irony' (for which read 'sarcasm', I think), 'my distaste for killing anything, even flies', 'my sharpness about people I don't like (usually because I'm frightened)', and, finally, 'my intolerance of the upper classes as a whole – and *most* rich people, unless they earned their money'. This last point – not exactly *de rigueur* for the wife of a Tory minister at that time – was to become a refrain in my teenage years because, though she came materially to depend on it, inherited wealth was something that caused my mother genuine ambivalence. She was probably a Roederer Cristal socialist at heart, and in her vario-focal utopia the Mr Whites (and possibly the Mrs Blacks) of this world would pour the champagne, and then sit down and join you. Whatever else these animadversions imply, Valerie must have been more than slightly disaffected with her personal life, which perhaps made her forthcoming resilience all the more remarkable.

My parents had never before visited Cliveden, which was then still a private house (when Harold Macmillan was told it had become a hotel, he replied, 'But, dear boy, it always has been one'). The first building there – dating from the *annus mirabilis* of 1666 – was a hunting lodge owned by the 2nd Duke of Buckingham, a Restoration rake who found it convenient for the pursuit of both types of venery. His principal mistress was the Countess of Shrewsbury, whose husband he killed in a duel while she looked on in admiration, disguised as a pageboy. 'The witty Duke of Buckingham was a very bad man,' wrote Alexander Pope, who noted that later he 'slept with her in his bloody shirt'. His verse portrait of the 'great Villiers' on his death-bed (in his 'Epistle to Bathurst') is one of Augustan poetry's most abiding images of decadence: 'alas! how chang'd from him, / That life of pleasure, and that soul of whim! / Gallant and gay, in Cliveden's proud alcove, / The bower of wanton Shrewsbury and love.'

Twice gutted by fire, Cliveden was rebuilt in the Palladian style in 1849 by the Duke of Sutherland (using Sir Charles Barry, architect of the Houses of Parliament), before being acquired by William Waldorf Astor, who gave it to his son Waldorf as a wedding present. He and his Virginian bride Nancy Langhorne – later the first woman MP to sit in the Commons, in 1919 – made it into one of the most sought-after country houses for weekend invitations, and the original 'Cliveden set' included Lloyd George, Charlie Chaplin, and F. D. Roosevelt. Bernard Shaw reckoned, 'It was like no other country house in the world . . . you meet everybody worth meeting, rich or poor, at Cliveden.' It was widely discussed in 1938, as rumours spread that regular house guests such as the Foreign Secretary and the editor of *The Times* were supporters of appeasement. The estate was deeded to the National Trust in 1942, but the family was allowed to remain there.

When Bill Astor took it over in 1952, then, this bower of love already had plenty of political connections. My father had known Bill (now the 3rd Viscount Astor) since his earliest days as an MP, but they were not particularly close friends – there had been a number of previous invitations, but it was not somewhere my parents were especially ambitious to visit. Also present at various points during that weekend were President Ayub Khan of Pakistan, David and Pamela Hicks, Johnnie and Jane Dalkeith, Dickie Mountbatten, Mary Roxburgh, and the painter Felix Kelly – a promising mixture of politics, landed gentry, and the arts. Some social harpies reckoned Bill and his third wife Bronwen (the former model Bronwen Pugh) were struggling to maintain a social set that could continue the cachet of his mother's, but altogether lacked the stylishness to manage it.

One symptom of this was thought to be Stephen Ward, a London osteopath who had been introduced to Cliveden by Bobbie Shaw (the loose-living son of Nancy by her short-lived first marriage). In 1950, Ward had begun treating Bill for aches and pains sustained on the hunting field, and now rented a house on the river – Spring Cottage, a converted mock-Tudor summer house, where it is said Queen Victoria used to like taking her tea. Ward, a clergyman's son, had graduated from the Kirksville College of Osteopathy, Missouri, and established a fashionable practice at 38 Devonshire Street, in London, where his 'healing hands' had been brought to bear upon Churchill, Gandhi, and Frank Sinatra. He was also a portraitist of some talent, and his sitters included Macmillan, Selwyn Lloyd, R. A. Butler, Prince Philip and other 'Royals', and Stanley Spencer in his Cookham studio. He was something of a social cocktail-shaker, and an addict of intrigue. My father described him as 'hugely charismatic', and found nothing in the least sinister about Ward, though they never saw much of one another – 'he was a closer chum of Bill's. He used to mob him up. He was partly a court jester, but also a go-getter of girls.' Ward's own, brief marriage had failed, and he now indulged his reasonably pornographic and voyeuristic proclivities, often by grooming up girls he called his 'bush-babies'. The usual analogy is with Professor Higgins, but in the case of Ward it seems that what initially attracted him to women was the fact that their virtue appeared already besmirched.

Many of the basic facts about what follows are by now ridiculously well known, but I have reproduced in particular a few details from my father's first draft of his statement to Lord Denning (1963). I am not sure how much of this his late lordship eventually saw, but it affirms that Astor had introduced him to Ward 'some time before 1950', when he, J, was still a bachelor and not an MP, and that even then he 'always had a lot of pretty girls about the place. I went, and sure enough found a number of very young models, starlets etc. I think that Maureen Swanson was probably one, who subsequently became Lady Ednam. I also noticed that Dr Ward had a receptionist who was quite remarkably glamorous.' J went to just one of these cocktail parties, then never saw Ward again until 1961.

To return to what is sometimes dubbed that 'fateful weekend' at Cliveden – on the Saturday night, Astor asked J if he remembered Ward, and he said he thought he did. The situation with the cottage, and the likelihood of pretty girls being around, were explained, and the magnanimous host added that he'd asked the Spring Cottage crowd up later to use the pool (originally built so Nancy would not have to swim in the Thames). At some stage, it seems that Astor brought Stephen Ward up to my parents' bedroom, as he had offered to massage my mother's neck: she 'found him creepy', and tried to get J to prevent it, but he said 'it would be ungracious to our host'. (However, when Ward suggested a reprise on the Sunday, V made an excuse and managed to avoid him.) After that Saturday dinner, Bill and my father arrived at the pool ahead of the rest, and saw two men and several girls. One 'who apparently had no bra on' was 'clutching a towel round her', and his lordship slapped her on 'the behind, in a playful sort of way and said, "Jack, this is Christine Keeler."'

'She was a very pretty girl, and very sweet.'

When my father first clapped eyes on her – possibly that is not the right verb – she was a darkly luscious girl of nineteen, an epitome of forbidden fruit with chamfered cheekbones, Slavic, slightly almond eyes (the legacy of her Red Indian blood, so they say), and a look that combined contempt with bewilderment. She appeared a veritable *poule de luxe* in the making, but already she had suffered a roughish existence. After a complicated adolescence in Wraysbury, Berkshire, that included inhabiting a converted railway carriage, and at least one unwanted pregnancy, she had gone to London and at length found work as a showgirl in Murray's Club, off Beak Street. This was a cabaret venue where showgirls like Miss K could appear on stage topless during the revue, provided they did not move, and remained a stationary backdrop to the dancers themselves. The club had a clientele for which rival establishments would have given an arm and a leg-over: it was a popular haunt for well-heeled overseas gentlemen and other aficionados of the twilit Soho world, and it may be that at times the showgirls could make a little extra cash. Ward fell for CK, and they began living together as friends, if not lovers. She was then briefly the plaything of Peter Rachman – 'Polish Peter', the ex-tailor whose name became a byword for exploitative landlordism – and shared digs with Marilyn Rice-Davies (a dancer rather than a showgirl, also the lover of Rachman) before returning to Ward in his house at Number 17 Wimpole Mews.

When I interviewed my father formally about Miss K, it was a cold February lunch-time and we were facing one another in his London flat, grasping a tumbler of Dutch courage apiece. It was not the most relaxing moment of my adult life, but he looked more *paterfamilias* than *senex fornicator*, imperturbable in his tweed jacket and slippers, the carefully knotted Paisley tie and benevolent, half-moon tortoiseshell spectacles. I gulped a hard jolt of gin when he replied, 'Well, I think I knew she was a call-girl. Because earlier I met her in a nightclub off Regent's Street.' So you had seen her elsewhere before Cliveden? 'Yes.' At a club called Murray's? 'Yes. I think I probably had a drink with her.' So, when you saw her again, did you recognize her? 'I didn't put two and two together.' Most unlike you.

Whether or not the above is true (it could be the result of collapsed memories, confusing Miss Keeler with some other girl he met at the club, for instance) there is little disagreement about the fact that *chez* the Astors they met up later for a drink. 'She was very simple and was obviously tremendously impressed by the colossal hall at Cliveden,' his statement continues. 'She kept on saying, "What a house!" I showed her one or two rooms off the main hall, and I certainly put my arm round her, but nothing else happened. I think Valerie and Bronwen had gone off to bed, and I do remember that there was some fooling around with the suits of armour in the hall. I think that I did put a helmet on her head.' Later, when he and Bill were enjoying a scotch and soda, the conversation came round to an appreciation of Miss K's charms, and his lordship recommended J to call up Dr Ward's home when back in town.

On the Sunday morning, Bill drove my father in a Land-Rover down to inspect his horses, and also to view an empty house on the river, because he and V were on the lookout for a weekend cottage. They dropped in on Ward's party on their way back to the main house, where 'a very grand lunch party' took place, with the Aga Khan as guest of honour. At the pool there were swimming races, where J perched Christine on his shoulders 'and we swam races and things and generally fooled about. After the swim I asked Christine if I could have her telephone number, and she said that I was to ask Stephen. Stephen Ward did seem very pleased to have met me again, and told me that his number was in the book and he would like to see me at any time.' One sentence in the draft to Denning nicely encapsulates the mixture of primness and prurience that underlay this whole episode: 'All the girls were very young, and very pretty, and very common, and I remember that subsequently my sister, Lady Balfour of Inchrye, who was there with her husband a week or so before, had said that she and her husband were absolutely scandalized that Bill should allow this man Ward to go up to the pool with all these common tarts.'

Unfortunately for all concerned, another of Dr Ward's eclectic circle of friends had come to join the Sunday fun. Captain Yevgeny Ivanov was working at the Russian Embassy, having arrived in March the previous year nominally as Assistant Naval Attaché. He had quickly established himself as a man about London, a party-lover, enthusiastic drinker, and a keen bridge player (his nickname was 'The Playboy of the Eastern World'). The catalyst to this friendship was, strangely, the *Daily Telegraph*: its editor, Stephen Coote, had been treated for lumbago by Ward, and despite the banal political chit-chat – 'his views would have seemed ludicrous to a mentally deficient child,' Coote robustly recalled – invited his osteopath to a bridge party. He also commissioned him to do for the paper some black-and-white drawings of the Adolf Eichmann trial then taking place in Israel, and Ward suggested that a similar series of portraits of the Soviet leaders might be interesting, but had difficulty obtaining a visa. On a tour of the *Telegraph* offices, Ivanov met the editor, and an introduction to Ward was effected at a subsequent Garrick Club luncheon. 'I had no idea of the existence of any young ladies,' sniffed Coote sanctimoniously in his memoirs, though 'there is always something unpleasant in being connected, however remotely, with a scandal.' Christ on a stick.

Ward was delighted with his new acquaintance, and the chance to attend Embassy parties. Ivanov – while not notably more charismatic or beguiling than many other foreign attachés – proved himself colourful company, and was soon on quite friendly terms with society figures like the Ednams, with whom he played bridge. But Ward was a fantasist in several respects, and liked to imagine himself as a political go-between (during the Cuban Missile Crisis, he seems genuinely to have felt he could defuse the situation with a few words in the right ears); he convinced himself that he was an agent for MI5, and while it is possible they strung him along because at some stage they thought to 'entrap' Ivanov (whose intelligence role was scarcely in doubt), the security services must have entertained strong reservations about the usefulness or reliability of Dr Ward, with his love of gossip, name-dropping, and naive political opinions. There remains considerable doubt over his affiliations, for what they are worth: on the one hand, certain parties have alleged he was helping to run Soviet agents, while others have suggested he had been a card-carrying member of the British Union of Fascists. Whatever the truth – I suspect he swung around like a weathervane, in fact – one can readily imagine the relish with which he viewed the prospect of a Minister of the Crown becoming swept up in the fishnet meshes of his pimping net.

On the night of Sunday 9 July, 1961, 'Eugene' Ivanov drove CK back to Wimpole Mews, polished off a great deal of either vodka or scotch (depending on whose account one believes, if any: they are both incessantly at variance) and either did, or did not, indulge in an energetic bout of recreational sex. Both parties contradict themselves and each other, and it is possible the highly trained sailor cannily refrained from intercourse for fear of becoming compromised, or else simply grew too inebriated to achieve his desired aim. Ward later claimed they had 'drunk between them two bottles of whisky', so it would have involved an heroic effort on the part of the attaché if he did manage to dance the Volga hornpipe before wobbling off into the night – and indeed the matter would be of minimal importance, had the ensuing furore not whirled centrifugally from the premise that, for the brief while that he was in contact with Christine Keeler, J was 'sharing her favours' with a 'Russian spy'. (The joke was that this time the Red was not under the bed, but on top of it.) My guess is that they never did have a fling proper, and that Miss K changed her story to say otherwise when later it sounded like an improvement, and she found herself selling it. The precise level of physical intimacy reached by these members of the cast does not eventually affect my father's transgression – and, *sub specie aeternitatis*, it looks like three-fifths of a row of beans – but it remains a curious nicety.

(In 1966, when Bill Astor died, his executors decided to forgo any further family connection with Cliveden. Earlier that year, Graham Gelder, a young registrar from the local hospital, who was the tenant at Spring Cottage, was found dead there, slumped over the sink. When Lady Astor had the place exorcized by a priest, Dom Robert Petitpierre, he claimed it was one of the most evil places he had ever visited.)

'I do not quite know how to analyse my feelings about this weekend,' wrote my father, 'except that I was extremely taken by Christine, whom I thought was Ward's girlfriend, but he did not seem to be particularly possessive about her.'

Two days later – on Tuesday 11 July – both my parents went to Number 13 Kensington Palace Gardens for a reception at the Russian

Embassy in honour of Yuri Gagarin, the first cosmonaut to return from space. My mother, in one of her most astral examples of millinery, was photographed shaking the hero's hand. J recalled that 'Ivanov came up to me and asked if we remembered him from Cliveden,' and asked if he could get us a glass of vodka,' and that Ward was there, too, with a girlfriend 'called Sally, who was one of the members of the bathing party at Cliveden'. This would have been Sally Norrie, who was originally 'procured' by Miss Keeler for Ward in a London restaurant. Despite his later claims, this was the only time my mother and Ivanov were to meet.

The amorous Minister meanwhile had naturally lost little time in giving chase to the fox. That week, he noted, 'I must have seen Christine once or twice, and I was getting her into a state where I could suggest having an affair.' It is likely that he visited her on the Thursday, after attending an Army Council dinner, because he recalled going round on one occasion 'in full dress'. On the Friday, my mother drove down to Shotteswell, in Warwickshire, to stay with my aunt, leaving the way clear. That Saturday J had to fly to a Territorial Army function in Castle Martin, and then back to Northolt; 'and I think that I must have planned to sleep with the girl that afternoon, when Ward was almost certainly going to be at Cliveden'. But bad weather delayed the plane, so 'I think it was the following day, Sunday July the 16th.' It was that afternoon when it all began.

Even in the immediate aftermath, there were to be disagreements about how long this 'affair' between the two really lasted; to me, my father was emphatically vague on this point – 'I only saw her I think three times, but it doesn't matter' (I thought it might, rather). The suggestions by Miss K that it had lasted much longer, that they had spent time together in France, that he had wanted to set her up in her own flat were dismissed categorically as 'absolute rubbish' – he agreed he might have suggested she 'get out of this dirty life' at some stage 'as a wild possibility', but no more than that. The exact dates for each *sveltina* are hard to establish, with only his ministerial appointments diary from which to work. (One of the illicit thrills of this clandestinity was not so much cheating on his wife as giving his secretarial staff the slip during such tight schedules; J fancied himself as something of a *camoufleur*.)

In a memo, my mother identified some likely days to have been the 19th (after a cocktail party they gave at the Royal Hospital, Chelsea, he going on to 'dine out somewhere and then vote'), the 27th (after a dinner of the Other Club, at the Savoy), or the weekend of the 28th, when V had taken the car to Kent, leaving him to attend celebrations for the 21st anniversary of the Intelligence Corps in the House of Commons.

In his draft statement, J maintained it did not occur to him that Miss Keeler was a call-girl – 'I simply thought that she was a very beautiful little girl who seemed to like sexual intercourse. She had told me that she had done a certain amount of modelling, and that she was now between jobs; that she was hoping to hear from her agent any day that she had another modelling job, or she might even go to America.' He also described her, dismissively, thus: 'She was completely uneducated. She knew absolutely nothing. She never read a book', though it's unlikely he would have been able to discuss much Pushkin, either, given his antipathy to literature. 'All she knew was about make-up and her hair, and about gramophone records and a little about nightclubs.' It's hard to believe J did not suspect what was going on *chez* Ward, though it would then scarcely have bothered him.

On one occasion, when my mother had their car, he borrowed my godfather John Hare's Bentley (it had a distinctive mascot on the bonnet) to take his *petite amie* for a spin. Another evening, she said that they could not be alone because 'some terrible old man who had loved her for a long time was going to take her to the cinema', and indeed a chap with a grey moustache, looking like a retired military man, did arrive (a 'regular client', the police later claimed). On another day, there was Hod Dibben – a man with teeth like wind-chimes, and unforgettable sideburns – and his wife, Mariella Novotny, 'who was a very beautiful dancer of some kind', one day to be the *genitrix* of a separate scandal of her own. The rest of the family were by now away on holiday in the Isle of Wight, so he took Christine for a drive and 'at some stage I called in to Chester Terrace, because I knew it was quite free.' ('It was a very curious thing,' he wrote in 1963, 'but she was extremely frightened of meeting anybody in the house.') There, he took her up to the bedroom, an especially intimate betrayal, which my mother always found hard to forgive.

'Certainly I never saw Ivanov at the flat,' he said, nor was there ever any question of Christine trying to get him to discuss security matters. 'Never. To start with, she wasn't trained enough to be able to make an approach. If she had been trying to do it, she would have chosen a moment for some pillow talk. And there was never *any* of that.' As Peter Ustinov put it years later, 'Such a preposterous idea might have held water in 1914 when a French general rendered forgetful by the delights of orgasm could have moaned, "Ten divisions – two of them mounted" into the attentive ear of Mata Hari.' The so-called 'security aspect' of this story was deliberately exaggerated by the Labour Party in 1963; however inadvisable the *liaison* might have been in other ways (the potential for simple blackmail was quite real), this idea was preposterous. Ward himself told Denning: 'Quite honestly, nobody in their right senses would have asked somebody like Christine Keeler to obtain information of that sort from Mr Profumo – he would have jumped out of his skin.'

Although he gave her a few paltry gifts – some perfume, a cigarette lighter she had admired – J claimed he never paid her money, other than twenty pounds as a *pourboire* for her mother ('it would have been a perfectly natural thing to do'). But when I asked him if he felt he had treated her like a mistress rather than a call-girl, he said, 'I don't think I know the difference.'

(When it eventually transpired that he had given Miss K some of the same scent – Femme, I think – which he used to buy my mother, V went up to the bathroom in disgust, and poured her own bottle down the lavatory. I doubt he was being unimaginative: as any old Sardinian perfumer could have advised – this is literally an example of common scents – it helps to avoid detection if your lover and your spouse both wear an identical fragrance.)

Just before driving down to Bembridge, on 31 July, Mark and I were invited to visit Montgomery of Alamein at his house, Isington Mill, on the River Wey in Hampshire. He took me by the hand, led me across the little river, and showed me the barn where, propped up against the wall, was the surrender table round which he had sat with the commanders of the enemy forces from Denmark, Holland, and North-West Germany. He later wrote to my mother inviting us again, adding, 'It is better to build boys than try and mend men.'

'On one occasion in August,' wrote my father in his 1963 statement, 'I took her to see an old friend of mine, Viscount Ward, and we had a drink with him. He seems to have forgotten the occasion.' Geordie Ward (no relation), who had been Secretary of State for Air until going to the Lords in 1960, was the sort of elegant gentleman with whom J quite often set out from Westminster late in the evenings for a little relaxation, and I doubt he would have been averse to making the acquaintance of his old colleague's lovely new companion. But 1963 was by then shaping up to be the Summer of Amnesia. Commenting on J's uncertainty about precise timings, Dame Rebecca West concluded in an article (*Esquire*, September 1964), 'It is a lesson to all young women over the age of twelve that he could not, in March 1963, remember whether an affair he had had in 1961 with an exceptionally beautiful girl had lasted one month or six.'

I was busy down in Bembridge with my Cerebos salt pourer in early August – we were staying with James Allason, at one time my father's Parliamentary Private Secretary, and father to Rupert, who was to write about espionage under the name Nigel West. On the 3rd, detained in London, my father paid a visit to his paramour, and she cooked him sausages and served coffee before making love in front of the television (I doubt that sort of thing happened very often at home). According to his account, Sally (Norrie) then came in for a bath, Miss K wanted to go into the bedroom, he demurred, and she replied, 'You're not sexy any more.'

After a brief trip to the seaside to check that the family was also having a good time – whatever else, that was *definitely* the summer of Hubbly-Bubbly – he saw her again on 8 August (dining afterwards with Sir Anthony Nutting, the Minister of State for Foreign Affairs who had resigned over Suez, a man of unusual intelligence and integrity, for whom J had great affection). He had made a date for the next day, too, but was informed by his secretary that on the 9th, at 4 p.m., he had to see Sir Norman Brook, Secretary of the Cabinet.

Such meetings usually signified security matters, or else a change in very senior civil service personnel. Brook said 'there was rather an embarrassing matter which he would like to get rid of very quickly.' He explained that MI5 was watching Ward's flat, and advised J to be careful; the security people did not think he was any kind of agent, but 'he may be a go-between of some kind, and he just thought he ought to tell me this and that Ward was not a very desirable person, before the recess.' (Ward said he told the security services on 12 July that Ivanov and the Minister had met, though Denning later dismissed this claim categorically.) At this juncture, J had no fear that some marital infidelity might be exposed, but rather surmised that he was being warned off any further association with Ward because of the indiscreet osteopath's friendliness with the Russian. He decided to cancel his assignation, and that same day wrote a note, the text of which was later widely published (I reproduce it here for the first time within copyright, by the way):

> Darling,
> In great haste and because I can get no reply from your phone –
>   Alas something's blown up tomorrow night and I can't therefore make it. I'm terribly sorry especially as I leave the next day for various trips and then a holiday so won't be able to see you again until some time in September. Blast it. Please take great care of yourself and don't run away.
>   Love J
>
> P.S. I'm writing this 'cos I know you're off for the day tomorrow and I want you to know before you go if I still can't reach you by phone.

There was now some concern that the telephone might be tapped, and J stated that he was then 'determining to break off the affair, but I did not want to write it in such a way as to make either Ward or the girl suspicious.'

His draft says, 'I never saw the girl again.' (By 1963, he seemed to think it might have gone on until December.) My own inclination is that he continued to visit her sporadically for a while – even, perhaps, partly out of defiance against the covert warning – but that certainly, by the end of the year, the excitement between the two of them had fizzled out.

In the latter part of August, my father took his wife on a hot holiday to Portofino.

That autumn, in the *demi-monde* where he had delighted to dabble, Miss K's social life was about to cause considerable complications. In October, she went to buy some drugs in a Notting Hill café from Aloysius 'Lucky' Gordon, a man with a history of violence; he obtained her telephone number and pursued her with rough love as she moved from place to place (including a flat in Dolphin Square, later the scene of some more inflammatory allegations).

In his speech about 'sleeping with an elephant', my father had not been far wrong: the lissom Christine Keeler herself was evidently no pachyderm, but it was just about two years before the consequences of his misdemeanour came trumpeting out for much of the world to see.

My mother once explained to me (ruefully, or perhaps tartly): 'He thought he could get away with it – after all, most of his friends did.'

———◆———

It was reported in January 1962 that J was one of the most widely travelled of all the Government's ministers, and this remained one of the aspects of his job that thoroughly appealed to him. Except when I occasionally saw him reading in bed with his breakfast tray – he took every paper every day, the counterpane protected by a voile covering, to fend off the newsprint – he was a man on the move: red ministerial dispatch boxes were carried in and out from waiting cars (I seem to remember a succession of glamorous Army *chauffeuses* at the wheel), even on the phone he would pace the room (there was a clunking, semi-miraculous device on his desk which allowed him hands-free talk on his 'scrambler'), and I was certainly impressed when he arrived in Kent one weekend by helicopter. They were both away in the Persian Gulf that month, on a most amicable visit to the Sultan of Muscat, who presented my father with a beautiful curved dagger of ivory and gold; V was granted the singular honour of sitting on the ruler's left at banquets, but was a little disconcerted by the custom of hurling scraps behind you for the servants to devour. They went on to East Africa and Zanzibar, bringing back many souvenirs around the theme of cloves. The nursery map was by now quite densely acupunctured with flag-pins.

Back home, the Secretary of State was under fire in the Commons for his Army Reserve Bill, and in March there was controversy over the BAOR (British Army of the Rhine) camps where some troops were reported to be feeling 'mutinous' over conditions; the German locals were requesting curfews because of antisocial behaviour by the military; courts-martial were in the offing, and morale was perilously low. (Ironically, considering all the troubles with the Rhine Army, the *Daily Express* noted that I had gone down with German measles.) One of J's more vociferous critics in the House was George Wigg (Labour Member for Dudley), who accused him of being dismissive of the real problems, which Wigg himself always claimed to understand because he had risen from the other ranks to become a colonel. A man with an openly professed detestation of all things Tory, Wigg was often twitted by his opposite numbers for his intransigent views ('Wiggery-pokery'), and my father made an enemy of him later that year.

This was over Kuwait, which had just been admitted to the Arab League and had requested the presence of British troops in June. Wigg's indignant claim then was that the military contingent had been so ill-equipped and suffering from exhaustion that, had they been required to go into action in Iraq as feared, there would have been a fiasco. 'I was a good target, and Wigg thought he could get one on me,' remembered J, admitting, 'they did have totally insufficient gear.' In a preliminary discussion, Wigg thought he had secured J's tacit agreement about how the debate was to proceed, but in the event he was trounced when J suddenly quoted from two letters of support from commanding officers. The texts of these had not been laid down in their entirety, and the livid Wigg (whose memory was unfortunately as elephantine as his ears) accused my father of not handling documents according to the Rules of the House. He felt he had been outflanked by a typical piece of Staff College duplicity, and (to adapt Wodehouse's truism) it is seldom hard to distinguish between a class-warrior nursing a grievance and a ray of sunshine. For my father, this was to prove a Pyrrhic victory.

In March, a photograph appeared of my parents at the Grosvenor House Spring Ball in aid of the mentally handicapped, gamely dancing the Twist.

'I try to be at home as much as possible,' said my mother in an interview, 'but I think it is wrong to put children before everything. They should take equal place with your husband.' She was also a firm advocate of boarding schools for boys, as it avoided the dangers of excessive mother love (an incontrovertible piece of educational philosophy); children had to 'learn early in life that you can't dodge unhappiness – that one is strengthened by obstacles.'

Following the sizeable government defeat at the Orpington by-election, on 13 July, Macmillan sacked one-third of his Cabinet; though not actually in the Cabinet, J was greatly relieved to survive this 'Night of the Long Knives', despite the iterative problems with the Army and its public image. In the red pencil he generally reserved for the more heartfelt of his notes, J wrote from the War Office to V: 'My Darling Darling – I suppose one thought hasn't occurred to you – the reason I haven't gone with the wind of change is largely because Mr Mac also didn't want to be without *your* side of our team, it's the sort of image he wants. I have my darling wife to thank . . .'

Whether or not it was because I was deemed to be developing a flippant interest in the *Eagle* magazine, or displaying wider signs of moral degeneracy, it was now decided that I should be looked after by a Christian Scientist governess, Miss Evelyn Lauderdale. She was a short, bespectacled lady with moulded graphite hair and an attractive smile of which, perforce, one saw relatively little, her view of the world being a rigorous one of divine love without much joy. She was strict without being fanatical, and would certainly not be mistaken for a children's nanny. It would be marginally unfair to say she was tough on fun and the causes of fun, but rolling marbles to demolish battle-lines of soldiers was not in her repertoire of activities. Instead, she taught me to knit and sew – this stopped fractionally short of me making all my own frocks, but that year I did give a surprising number of blanket-stitched felt log-gloves as Christmas presents. She drank cups of hot water with each meal, even in summer, and invariably wore flat, lace-up shoes.

Each morning and evening, there was an hour of Bible study, pondering the set text for the day. There were no concessions to children in this programme, and if the passage was especially opaque, 'Laudie' would read it aloud – the Revelation of St John the Divine, for instance, or one of the choppier sections of the Psalms – but otherwise we would take it in turns. Thus I was apprenticed to cubits and wormwood and potsherds and foreskins and the voice of the turtle; I was especially taken with 'him that pisseth against the wall', the village oiks in Kings who taunt the Prophet ('Go up, thou bald head') and are dismembered by bears, and the horse that smelleth the battle from afar and cries, 'Ha ha.' I learned the Creed, the significance of the Cross (it is the egotistical 'I', crossed out, its shape prefigured by the vertical banishment of Satan's fall, and the horizontal expulsion from the Garden of Eden).

Laudie – I think the nickname was merely fortuitous – also favoured longish but plain-spoken prayers, that invariably began with a rapid 'Oh Lord', to the extent that I began to form a slightly louche mental image of a deity named Olord, whom I could address without quite the same degree of awe as my governess brought to bear on her version of Jahweh. (In times of bewilderment for a number of years to come, Olord was a source of succour and comfort until, when I was a teenager, he morphed into Hughie.) As it happened, I was invited to supplicate on my knees for forgiveness with commendable frequency. On one occasion, when only the twin mini-packs of corn-flakes were left from the new-fangled Kellogg's Variety assortment, I ventured to say over breakfast that I did not much like them: in a world of starvation, this was a sin for which one atoned verbally, in tears, on one's own. (I still prefer Ricicles, I'm afraid.)

Whenever I said something that exasperated her, Laudie would give a thin sigh, remove her glasses, and begin to clean them roundly, thoroughly, with a small handkerchief kept up one sleeve. Without the lenses, her eyes seemed somehow flatter, and watery like tinned grapes.

My mother, who fiddled for much of her life between various wavelengths of Christianity, had considerable regard for Miss Lauderdale – and quite right, too – whereas I believe my father gave her a fairly wide berth. Her legacy to me was that I soared (humbly, of course) towards the top of most divinity exams for the rest of my schooldays, and, although lapsed and rusty in many ways, at the age of twenty-three I was still sufficiently equipped with chapter and verse that I could drive a religious maniac from my bedsit by reciting fluently from Ecclesiastes. I tell you, the training was worth it.

There were two areas where I conspicuously failed to show much progress, and, perhaps significantly, neither of these lay within my governess's remit. First came the bizarre family tradition of learning to ride horseback in Hyde Park. The stables behind the Royal Albert Hall run by Miss Dixon were doubtless a faintly modernized version of Mister Meades's old establishment, and the pony I was assigned was called Goldie; twice a week we traipsed forlornly on a leading rein along Rotten Row, being photographed occasionally by tourists (I had the smartest of jodhpured outfits, of course, and now realized what was the significance of that horse in the window of Rowe's). I was uncomfortable in the saddle, and have always been slightly scared of horses, so these lessons showed very gradual evidence of proficiency, but at least we proceeded so slowly that there was no danger of serious injury. Failure at the piano was more excruciatingly obvious. Each Tuesday, I had private lessons at the nursery upright from a tall, curly-haired musician called Mr Tubbs, who sported a nicotine-stained forefinger (for Christmas I presented him with a box of Swan Vestas, rather than anything I had sewn). He was most patient, but it must have been clear I had a tin ear for classical music (it has always made me feel uncomfortable and weary, a trait inherited from my father); like the poet, Pope, I 'preferred a street barrel-organ to Handel's Oratorios'. I could only locate 'middle C' by searching for the keyhole in the wood. I can definitely recall a four-line piece for the right hand entitled 'Ribbon Road', which took me several months to master; small wonder Tubbs was on sixty a day.

The school I was now attending was Hill House, a looming Victorian building of ruddy brickwork situated on the corner of Pavilion Road in Knightsbridge. It had been founded, and run, by Lt.-Col. Stuart Townend, a Monty-style martinet who was until quite recently still to be seen scouring the doorstep each morning in his shirtsleeves. His wife, Beatrice, seemed an alarming creature, overly made-up and with garish *coiffure* (it was rumoured that she drank, having been terribly burned trying to rescue a child from a fire); their son Mr Richard, a limp individual, was the head of music. In later years, the school became so popular – especially for children of overseas and diplomatic families – that it proved impossible to cram all the pupils into the building at the same time, and charabancs of them were to be seen heading off around London on various expeditions, like aircraft stacking for a landing-slot. In 1962, numbers were more containable, and when we were given our marching orders we went on foot, in a good old-fashioned crocodile, accoutred in russet corduroys with caramel-hued sweaters, and caps which we doffed in synchronized gratitude to motorists who allowed us to cross.

Laudie would take me there on the bus, which we boarded by the handiwork showroom of the Royal National Institute for the Blind, opposite the Portland Hospital; much of the journey would be given over to improving commentaries about the passing scene, the iniquity of football pools ('Zetters' proclaimed the side of many buses), the impractical vagaries of fashion ('all these women wearing thin boots!') and the health dangers of many advertised products. Like most children, my fancy was graphically taken with billboard images, and I determined, as soon as possible, to smoke Weights and exclusively drink Mackeson, as prompted on the illustrated school run.

My constant school friend and companion was Jamie Chatto (we were equally incompetent at hoofing footballs on the Duke of York's playing-fields, and once covertly tried on Miss Ferguson's leather gloves in Form Four); his was the only other house in London where I went to stay, a cramped, bustling family home in Chelsea, where his gran sat in a chair in her cardigan, the doorbell was constantly rung by passing thespians, and the place was full of dogs, cooking and background television. If not away on tour, Jamie's father Tom would crack jokes in various gravelly voices – he was a consummate character actor, often depicting detective inspectors in belted raincoats – and we were allowed to go unescorted to the corner shop to buy bubble gum and collect Confederate Army cards and read *Marvel* comics on our bunks and stay up remarkably late. I never had to play on my own, and there were complicated games of make-believe with Jamie (shy, musical and with a strabismic sense of humour) and his younger brother Dan (who once played the Milky Bar Kid on the box, and ended up marrying into the royal family). It was a household quite unlike ours, my own epitome of forbidden fruit, and for many years I went there eagerly, whenever I could.

On my seventh birthday, I was treated to a front-row seat for the State Opening of Parliament; having been in a box for the Trooping of the Colour, I was beginning to enjoy some propinquity with pomp and circumstance, and was only mildly disconcerted that none of these splendid gentlemen later attended my tea party – though Bustie saved the day by dressing up as some kind of Lord High Chamberlain, complete with a chain of office that sported the foil-wrapped lid of a baked beans tin.

Meanwhile, developments in the Cimmerian parallel world were proceeding with less protocol and regalia. Miss Keeler had finally dropped Lucky Gordon in favour of Johnny Edgecombe, another excitable West Indian (he was not a Jamaican, but originally a merchant seaman from Antigua). The two swains fought on more than one occasion, but during a lively skirmish on 27 October at a Soho club called All Nighters, Lucky sustained extensive knife-wounds that required stitches. His assailant went into hiding, but approached Miss K – who, with Mandy Rice-Davies, was now installed back in Wimpole Mews – for assistance in finding himself a nifty lawyer (rightly surmising she might be acquainted with some). She declined, so on the morning of 14 December Edgecombe turned up at the mews, tried to force the door, and discharged his pistol before making off in a waiting minicab. 'Les Girls' rang Dr Ward in his surgery, but the fracas had been observed by a schoolgirl returning from hockey in Regent's Park, who ran into nearby consulting rooms and alerted the police. The *pistolero* was arrested, and charged also with the attack on Gordon; the papers, attracted by its spicy mix of race, drugs and girls, ran the story.

Fired up by these events, Miss K now embarked on a round of storytelling that was to persist for decades. She spoke to detectives, journalists, and lawyers (in particular, one Michael Eddowes, a solicitor who was a patient of Ward's). The ghost net was being anchored in place to catch its first full tide.

Christmas was always a performance of lavish theatricality at 3 Chester Terrace, a decorative occasion to which my mother rose superbly. Large Harrods cartons were lugged up from the basement, and the house was transformed with tinsel and baubles from many countries of origin. The tree in the drawing-room was surmounted by a handmade angelic fairy given to her by the dressers of Drury Lane, and at its foot would be an obscene agglomeration of presents. We always went to church – St Peter's, Vere Street, where there was an excellent young vicar called Geoffrey Rawlins, a Gregory Peck look-alike who later became a star pupil of the portraitist Annigoni – and then we were invited down to the staff sitting-room for a seasonal glass of cream sherry, where Bustie proposed a respectful toast (he stuck to ginger ale, having some time before already drunk enough alcohol for one lifetime). Once it was dark, he would knock on the French windows in his full Santa fig and deliver yet another sack of gifts. We all had a very merry Christmas in 1962, but – in the late Dr Hunter Thompson's unexceptionable phrase – the weasels were closing in.

———•———

Philip Larkin may have chuckled ingeniously that this was the year when sexual intercourse began, but 1963 does now genuinely look like something of another *annus mirabilis* – watershed or not – with iconic events like the Great Train Robbery (for some reason regarded with fond nostalgia by the British, though the driver had his brains beaten so viciously that he was never able to work again), and the assassination of JFK, to say nothing of the invention of friction welding or the demise of Georges Braque. It began with a lethally cold winter, one of the most severe since 1740: then, a Frost Fair had been held on the frozen Thames, and one woman slipped through, was decapitated, and her head scudded across the ice between the revellers. There were no such mishaps at Oxford, where cars were able to drive across the river, though it was reported that one Dartmoor family was marooned for two months, and forty-nine people died from the cold (as did a zebra at Whipsnade). We were certainly snowed-in over New Year at our rented Kentish oast house, though not to the extent that my mother had to leap from a first-floor window with her shovel, as suggested by one journal of record. I was able to achieve my heart's desire by walking to the sub-post office in Frant and spending ninepence on a transparent Bic ball-point that, like my teacher's, had green ink.

My father flew to the United States for discussions with Cyrus Vance, and to inspect various army units; there was an official reception at Fort Bragg, and he was made an Honorary Trooper, 82nd Airborne Division. It is unlikely that his private views on the standards of the American military would have been aired, and I think his overall interest in gadgetry made these visits altogether intriguing. Apart from his position as one of the three Service ministers (Lord Carrington was in charge of the Navy, Hugh Fraser the RAF, and Peter Thorneycroft overall Minister of Defence) my father garnered a little extra respect from his hosts for having served with MacArthur as a one-star general. He secured the assurance of the Kennedy administration that it would assist in getting the Polaris missile system into service, and that there would be closer consultations in the future. At a press conference on UK defence policy in Washington, J was asked if he would be able to explain the recent Nassau Pact to the electorate, and his reply ('to much laughter') was: 'I have every confidence in the Government of which I am a member to explain anything.'

This was to be tested to near destruction by the events of the next few months, which created a cat's cradle of barbed wire. Having first approached the reporter Peter Earle, Miss Keeler – whose lifestyle, understandably, required cash to be earned by a variety of available means – had eventually been paid the sum of £1,000 by the *Sunday Pictorial* for her story, which included producing the so-called 'Darling' letter. When this paper approached Ward for an interview, he became alarmed. Before any such story actually appeared, my father was requested to meet the Attorney-General (Sir John Hobson) late at night on 28 January; it was the latter's duty in the face of any such allegations to enquire whether a minister was considering a libel action, and to offer his professional assistance. Hobson (also Harrow and Brasenose College, as is always pointed out, though no relation of V's) repeatedly stressed the need for my father to be frank and truthful at this stage, and was categorically assured the story was false regarding any sexual involvement. J admitted to having written a note immediately after his talk with Brook, but claimed the appellation 'Darling' signified no degree of especial intimacy as a form of address in the theatrical circles wherein he and his wife were used to moving. Hobson retained his doubts – 'He thought it rather odd,' in Denning's throwaway phrase – and discussed the situation with Sir Peter Rawlinson, the Solicitor-General.

That evening, my father had also asked the Director-General of MI5 to come and see him. 'Roger Hollis actually came round to the War Office, and said, "Do you know those people? They're dangerous." I told him there was no connection with Ivanov; all I knew was that he liked playing cards. I was making an off-centre suggestion, to make my relationship with Miss Keeler look less alarming.' Though J later indicated this was never the case, Hollis was under the impression my father hoped the security services might be able to prevent publication, possibly by issuing a D-notice. (Had Ivanov been recruited by MI5, this might have been feasible.) After obtaining J's assurance that there could have been no leak – even though Miss Keeler was noted as having already told them Dr Ward suggested she might ask my father sensitive military questions – Sir Roger seems effectively to have backed off and left any remaining investigative work to the police. (My father later told me, 'MI5 were pretty lax. I don't think they did their work very well. But it may have been Macmillan not wanting to uncover anything further.') The next day, Ivanov departed for Moscow.

The position Hollis seems to have taken was that his concern was not the sex-life of ministers but the 'Defence of the Realm', and that now Ivanov was safely back on home turf the security risk potential was over. He issued a directive that 'Until further notice no approach should be made to anyone in the Ward *galère*, or to any other outside contact in respect of it. If we are approached, we listen only.'

On his birthday (30 January) J's horoscope was cast in the 'Lord Luck' column of the *Daily Express*: 'Greetings to John Profumo, Secretary of State for War, 48 today. Strenuous but profitable year. Professional prospects highlighted.' So much for the crystal balls of Fleet Street.

On 1 February the possibility of an affair was noted in the Prime Minister's papers: J was alleged to have been involved with a girl code-named Kolania, and the Cliveden–Ivanov connection was also made. One of Macmillan's private secretaries, John Wyndham (later Lord Egremont), sent a memo to the Prime Minister's office noting the imminent appearance of the newspaper article and, although his PPS, Tim Bligh, went to discuss the possible repercussions with J, it seems the Premier himself (who was in Italy) chose to let the matter be. The story still had not broken, though the *News of the World* published a picture of Miss K, saying she was to be a witness in a shooting trial (3 February). My father instructed as his solicitor Derek Clogg, a senior partner in the firm Theodore Goddard, further protested his innocence to him, and they met with Hobson, assuring him they would sue for libel if necessary. In Macmillan's absence, J was interviewed on 4 February by the Chief Whip, Martin Redmayne, and asked him if it was felt he should resign; providing the allegations were untrue, came the reply, then most definitely he should stay. It was still considered unnecessary to trouble the Prime Minister further with the matter.

Meanwhile (having drawn a blank with the security services) different attempts were naturally being made to dissuade Miss K from publishing her story. During the first week of February, her solicitors and Clogg were discussing the legal position of her existing newspaper commitments, and eventually a figure of £5,000 by way of compensation was arrived at, should she withdraw from her contract. This was partly to enable her parents to buy a house, she explained, and to ensure that she would agree to lie low after the Edgecombe trial. As Miss K herself later pointed out, had she been intent upon attempting blackmail, it would have been for a far greater greater sum than that. 'Let no one judge her too harshly,' wrote Denning. 'She was not yet 21. And since the age of 16 she had become enmeshed in a net of wickedness. I would credit her, too, with a desire only for a fair recompense and not an intention to extort.' In the event, the money was not paid; on 28 February the *Sunday Pictorial* informed her they were backing down, that particular settlement was nullified, and the article did not appear. (It contained one rather sad phrase, in which she wrote of J, 'it is true he did not take me out much.')

Instead, the paper had negotiated for a Ward piece they could run once Edgecombe's trial was safely over. Before then, however, Ward had cause to contact the police and claim that there had been stolen from his possession two photographs which, if made public, might 'bring down' the Government. At this stage, I suspect, he was still able to savour the intrigue and spectacle which perhaps he fondly felt he was orchestrating.

It looked as if J's hand might be forced on 8 March, with the appearance of the latest issue of a typewritten newsletter entitled 'Westminster Confidential', circulated privately to several hundred subscribers. This alluded to certain girls who were peddling their stories, 'a letter, apparently signed "Jock" on the stationery of the Secretary for W+r', a 'Negro', a 'famous actress wife', VD and a Soviet military attaché. On 13 March Tim Bligh wrote a 'Private and Personal' memo to my father from Admiralty House (the Prime Minister's offices in Whitehall were being refitted): 'Dear Jack, I attach a copy of a publication which came into my hands via the Chief Whip this morning. I have sent a copy to the Attorney-General and asked for his advice. I thought you ought to see it.' Hobson agreed that it was, on balance, not worth taking action against a publication with a relatively small circulation, but he wrote to Bligh (regarding J), 'It may become increasingly difficult for him to maintain his position much longer.'

Given the virulence of parliamentary and media rumours, even then, it was hardly surprising that a number of my father's friends asked if he would like to take them into his confidence. Selwyn Lloyd was one, as sympathetic and distinguished a colleague as one could wish to have, yet J blithely assured him there was nothing untoward in these stories. (It is said that this later influenced the Prime Minister's attitude towards his minister's denials, because he knew Selwyn was such a close personal friend.) Randolph Churchill was another who, reckless of the possible offence caused by speaking his mind, proffered advice; from personal experience, he could envisage the sort of trouble in which my father might stupidly land himself over a fiercely desirable girl. But his wartime pal was equally stubborn, and would not budge. The Japanese have a term for political scandal, and attempts to disguise it: *kuro kiri* means 'black mist'. Although the extent of the disaster could not then have been foreseen by any one person, there must have been plenty of people all over London who at that time, in their joint and several ways, suspected that something was about to go spectacularly wrong, and that from several quarters there was black, mephitic mist arising.

John Edgecombe's trial began on 14 March at the Central Criminal Court, before Mr Justice Thesiger and a jury. When Christine Keeler failed to turn up as a Crown witness, the accused was acquitted of the charge of attempted grievous bodily harm, but was given seven years for possessing a firearm with intent to endanger life. The next day, the *Daily Express* ran an ingenious teaser to the effect that John Profumo had offered to resign – 'War Minister Shock' – carefully not cross-referring it to their item alongside, a report about the mystery concerning Miss Keeler's whereabouts. (There were illuminating pictures of her on an inner page 'from which most people could readily infer her calling', as Lord Denning later described them *ad unguem*).

The coincidence of the model's convenient disappearence, and stories that circulated about the Minister's possible involvement, brought matters to a head in the Commons at eleven in the evening on 21 March when George Wigg – using parliamentary privilege, and supported by Barbara Castle, the Hon. Member for Blackburn – invited the Home Secretary to deny the rumours ('Everyone knows to what I am referring'). It is from this moment that the 'tick-tock', or back-story, to my father's political nemesis effectively ends: now, he was heading face-down into the fertilizer.

(George Wigg later became Paymaster-General, and, as Lord Wigg, he was in 1976 charged with kerb-crawling, using insulting behaviour, accosting women and endangering the peace. His defence before the magistrates was that he was endeavouring to purchase a newspaper. I just thought I would mention it.)

That evening, J was dining at the Other Club (an exclusive cross-party political coterie founded by Churchill) and my mother had gone to the theatre. She then left their car for him on the forecourt of the Commons, and took a taxi home, but seeing a crowd of photographers around Chester Terrace, she realized something was amiss. She called from a nearby hotel phone to warn my father, only to find he had Martin Redmayne with him in the House. She went to join them, and the Chief Whip again outlined the situation in which the Home Secretary, faced with such pointed questions, now found himself. J had already again denied the allegations, and Redmayne assured V that there were not going to be any resignations; they were told to return home, brave the press gang, and get some rest. This they did. 'I was so tired, so defeated,' recalled my father, 'I wasn't up to what followed.' They both took a sleeping pill (*miserabile dictu*), and went to bed just before one in the morning.

The debate in the House did not conclude until 1.22 a.m., and there was then an impromptu meeting of five ministers – Iain Macleod (Leader of the House), Bill Deedes (Minister Without Portfolio, who had been in the Commons when the question was first raised), Redmayne (who counted as a minister), Attorney-General Hobson and Solicitor-General Rawlinson. It was no preordained troubleshooting tribunal, but an improvised quorum which, with the Prime Minister's agreement, decided that this would be an apposite moment to issue a denial: it would be less messy than any libel action, and it was thought advisable to act before the weekend papers promulgated the rumours any further (it was now Friday morning). My father was accordingly summoned, but they could not rouse him by phone. Redmayne therefore sent an assistant who contacted them from the local police station and eventually fetched him by car, just before 3 a.m.

'The photographers were still beating on the door and making an awful noise,' said my mother. This was the first time I had ever heard that disconcerting, deep sway of male voices below my bedroom window but it is something I also remember well on several other occasions. A little later that year, it woke me up and I came down the stairs in my pyjamas to see a man from the crowd attempting to force his way through our front door, shouting at my mother, 'You have the manners of a pig.' Bustie was using his considerable weight to put the chain on the lock, and my mother's defiant retort to the intruder is memorable for its quaint phrasing – 'Leave us alone, or my man will give you blows!' Fortunately, it did not come to that, though the stalwart Brisco would not for a second have blenched.

My father was 'very woozy' from the pill, as more than one of 'the Five' later attested (only Rawlinson emphatically denied seeing any evidence of grogginess). There was a delay while his solicitor, Derek Clogg, arrived; he had to ascertain there was no discrepancy between what he had been told by his client and the contents of any statement (he was primarily a divorce lawyer, who, three years later, was sued by his wife on the grounds of his adultery with a model). Commentators have sometimes accused the Five of being naïve in their handling of that meeting – Dame Rebecca West recommended on television that they 'should be smacked and sent to bed without any supper'. The principal intention, however, was not to further cross-question their colleague, but to draft a refutation in response to the specific questions put to the Home Secretary. Macleod's biographer records that he did baldly ask, 'Look, Jack, the basic question is, "Did you fuck her?" ', and J seemed to recall a remark, 'Something like that, yes.' His tack all along was to concede that everyone was going to find it almost impossible to believe, but none the less he had not in fact been sexually involved with this girl. In his mind the priority was to deny (truthfully) the security allegations and any suggestion that he was complicit with CK's recent disappearance; he regarded the adultery as something of a side issue, though this led to the crucial mistake of including that in his public denial. Much later, the rebarbative Wigg asked – justifiably, under the circumstances – exactly what the Five thought J and the girl were doing, then: 'Meeting in order to practise the latest stitches in embroidery? To discuss the subtler points in the Higher Catechism? Or what?' Lord Lambton (family motto, *Le Jour Arrivera*) also scoffed, 'But what did these people say when they went to interview little Jack Profumo that night? Had Little Jack been to bed with Miss Keeler or not? They were like frightened mothers.'

This overstates the case, but one must remember that the Government at that time was uneasily awaiting publication of the Radcliffe Tribunal report on the Vassall case: William Vassall, an Admiralty clerk, had been jailed for eighteen years for spying for the USSR after being caught in a homosexual 'honeytrap', and this had led to the resignation of Tom Galbraith, Under-Secretary of State for Scotland, over rumours that were proved to be unfounded. They did not want to engineer a repeat performance and, rather than being gullible, it must have seemed frankly unthinkable that a minister would continue so brazenly to lie to his colleagues at this level. He was definitely not thinking straight, and it is true that they probably hustled him: Bill Deedes once charitably stressed they had been 'in a desperate hurry', probably creating a set of circumstances which made 'the truth extremely hard to tell'. Nevertheless, my father made a very poor decision and stuck to his story. 'It was a terrible moment to have faced me with this. I felt I couldn't tell the truth at that stage. I thought it was all going to go away from me in a while. It would have been beyond my political ability to own up to them – having got that far telling lies. One more wouldn't have mattered so much.' By any standards, this was a fairly spectacular mistake.

A handwritten draft was prepared for his consideration. He cavilled at the phrase admitting that he had been 'friendly' with Miss Keeler, but they insisted on its inclusion, and a final version was then typed by Deedes, and approved. Exhausted, my father arrived home just before five in the morning, where my mother was waiting up for him with Blackie the cat in her lap.

I have heard it said that she must have known the truth, having seen the alluring 'model' for herself, but I am certain at this stage, despite everything, she believed her husband ('How Green Was My Valerie', as a subsequent wag put it). Late that night, on a piece of House of Commons paper taken from his desk at home, she proudly wrote:

> My Darling Husband,
> You may not have time to read this – but if you do: it's only just to say that for eight wonderful years I have borne your name – but *never* have I looked forward to doing so as I shall from now on.
>   Your devoted wife – Valerie 'Pidge' Profumo

In her interview with Tom Denning, V later suggested that, had the urgency of the situation not been so critical, with a little more breathing space they might as a couple have arrived at a different decision, and J would never have signed such a statement. I am not so sure. While not quite subscribing to the view that he was more scared of his formidable wife than he was of incurring the displeasure of the Commons,

I think my father was so enmired in his story that he would by then only have owned up to one person: the Prime Minister himself. It may indeed be wondered why Macmillan did not confront him face-to-face, and the allusion (first used by Lambton) to a telescope being held up to the blind eye seems plausible. Perhaps he did not want to believe the worst, or maybe he already knew? 'There is no ground whatever for suggesting that the Prime Minister knew Mr Profumo's statement to be untrue,' insisted Denning, but it has been mooted that the Premier let J proceed anyway, in the hope that his denial at such a high level would force the scandal-trufflers to back down.

The specific point in the report at which this is addressed is paragraph 186: 'It appears that early in March, 1963, Mr Profumo said words to this effect to a friend. "I've got involved with a girl. I wrote her a letter. The *Sunday Pictorial* have got it and it can now come out any day. I've had to tell Valerie, the PM, my boss."' Denning says this friend took it to mean that there had been an illicit association to which he had confessed, and so appraised another friend who was a Tory MP. In fact, the report explains, the remark really meant that his innocent friendship with a girl was being misinterpreted and was about to cause him trouble, and that was what he had told V and (via his secretaries) the Prime Minister: 'It is, I fear, such misunderstandings as this which have led to most unfounded suggestions.'

I had been mildly interested in this detail, but assumed it was one of those lost leads in which the saga abounds (the ghost net sweeps up its fair share of red herrings), and certainly my father never suggested that the Premier knew in advance that any part of his statement was untrue. Then, when I was finishing the first draft of this book, I happened to meet a man in a South London garage, who overheard my name and introduced himself. His mother had been a serious girl-friend of my father's in the 1950s (I had seen her photograph in his album – a French girl of extraordinary beauty) and I effected a reunion between them next time she visited London. She revealed that she had been the 'friend' in question, and had dialled J's number at the War Office for fun on the very first day you could make telephone calls direct from Paris to London (I'm not sure why she had this number in the first place); he had said he was busy, then called her back later and it was her understanding that he had confessed all to Macmillan. Denning had requested her evidence for his inquiry, and a plane ticket had even been sent, but she was at that time undergoing a complicated divorce and was advised not to become involved in case it interfered with getting the custody of her daughter. She remained convinced that the Prime Minister had encouraged J to proceed anyway, and then let him take the rap. However, when she tried to remind him of this, as we all sipped champagne some forty years later, my father met the lovely French lady's account with a puzzled shake of the head, and seemed to feel the whole business had indeed been another of those misunderstandings.

Accordingly, just after eleven o'clock on that Friday morning, John Profumo stood up in the House and asked permission to make a personal statement – this is a parliamentary device that does not permit any further cross-questioning or debate. In it, he said he had not seen Miss Keeler since December 1961, had no idea where she was now, and any suggestion that he was connected with her absence from the Old Bailey was untrue (so far, a true response). He asserted that – apart from the Cliveden weekend – the only other occasion he (or his wife) had met 'Mr Ivanov' was at the Gagarin reception (also correct). He admitted: 'Miss Keeler and I were on friendly terms' (yes), but continued, 'There was no impropriety whatsoever in my acquaintanceship with Miss Keeler' (the crucial lie), adding, 'I shall not hesitate to issue writs for libel and slander if scandalous allegations are made or repeated outside the House.' He sat down again next to the Prime Minister, who clapped my father clubbably on the shoulder. In Denning's words, he and his ministers 'could not conceive that any of their colleagues would have the effrontery to make a false statement to the House.' My mother watched these proceedings from the Speaker's Gallery. Immediately afterwards, the House began an earnest debate concerning estate agents.

The Secretary of State for War went straight to Sandown Park, where he accompanied the Queen Mother to the races – it was the Grand Military Gold Cup, and this was one of his official duties. ('Lucky John Profumo' ran the banner headline in the next day's *Daily*

Sketch: they reported he had backed an Irish horse at 10–1 that was the winner in the three-thirty.) That evening he attended a dinner-dance at Quaglino's for the Hatch End Conservative Association, addressed them to rousing applause, and then danced with V to 'The Green Leaves of Summer' (they were to grow sere and yellow, ere long).

At this stage, the British press did not dare publish further allegations, but on the Continent there appeared many amiable references to '*le minister et la jolie fille*', or '*le ravissant mannequin Londonien*' (amazingly, 'model' has to be masculine, but then so is the French for vagina), and the Italian view was that '*Tutta l'inghilterra parla di Christina*' – though not at Number 3 Chester Terrace, I think. On the 25th, Miss K was tracked down in Spain, where she said she would like to remain, though four days later she flew home in dark glasses and a fetching sheepskin jacket. Apparently endorsing my father's statement, she told the *News of the World* that her relationship with the Minister was 'a friendship no one can criticize'. Later, she was fined forty pounds for failing to appear in court.

In a letter from the Royal Courts of Justice, dated 26 March, the Attorney-General wrote to my father, thanking him for his own kind letter, and stating: 'I hope the thing is now dead . . . If anyone tries to play the "Ivanov" bit, you ought to say with complete truth and accuracy that you ceased to see her and Ward from the moment you discovered that she was getting on friendly terms with him.' The 'thing', however, was very much alive.

During the first week of April, the straws on the wind began coming in bunches (by early summer, there was to be a bale on the gale). In a move that was going to make life pretty awkward for some years to come, J instructed his lawyers to initiate proceedings in France against the magazine *Paris Match* for suggesting he had been involved in La Keeler's disappearence; they retracted, and copies of the relevant issue were withdrawn before reaching Britain. A writ was also issued against the UK distributors of *Il Tempo* magazine for making a similar connection, and he received an apology in the High Court, plus token damages of fifty pounds (which was donated to an army charity). The very act of suing served as an effective deterrent to many, but this did not prevent *Private Eye* from making references to Sextus Profano, 'Chief of the Praetorian Guard'.

On 4 April, the police began taking statements with the aim of putting together a case against Stephen Ward, whose activities were deemed thoroughly worthy of investigation (he was eventually charged with living off immoral earnings). During the course of their enquiries, they interviewed Christine Keeler on more than thirty occasions, and she signed a statement to the effect that she had been the Minister's lover (providing a plausibly detailed description of the interior of our home), and that Ward had asked her to get information about 'The Bomb', though 'it was ridiculous and could have been made in a joke.' Throughout what Denning labelled an 'unprecedented situation' – adding, 'we have no machinery to deal with it' – the various authorities failed to keep one another usefully briefed. MI5 may have already known that the Minister had been sleeping with the girl (and was therefore lying), but by then this was no longer deemed to constitute a security breach, whereas the police felt they had strayed into moral issues, which were not their brief either. Matters were perhaps not helped by Miss Keeler's mercurial nature when giving testimony, sometimes (then and since) changing her replies according to what she felt she was expected to say – I am tempted to call this the behaviour of a mannequin-depressive – but there can be little doubt that, with proper co-operation, the entire situation could have been managed in a more efficient manner. Conspiracy enthusiasts, with their Procrustean proclivities, have other explanations for it, I know.

At this stage, my father had every reason to believe that the storm had blown over; and of course he was continuing with his duties as if it had. On 22 April, he attended the ball to celebrate the wedding of Angus Ogilvy and Princess Alexandra (serene daughter of his erstwhile inamorata Princess Marina), and dined with the Queen Mother. Two evenings later he was sitting at the top table of the Rose Ball in the Grosvenor House, along with Douglas Fairbanks Jr, and that weekend was spent at Chequers, part of a policy meeting of twenty-eight ministers to discuss the run-up to the autumn election (an event in which J's legacy was to feature rather more prominently than he might have wished).

Understandably, Dr Ward felt he was now under irksome pressure from the police, and on 7 May he made an appointment to see Macmillan's PPS, Bligh. He suggested there was 'a great deal of extremely explosive material' of which he had knowledge, and claimed he was fed up with covering for J, for whom he had 'made a considerable sacrifice'. He was evidently hoping that the Government would call off their investigation if he agreed to keep quiet, but there was no deal. He wrote plaintively to the Home Secretary, saying his friends and patients were being harassed, and indicated, 'I intend to take the blame no longer.' He wrote *inter alia* to Wigg and to Harold Wilson, pointing out that the Minister had lied, and as a direct consequence of having tried to shield him it now looked as if it were Ward himself who 'had something to hide'. In the week of 20 May Wilson copied this letter to the Prime Minister, and from the start he was canny enough to insist on the security risk factor. I don't suppose he or Wigg genuinely believed that had been a danger, but they had definitely scented blood.

On the 17th, Miss Keeler appeared in Cannes to announce that filming was to commence next month (in Copenhagen) of *The English Dolce Vita*, a feature film starring herself. My mother was photographed in a line-up of supporters for a charity show at the London Palladium – 'D-Day with the Stars' – alongside Anna Neagle and Harry Secombe. That entertainment was scheduled for 6 June but on the night she was otherwise engaged.

No doubt with some reluctance, Harold Macmillan acceded to the Labour leader's request, and agreed to have the security services reconsider the matter. He finally discussed details with Hollis and heard of Keeler's allegations to MI5 (back in January) that Ward had suggested she try to elicit information from J about 'atomic secrets' – specifically, the timing of delivery of nuclear warheads to West Germany. This was something (reported Denning, with no discernible incredulity) that 'he and his office had not known before'. On the 29th, Macmillan instructed Reggie Dilhorne, the Lord Chancellor, to conduct an investigation specifically into the security aspect of the affair, and then left on the overnight sleeper for the Highlands of Scotland (Parliament was adjourning for the recess over Whitsun). For the first time, in his absence he handed over to R.A. Butler, his deputy. (My father had no very high opinion of 'Rab': 'it wasn't that he was ambitious, but his manner was so off-putting, and he simply wasn't good enough with *people* – he couldn't control them, not even me!')

On 31 May, amid much activity from the paparazzi, my parents flew off to Venice for a holiday. They stayed at the Cipriani, which (rather strangely, it always seemed to me, all things considered) remained their favourite hotel thereafter. Before they left, my father had been given yet another opportunity to indicate whether the Dilhorne inquiry might discover any flaws in his statement, but he had held his ground. Knowing he would be questioned the following week, he realized he had to confess to his wife during their Italian sojourn. 'By that time it was perfectly clear to me that it was no good me covering it up any more, because the goose was cooked, so to speak.' Having a Bellini cocktail before dinner that first night, he finally told her the truth. 'She was very good about it. I just owned up. She said, "Well, I don't know what the history of all this is, but from what you tell me now you are a hot potato, so you ought to go back and make the best of it. Don't go on like this. We had better get back." ' (Somehow I doubt this is a verbatim recollection of the exchange, but in his nineties my father preferred not to revisit this scene too closely.) On the Saturday morning, Dilhorne put through a call and told him the game was up, and they had best return sooner than planned. This they did on Whitsun, avoiding the air route which would have attracted obvious attention. It was a desperate homecoming. After a long gestation, the elephant was about to calve.

Following a day of preparation and consultation with loyal friends such as John Hare, my father went to see Tim Bligh and the Chief Whip on Tuesday 4 June (the anniversary of the Fall of Rome). He wrote Macmillan a resignation letter in which he had to admit his lie, misleading 'you, and my colleagues, and the House. I ask you to understand that I did this to protect, as I thought, my wife, and family . . .' He repeated that there was 'no truth whatever in the other charges', but that he had lied about the impropriety, and therefore 'cannot remain a member of your administration, nor of the House of Commons'. Rab Butler put a police guard on Chester Terrace overnight.

Harold Macmillan was staying at Ardchattan Priory in Argyll when this letter was read to him. Apparently, his first reaction was, 'Well, thank God it's a woman, this time.' His reply, which was dated the 5th and was released to the press that evening – along with my father's letter – was free from reproof, but also conspicuously made no mention of services previously rendered. He spoke of his 'deep regret', and the 'great tragedy' for family and friends, and ended 'yours very sincerely'. The resignation was accepted, and the Fall of the House of Profumo seemed complete; the head waiter had done something unspeakable to the soup, and there was definitely to be no tip. Of all this, at the time, I knew nothing.

On the morning of 5 June I went back to Hill House as usual after half-term, but was told to inform my teacher I was to leave at break-time for an appointment with the dentist. I could tell that something not quite right was happening – a lopsided feeling setting in – when Mrs Townend herself collected me from the classroom and took me up to the private flat, fed me a cup of warm milk, and gave me a book about Mozart. It had a cover of thick, golden linen, and she said it was a present because she knew I enjoyed my piano lessons with Mr Tubbs (somehow I associated the hue of the book with his nicotined digit and hair). I had never before been alone with her – nor had any pupil, so far as I knew – and I sat on the edge of the sofa, but simply could not look her in the eye. The thickly applied make-up seemed a clown's face, the kindly attention a skewed version of what appeared maternal. A car came with Laudie (she could not herself drive), and we went to my uncle's house in Kensington. 'There's a surprise for you,' she said gently, 'we don't have to go to Dr Sturridge after all.'

In the conservatory overlooking the garden of End House were my parents, and various members of our family, sitting on the painted cane chairs under the thin and shifting sunlight. Mr White was dispensing sherry from a decanter into slender glasses, and on the round table was a stoppered Thermos jug of hot consommé, with two plates of chicken sandwiches – the white bread quartered into triangles, and, of course, the crusts cut off.

My mother was wearing a burgundy-coloured cardigan – cashmere, I imagine – with rimless sunglasses, an unusual combination for London. I sucked on my orangeade. She said, 'Daddy's decided to stop being a politician. He told a lie in the House of Commons, so now we're going to have a little holiday in the country. All together. Now, doesn't that sound fun?' The slipstream of Mr White's cologne caught me as he cruised by with the amontillado. I swung my legs with excitement: there I was, fizzing with the thrill of missing school, and my parents must have felt they were on a tumbril. Life was never better, as Larkin was to surmise. My Aunt Maina lit a Du Maurier cigarette, and squinted at me through the smoke.

In good time, before the announcements were made that evening, we fled to the country in our ice-blue Jag.

If there is one perspective on this sublunary world that appeals to my gallows humour and makes me believe that the god Hughie is not just an inebriated minicab driver, it is the concept of 'historical comedy'. I was first alerted to this by my Oxford tutor, the percipient ironist and poet John Fuller. The phrase derives from historian Lewis Namier's study, *England in the Age of the American Revolution* (1930), where he explores the often absurd or trivial origins of historically important developments, and how we are all brought low by our limitations. In this book he observes that only the truly humble can be lifted 'beyond the realm of historical comedy', as those who believe themselves to be in powerful or manipulative situations tend to forget the normative values of everyday life and the fact that to others there are always more important matters to be getting on with. To the wife of the man who has a heart attack in their box at Covent Garden, it is a cataclysm; to the buff in the audience below, it is an irritating interruption to an evening's opera. (There is something of its essence in the question, 'Yes, but apart from that, Mrs Lincoln, how did you enjoy the play?')

The spirit of historical comedy suffuses W. H. Auden's poem

'Musée des Beaux Arts', too, where he praises the Old Masters for rec-
ognizing that terrible events – in this case, the Fall of Icarus, as
depicted by Brueghel – occur apparently anyhow, when ordinary
people are just taking a walk or tilling their fields, or frankly couldn't
much care (like the torturer's horse, scratching its 'innocent' behind
on a tree). The painting shows the legs of the legendary Icarus (who
flew too near the sun and melted the wax cohering his artificial wings)
just disappearing into the sea, but nobody paying much attention. It
was just another bloody hot day in Ancient Greece, and there was
work to do – a trug to be filled with olives, a couple more wretches
to be flayed. There was no time to notice the disastrous, let alone to
become involved.

So, however agreeable, this is not a *Weltanschauung* that is going to
make you laugh aloud; it makes me smile, now, to think that my chief
experience of that turning-point in all our lives was the taste of
chicken sandwiches and freedom, but I do not believe my father was
much amused when, just to round off his week nicely, he was stopped
for speeding the next day *en route* for our hideout, and later given a
fine of four pounds, plus an endorsement.

V

The Thing Which Was Not

L ET US NOW afford the family members of the cast a brief inter-
lude to get their breath back, and consider the wider situation.

What ensued in the international media, I can only describe as a
veritable shitstorm. There was a great, persistaltic explosion of activity from the world's press, and I have five entire cuttings books for the
rest of 1963 alone. Considering this was essentially a British political
convulsion, the extent of the global response was virtually unprecedented; from the *Bootle Herald* to the Lebanese *Al Siassa*, it all
seemed nearly too good to be true (and of course much of it was not).
To my beleaguered family – whom I am going to leave in suspended
animation for a while – this slew of unrelenting comment, exposé and
speculation that dominated the next few months meant that events
hurtled by as if high-lit, queasily, in a stroboscopic flurry.

Apart from the many 'I Lied' resignation headlines on 6 June 1963
there was a chance for some of the other *dramatis personae* to have their
say. The *Mirror* reported that Dr Ward was wearing pyjamas and had
taken to his bed with a paperback thriller, explaining, 'I feel sick and
ill with the worry of it all' (two days later he was arrested). The Prime
Minister, disembarking imperturbably at Oban from a cruise to Iona,
turned to his wife Lady Dorothy and said, 'I think I had better push
on. I have a lot of telephoning to do.' From her vantage-point in the
Mayfair Hotel, Marilyn Rice-Davies announced, regarding the latest
developments, 'I am not surprised.' Harold Wilson – perhaps fum-
bling for the hankie in his Gannex pocket, to staunch the crocodile
tears – described it as 'a sad affair'. For the time being, the Soviet
papers kept their silence.

That Sunday, Miss Keeler (who had just been accused in court by

Lucky Gordon of giving him VD) published a story in the *News of the World*: 'I knew he loved Valerie. I didn't want to take him away from her. Yet I loved him terribly.' The paper was said to have paid her £23,000 for her trouble, then a small fortune. John Freeman, a Brasenose contemporary, described J as 'cheerful, generous, silly, self-indulgent. But not wicked.' The 'Darling' letter was reproduced by the *Sunday Mirror*, so there was plenty to tut about over the Golden Shred.

Macmillan finally bagged up his niblick on the 9th and headed south, taking the Gleneagles sleeper. In Alabama, the Affair took precedence over details of the latest Ku Klux Klan activities. A nightclub called the Astor offered Miss K £2,000 for a month's worth of appearances; speaking to the *Express* about my father, she regretted that both their careers were over. 'It *is* a Moral Issue', *The Times* assured its readers on the 11th. (Sir William Haley, the editor, was known around Whitehall as 'Halier than Thou'.) The Continental papers – while enjoying the spectacle of a Britain so discomfited by the truth about lasciviousness – could not ultimately see what all the fuss was about, visiting your mistress for a *cinq à sept* being an integral part of the European political lifestyle. One Lausanne paper, *Pour Tous*, elegantly explained how '*le malheureux minister de guerre britannique qui, pour quelques agréables moments passés avec Christine Keeler, voit toute sa longue et brillante carrière politique irrémédiablement brisée*'. When told of the resignation, Godfrey Golder (who had been a young chauffeur at Avon Carrow) replied levelly to reporters, 'Well anyway, he'll always be my Mister Jack.'

This Christian spirit of acceptance was not universally in evidence. In a remarkable outburst on BBC's *Gallery* programme (13 June) Lord Hailsham, the Lord President of the Council, fulminated that 'It is intolerable for Mr Profumo in his position to have behaved in this way, and a tragedy that he should not have been found out, that he should have lied and lied and lied; lied to his family, lied to his friends, lied to his solicitor, lied to the House of Commons.' (I have always liked that extra stroke of indignation, from a QC, about misleading the lawyer.) In his denunciation of my father's immoral conduct, he spoke for many, in and outside Parliament.

There was much (understandable) gloating from the Opposition, though the ever-principled Tony Benn considered this both unseemly and inadvisable, noting in his diary that 'it's a bit like wrestling with a chimney-sweep.' Another voice from the Labour benches actually came to the former Minister's defence. Reggie Paget – who had piped up in the original Commons debate and suggested that J's acquaint-anceship with such a pretty girl 'was a matter for congratulation rather than enquiry' – was the Member for Northampton, who sometimes appeared in the Division Lobby in his hunting breeches, and had the reputation for being the slowest speaker in the House. 'From Lord Hailsham,' he countered, 'we have had a virtuoso performance in the art of kicking a fallen friend in the guts . . . When self-indulgence has reduced a man to the shape of Lord Hailsham, sexual continence requires no more than a sense of the ridiculous.'

'I have never known a man to be so insulted and abused – not even Hitler,' complained 'Boofy' Arran to the *Daily Mail*, from St Tropez. 'It's so damnably un-British.' Not everyone was quite so *à moment*; on the remote Hebridean island of Muck, where newspapers were scarce, a fisherman was listening to the saga on the wireless, and said, 'To think of the shame! I didn't know that Christine Keeler was a Coll girl.'

The ingenious denizens of Fleet Street were not so much febrile as virtually on heat. There was some initial talk of personal tragedy and a little lip-service of sympathy, but the temptation to follow this up with a good going-over was (perhaps understandably) too much to resist. These days in Britain, we have become so familiar with this sort of press-gang-bang that it's hard to conceive of a time when it was still rare; the media were also riled by J's earlier threats of litigation, and this was a further chance to smack back at the Government for its recent reprimand over the coverage of Vassall. It did not take long for certain metaphors to become standard – bombshells, skeletons in closets, black sheep were among the favourites – and several history graduates among the Fourth Estate made learned and salacious allusions to the Parnell Case that had dogged the Gladstone administration. There were calls for Macmillan's resignation, and the security aspect of the scandal was frequently raised, though everyone was careful enough not to accuse my father of anything treacherous. Once it looked as if this angle was going to prove a dud, the mendacity was what most pundits insisted upon. The Eleventh Commandment was much quoted: 'Thou Shalt Not Be Found Out.'

'Moral indignation is jealousy with a halo,' wrote H. G. Wells, and predictable outrage of several types was to emanate from pent-up ecclesiastical quarters, to whom the miasmic unfurling of this saga must have appeared a God-given opportunity for indignant pontification. During several Saturdays to come there was much extra midnight oil burned in the vicarage studies as sermons were prepared in laboriously preceptive mode. The admirable Methodists tended to preach forgiveness, but many were the other tub-thumpers who saw this affair as a symptom of general swinishness, hypocrisy, and corruption. The 'evidence of national corruption' school of thought may now look rather absurd, but it had powerful adherents at the time. Dr Mervyn Stockwood, Bishop of Southwark, provided what was effectively the caption to the entire month of June, when he spoke rousingly of 'the smell of corruption in high places', and called for a cleansing of the national stables. 'Profumo is a stinker', concurred the coruscating punsters on *The People*. Never perhaps was the saying apter: 'Humbuggery is the true *vice anglaise*.'

My father applied for the stewardship of the Chiltern Hundreds (MPs cannot resign directly from the House but have to be first appointed to this ancient sinecure), sent back his Seals of Office to the Queen to avoid her the embarrassment of his personal visit to the Palace, and had his solicitors issue a statement stressing his 'profound remorse'. On 20 June he was formally censured in the House for his misdemeanour. On the day of their debate, it was reported that the House of Commons Library had returned to its publishers Colin Wilson's previously ordered book, *Origins of the Sexual Impulse*, with a slip that read, 'Not suitable for this library.'

It was a time of whores, and rumours of whores; and before too long this Feast of Fools atmosphere led inexorably to gossip about the royal family. On the 24th, the *Mirror* ran a headline in Second Coming type – 'Prince Philip and the Profumo Scandal', helpfully explaining that although Ward had done a portrait of the Duke of Edinburgh, any suggestion of his involvement constituted the 'foulest rumour' around, and assuring readers that it was all 'utterly unfounded'. It didn't help when Miss Rice-Davies later implicated Douglas Fairbanks ('because I didn't like him,' she explained of her quondam lover, to whose charms she had succumbed in his Dorchester suite), since he was widely known to be a favourite with certain Royals. One must feel confident that the Duke would never have moved in such twilit or nether-worldly circles, but, all the same, my father remained convinced that he never forgave him personally for this unwarranted media association.

In this festive, open-season frenzy, the saucy seaside postcard aspect of the English national character seems to have responded to the unusual turn of events as if it were suddenly a licence to have a bit of fun. The Dundee *Courier and Advertiser* reported that the judge at a fancy-dress parade in Carnoustie had awarded first prize to two children dressed as the Minister and Miss K. Every cartoonist thought it was his birthday, and soon there were plenty of bad jokes doing the rounds. There was also at least one excellent limerick:

'What have I done?' cried Christine;
'I've ruined the Party Machine.
To lie in the nude
Is not very rude,
But to lie in the House is obscene!'

Jack Profumo had become a household name. Paul Muldoon – in his poem about adolescence and hypocrisy, entitled 'Profumo' – describes how in his house the *News of the World* was hidden: 'My mother had slapped a month-long embargo / on his very name.' Probably my favourite quotation is from the August issue of the magazine *Chemical Products and Aerosol News*, which related how Commendatore Elio Paglieri – a successful Italian perfume manufacturer – had decided to withdraw and redesign his products destined for the English market so that 'no ambiguity shall be implied or inferred' concerning the word 'Profumo' on his labels.

While my parents are still in freeze frame, there are two codas to the resignation which belong here, in the immediate aftermath of the summer of '63.

As Secretary of State for War, my father inspects a Guard of Honour provided by the 2nd Battalion, 2nd King Edward VII's Own Gurkha Rifles, at Effingham Hall, GHQ Far East Land Forces (January 1961)

A meeting of Harold Macmillan's ministers at Chequers, April 1963. My father stands in the back row, fourth from the left, behind Edward Heath

Left: Valerie and Jack dancing the twist at the Spring Ball for the National Society for Mentally Handicapped Children, Dorchester Hotel, London (March 1962)

Below left: Bill Astor and Dickie Mountbatten, photographed by my father at Cliveden, 9 July 1961

Below right: A drawing of Christine Keeler by Stephen Ward, inscribed, 'To dear Christine at Cliveden' (1961)

"Frightfully Sorry, Really"

MACMILLAN

PROFUMO

©1963 HERBLOCK
THE WASHINGTON POST

Left: Perhaps the most eloquent of all the cartoons following my father's resignation from the Government in June 1963

Below: My mother meets Yuri Gagarin, the first cosmonaut to return from outer space, at a reception in the Russian Embassy, Kensington (11 July 1961). Also pictured is Mrs Soldatov, wife of the Russian Ambassador

Top left: My mother and Randolph Churchill in pensive mood at his house in Suffolk during 'Operation Sanctuary', June 1963. The photograph was taken by my father

Bottom left: On 8 July 1963, my mother opens a new home for the mentally handicapped at Dymchurch in Kent. Frank Longford (*right*) is making a speech

Right: The author, aged seven, with his father on the banks of the River Borgie, Sutherland, (August 1963)

Below: Mark, our mother, and me on the River Thames near Windsor, for my ninth birthday. Photographed by my father (October 1964)

Left: At the entrance to the Dower House, our home in Hertfordshire (May 1967). *From left to right*: Mrs Waller (the cook), 'Bustie'(the butler), and Marjorie (the housekeeper)

Below: My parents with Jo-Jo the spaniel, outside the Dower House (August 1968)

With his first public speech since his resignation, my father opens an exhibition of paintings by inmates of Grendon Prison (of which he was a governor) at Toynbee Hall, in the East End of London (November 1969)

My parents welcome HM the Queen Mother to Toynbee Hall on 13 April 1976, when she came to open Sunley House

My father, his first grandchild James, and my wife Helen, on a visit to the Old Barn House, my parents' final home, in Hampshire (Summer 1985)

In the last picture taken of them together, my parents leave St. Margaret's Church, Westminster, after a memorial service for Maureen Dufferin (summer 1998)

The author and his father relaxing in Perthshire, August 2000

The trial of Stephen Ward (which began on 22 July in the Old Bailey) does not form an integral part of my family memoir; my father was not involved in the proceedings (though some people persist in thinking he was before the courts at some stage himself) and the story has been so thoroughly documented that I am not even tempted to treat it to a shampoo and set. Certain details, however, typified the ambience of those extraordinary months. There was of course Mandy Rice-Davies's now near-legendary utterance which brought the house down at the previous Magistrates Court hearing, when responding to the news that Lord Astor had denied ever sleeping with her ('Well, he would, wouldn't he?'), and also the revelation by Vickie Barrett – really Janet Barker – that the going rate for flagellation at Bryanston Mews was one pound sterling a stroke (prompting the saloon-bar quip, 'At the third stroke, it will be three pounds precisely').

At the time of his trial, Ward was urgently trying to raise funds, and there was an exhibition of his drawings at the Museum Street Gallery. Just before closing time on 28 July an unidentified man entered and bought thirty of the pictures, including all those with royal connections. It was rumoured that this might have been none other than Anthony Blunt (later famous as a traitor, but then known for his art-historical expertise) acting as an intermediary to spare the Royals from any further embarrassment; actually, it was someone from the *Illustrated London News*, the magazine that had originally commissioned them.

Stephen Ward killed himself on 3 August, having taken an overdose of Nembutal. His last letter (to his friend Noel Howard-Jones) was very English, and quite moving – 'The car needs oil in the gear-box, by the way. Be happy in it. Incidentally, it was surprisingly easy and required no guts.' It contained the sentence that still wheels over his story – 'I am sorry to disappoint the vultures.' In their rabble-rousing profile of him, the *Daily Sketch* writers demanded, 'How sleep tonight the ones who knew him well?'

I asked my father what he thought about Ward: 'He was badly served in the long run, poor man. I really don't think he deserved to kill himself.' Depending on your views about suicide, I think it is one thing to feel sorry for Stephen Ward but to portray him as heroic – as certain parties have sought to do – does take some imagination.

It quickly became a commonplace in print that tragedy and farce were becoming admixed with bizarre frequency. In August, there was an unseemly scramble for the by-election at Stratford-on-Avon, where the dozens who applied for nomination papers included a prisoner serving time for causing malicious damage. The Labour candidate was actor Andrew Faulds, brashly bearded for his role as the villainous Carver in *Lorna Doone*, and his opponents included David Sutch (not yet 'Screaming Lord'), a 22-year-old former plumber's mate who stood as the official National Teenage candidate and whose proposals included abolishing the dog licence. In the heartlands of his old constituency, John Profumo still had such a strong personal following that there remained quite a few who believed he would have been re-elected if he had stood straight away as an Independent. 'I blame it all on the girl,' wrote one supporter, to the *Banbury Guardian*. 'Mr Profumo was always such a gentleman.' But there were lines to be drawn, even in those days. 'It wouldn't have mattered,' explained one gentleman-farmer, 'if he had just gone to bed with the wife of another Conservative MP.' No indeed.

In the event, Angus Maude took the seat with a ten-thousand cut in majority. From the Tory perspective, it could have been worse.

When the *Sunday Times* asked C. S. Lewis for his views on that summer's hottest story, he replied, 'I only started reading the Profumo case halfway through, so I'm a bit vague about the plot.' Since then, there has been such a volume of comment – much of it screaming gin and ignorance – that the plot can indeed be sometimes quite hard to remember. I have no intention of embarking on some *tour d'horizon* of the literature here, but I must say that, having surveyed many versions of this story in the line of duty, the Denning Report, however idiosyncratic, still appears the soundest guide.

I happen to be an admirer anyway of the prose style of this High Victorian ethicist, his opening gambits in particular ('It happened on the 19th of April 1964. It was bluebell time in Kent . . .' is the most famous). His report is a pawkily dramatic piece of writing in places, and remains an intriguing read. I agree with Wigg's remark, 'And what a journalist was lost to Fleet Street when Lord Denning opted for the Law!' He began his inquiry on 25 June and insisted on hearing evidence in private. Mandy tipped up late for her interview, owing to a hairdressing appointment, but declared, 'Lord Denning was perfectly sweet. He's quite the nicest judge I've ever met.' (One dare not speculate under what circumstances she encountered the many others.) Miss K also recalled his kindly manner, and decided 'he resembled a farmer'. One must presume this was intended as a compliment.

Not least by farmers, the appearance of the report was awaited with widespread eagerness. On the eve of publication, the editorial view of the *Fertiliser and Feeding Stuffs Journal* was: 'It would be quite ridiculous to suggest that Mr Macmillan is in any way responsible for the stupid conduct of Mr Profumo or, indeed, of another Minister should anything of the kind be discovered in Lord Denning's report. To believe otherwise would be just stupid.' Amidst the clatter of cascading cattle-cake, the robust voice of Middle England thus made itself heard.

The Government Stationery Office in Kingsway opened early, at 12.30 a.m., on 26 September and the report became a national sensation, and a brisk bestseller both at home and abroad. One hundred thousand copies were sold in the first few days, and there appeared a pirated edition in Stockholm containing 'unsuitable pictures'. The tea-drinking, Panama-toting Tom Denning joined the pantheon of the people's pin-ups for the year. When Harold Wilson had an early opportunity of reading the report, his immediate reaction was that there wasn't much in it (glossed as 'Well, not much in it for me,' by Macmillan). Others at Whitehall joked that from now on they would have to date things BC or AD – Before Christine or After Denning (it is sometimes said the designation was his lordship's own).

Although in some quarters it was inevitably accused of being a whitewash by 'the Establishment', the report was perceived as pretty fair by most *bien pensants*. The Prime Minister was certainly relieved – as were the security services, which were effectively exonerated. Denning stated emphatically: 'I do not think the Security Service should be blamed for not doing more', but this was a view not widely shared outside Government circles. On publication, John Hobson (the Attorney-General) wrote a resignation letter, feeling indignant that Denning had indulged J and V at the expense of 'the Five' ministers, who were reprimanded for not having been more hardbitten. Macmillan dissuaded him from this decision. It is true that Denning was well disposed towards my mother, and they remained on good terms for the rest of his life. He was quite rightly emphatic, though, about the extent and variety of my father's deceptions, pronouncing unequivocally, 'His disgrace was complete.'

If he seemed sympathetic towards Christine Keeler, Denning was hard on Ward. In his opening sentence – 'The story must start with Stephen Ward, aged fifty' – there was even an inference that the man was old enough to know better; 'he was at the same time utterly immoral,' ran another description, with an allusion to his 'vicious sexual activities'. One cannot help feeling there might have been something personal in the vehemence with which he assessed 'the most evil man I have ever met'.

Despite its overall concinnity, and the clarity of phrasing in particular, the report was simultaneously responsible for some of the confusion surrounding the plot *tout court* of the Profumo Affair, particularly for the items in Part Four – 'Rumours Affecting the Honour and Integrity of Public Life'. To this we can partially owe the impression of Westminster and the West End as a hotbed of intriguing diversions – so deftly evoked in Tom Stoppard's agreeable farce *Dirty Linen* (1976), with MPs dining clandestinely at the Coq d'Or, and the alluring central character of Maddy Gotobed (a role interpreted in the Southampton production of 1981 by the actress Mandy Rice-Davies). Denning was following up rumours that several folk 'in high places' might have been involved in compromising situations: the 'other minister' found to have been frequenting prostitutes turned out to be Ernie Marples, Minister of Transport, while the allegations of homosexuality concerned Denzil Freeth, MP for Basingstoke (who resigned from the Ministry of Science, but always denied the suggestions). As a consequence, there was an entire supporting cast with which the Profumo Affair became inextricably commingled in the popular memory.

The Duchess of Argyll divorce case gave rise to certain lubricious details, for instance. This was already up and running, having begun back in 1959, though it climaxed, as it were, in '63; and indeed when the news of my father's resignation broke, the Duke of Devonshire (then Minister of State at the Commonwealth Relations Office) was reported as saying, 'First Argyll, now this. I never thought I should be ashamed of being both a Duke and a Minister in the same week' – his own predilection for hired help was of course not revealed until some time later. Denning had called in the promiscuous Margaret Argyll's diaries because there were allegations that the so-called 'Headless Man' receiving oral succour in an 'improper photograph' might have been a government minister. The suspicion was that it was Duncan Sandys (who duly had to submit his lower physiology to examination by an urologist), but in the end a simple handwriting test established the identity as that reliable performer, Douglas Fairbanks Jr. An entirely separate conundrum – the 'Man in the Mask' – concerned a supposedly risqué dinner party, though these penny dreadful person- ages occasionally become conflated.

The concluding function of the report was to assure the nation that, despite the shrillness of accusers on every side, all was essentially well in Albion. At that time, plenty of decent people still liked to believe what judges said, and Tom Denning's *ex cathedra* pronouncement to the effect that the body politic was by no means corrupted – 'There has been no lowering of standards' – was greeted with considerable relief by many, who could now continue to shop for cornflakes and coley fillets with one less thing to worry about.

The *New York Herald Tribune* sagaciously summed it up: 'Britain, which has survived wars and pestilences, blitzes and Colonel Blimps, has also survived Miss Keeler.'

Although political history *per se* has never been one of my favourite subjects, one of the few British authors who has my undivided admir- ation – Jonathan Swift – was a swingeing political satirist. Any scholar of his voluminous canon needs to be deeply familiar with the polit- ical background to the reigns of Queen Anne and the early

Hanoverians (something of a black hole for many of us). Despite three years of unconsummated doctoral delving into the life and times of the egregious Dean – who, widely celebrated for his authorship of *Gulliver's Travels*, one of the most reprinted works in our language, nevertheless profoundly disliked children – I would still choose him as my literary hero (unalloyed enthusiasm for an author does not always emerge unscathed from protracted academic research). He was a forbidding moralist, rigorous punster, stalwart friend, courageous libertarian, and sexually complicated Anglo-Irish clergyman, who published some of the most scabrous and physically graphic verses ever written, lived frugally and was charitable to the poor and deranged, missed out on high office by offending the grandees of England, and died lonely and old, treated as a lunatic, 'a stranger in a strange land'.

I mention this not merely in homage to the man who refined the literary digression long before Sterne got his hands on it but because when I consider the colourful shenanigans of 1963 I often think what sport my cynosure would have made of it all. In Chapter Four of the last Book of *Gulliver*, he treats us to a survey of the land of that ultra-rational equine race the Houyhnhnms; as their whinnying name implies, they are not remotely like us ('who-in-humans'), not least because in their society there is no concept of lying. Introduced to the idea, they could only designate it as 'The Thing Which Was Not'. To my mind, this is what lies at the heart of the Profumo Affair, and it is a phrase quite useful as a touchstone for modern life. How often has a gas-fitter, windshield mechanic, or pencil-sharpener repairman begun to explain to you his manifest botch and bungle with the self-exculpatory Neo-Estuarine utterance, 'Well, what it is, is . . .', and you have known, *instanter*, that he or (less likely) she was actually telling you The Thing Which Was Not?

For several years now there has been a bulky huddle of books sprawled in the corner of my library, sullying my Axminster; these are works devoted to, or tangentially commenting upon, the events surrounding my father's fall from grace, and though I see no need to furnish any kind of overview, or Bovrilize the sundry rip-snorting theories that have been on the hoof since 1963 – guzzled up, *à bouche ouverte*, by sections of the reading public – it is worth noting how swiftly various commentators made it into print. With a rapidity truly impressive for the technology of the day, *Scandal '63* (by Clive Irving, Ron Hall and Jeremy Wallington) was rushed out in record time in September of that year, pipping Denning to the post; it was quite a creditable achievement, less hysterical than some subsequent efforts, and certainly less politically biased than another quick-fire product, *The Profumo Affair: Aspects of Conservatism* by Wayland Young. Iain Crawford's *The Profumo Affair* and *Stephen Ward Speaks: The Profumo Affair* by Warwick Charlton and Gerald Sparrow both appeared within the next few months, but contained significant errors. By the time Ludovic Kennedy's outspoken, but ultimately implausible, volume *The Trial of Stephen Ward* appeared in 1964, Cyril Connolly (in a review) reckoned it was a subject of which 'most of us are thoroughly sick', though the wider public appetite showed scant signs of abating.

Perhaps more intriguing than such punditry were the works of the girls themselves. From her Kensington abode, Miss Rice-Davies produced *The Mandy Report* (1964), a colourful opuscule costing 3s 6d; she invited Denning, Astor and the Premier to her publishing launch on New Year's Eve, proclaiming, 'It is time to let bygones be bygones', but none of them attended (neither did my father, but it was his wedding anniversary). She wrote of the ex-Minister that Christine was 'proud of him, but for myself I wondered what she could see in him. To me he did not look bright enough to be in the Government.' Reviewing this book, the waspish John Sparrow, Warden of All Souls, concluded, 'Her confessions are worth their weight in mink.'

With her spun-sugar hair-do and pert, pug-dog looks, Mandy was always the sassier of the two 'girls', and soon proved herself both entrepreneurial and articulate. She once described herself as an 'adventuress', and this seems fair: she went on to become an actress and nightclub performer, and wrote several books, including some fiction and her memoirs, *Mandy* (1980). Although at the time she was little more than a cute young soubrette she turned herself ingeniously into a sleek courtesanal figure, who spoke several languages, drove smart cars, and had a head for business. Apart from her remark about Astor, she was responsible for a number of additional *bons mots*: she styled herself the new Lady Hamilton, and told the world, 'I'm looking for another Lord Nelson, only taller.' On another occasion she refused to comment on media coverage, saying, 'Like royalty, I simply do not complain!' I feel sure she was a most pleasurable companion, but, despite the fact that she and Miss K are invariably twinned in the popular line-up, Miss Rice-Davies and my father did not know one another.

There have been several versions of Christine Keeler's life, all hard-luck stories shaded with paranoia and in places prinked with vindictiveness. Early on, she was intent on bringing down the Tory administration, apparently, because of the way in which she was spurned. Her shambolic finances have made storytelling a regular way of earning some cash, and I entertain no especial animus towards her, though at times the reek of *crambe repetita* is a little unappetizing. There is a touch of the Ancient Mariner about her tale – 'It wasn't fair . . . He never lost anything. I had nothing' – which has ceased to play well, but occasionally she appears as fed up with the whole subject as some others are. 'What was this affair that became tainted by the filthy minds of the creeps in their two-up, two-down, semi-detached suburbia?' she wrote in 1989, a sentence silvery with the ring of true resentment. The latest book, *The Truth at Last*, contained the revelation – hitherto kept incredibly under wraps – that my father had impregnated her and she had to undergo a perilous abortion, and also that Dr Ward was in the pay of the KGB (it was surely then strange that he was just prosecuted as a pimp). She and I have never met, though more than once I did walk past her in the King's Road and I entertained a sudden impulse to introduce myself, but was never quite sure as to the precise etiquette.

It is quite poignant to re-read how, at the time, Miss Keeler was adamant not to be labelled a call-girl or prostitute. She tried to insist on the appellation 'model', but some reputable modelling agencies objected, and the head of one said his girls would refer to her instead as 'the well-known journalist'. Rebecca West astutely noted how Mandy revelled in her notoriety, whereas Miss K was always anxious about her supposed reputation; when questioned by Mr Justice Marshall as to why she had sold her story the first time around, she explained, 'My reputation had gone, and I had to think of the future,' and she once told Simon Hoggart, 'I'm sure Jack Profumo wouldn't have gone out with a scrubber.' (I doubt if it ever crossed his mind that he was 'going out' with her in the first place).

Although in later years the sultry slinkstress became wire-haired, rusty-voiced and matronly (her name was eventually Mrs Sloane), Christine Keeler was the really lovely one, with her hourglass figure, zip-up dresses, Anello & Davide boots, and that alluring moue. Her harsh private life has been unstable and benighted, and has stolen away that beauty which one summer caused crowds of lustfully voyeuristic men to jostle her, and jealous women to vilify her very appearance in public. Unlike Mandy, she was terrified by these mêlées, and, perhaps because she refused to acquiesce in the overall process, was never the one the nation took to its heart. (As recently as 1995, she was apparently sacked from her job as a school dinner lady when the Head discovered who she 'really was'.) Imprisoned in Holloway for nine months for perjury in the trial relating to Lucky Gordon, she was said to have received hate mail that included threats of acid attacks. She never quite twigged how to play the press for profit, and her sense of self-worth seems to have been so low that she always allowed herself to be treated as a disposable asset. 'Sex for Rachman was like brushing his teeth,' she once remarked, 'and I was the toothbrush.' Her yearning for respectability – rather than embracing the situation, like Mandy, and making 'a vineyard of the curse' – is one of the more illuminating aspects of this sorry affair.

It is an index of just how ill-served Miss K was by the whole business that even when *The Christine Keeler Story* came to be filmed, she was not allowed to appear in it herself; Equity denied her membership for the original project, and eventually it was shown to an appreciative audience in Copenhagen. John Drew Barrymore, son of the great actor John, interpreted the role of Dr Ward, and it played to packed houses in the Middle East, but it was refused a British certificate. On the Continent, it was vociferously denounced by the Cardinal of Paris, who later died in the residence of a young lady called Mimi Santoni.

I wish I knew for sure why, forty years and more later, when it comes to parliamentary scandals 'Profumo' is still awarded the Best in Show rosette, despite the sprawl of subsequent contenders, and its stimulus endures where more recent *esclandres* appear decaff versions. If it has, as I've suggested, become some kind of industry standard, it may be in line with Mark Twain's dictum that 'History never repeats itself; at best it sometimes rhymes.'

There have been many ingenious analyses of this enduring resonance, and I wouldn't give you a flying fig for most of them. Some things are simply dead centre – they are boss, the cat's pyjamas, paragons, nonpareils – and when you have a specimen so excellent of its type, why murder to dissect? You don't have to be coping with the Von Trapp family to have a list of favourite things: mine would include Raquel Welch, Meerlust Chardonnay, the Discworld series, Kurt Schwitters, Cohiba Exquisitos, Bogdan fly-reels, Iggy Pop, Horlicks, Aston Martin DB 9s, Noxzema cocoa butter shaving foam, Robocop, violet crèmes and Ralph Lauren chinos. On one level, such epitomes just *are*.

The Profumo Affair was partly a potent mix because it had so many tasty ingredients; sex, lies, drugs, espionage, violence, race, hypocrisy, and a complicated class element – an 'upstairs-downstairs' dimension – which seems now peculiarly of its time. There was something for everybody, and it was built to last. Apart from the man who lent his peculiar name to the whole shebang, it's a *comédie noir* involving vaguely stereotypical characters – the Doctor, the Lord, the Spy – that could derive from some variant of Cluedo, and the principal players – whom Harold Wilson dubbed 'this dingy quadrilateral' – were once rightly identified as looking like 'refugees from some parody saga of Greene-land'. In other words, it is an intensely British period piece, though there was an American offshoot – 'Operation Bowtie' – that investigated the possible involvement of Kennedy and his circle.

It is one thing to feel it brings into focus something of the era – it is often clipped together with pop music, miniskirts, Lady Chatterley and the Pill – and indeed, the photographs do partly embody the black-and-white look of those years (not least CK in her chair, an iconic image aped by Joe Orton, Barry Humphries, the Spice Girls and the Simpsons); but I am less convinced that in itself it constituted a genuine watershed in British history. Rather than being a liberating business that helped to usher in the Permissive Society, if the Profumo Affair was a *Zeitgeist* it actually harked back to an earlier, more repressed age, before the go-go, tutti-frutti psychedelia and parties where hairdressers socialized with debutantes, or whatever the new symptoms were; it belongs to the time when people wore hats, and policemen had stripy wristbands to direct the traffic, and there was smog, Spam, skiffle, National Service, and 'something for the weekend'. The divorced were disbarred from the Royal Enclosure at Ascot, and a princess seen brushing lint from a man's lapel was deemed perilously intimate. It has become something of an idée fixe that my father's behaviour was instrumental in changing the heartbeat of our society, but though I can see it may have helped to tear at the protective layers that had been swaddling the old order of things, I don't think we can date the decline of an entire culture of respect (as some would have it) to the events of 1963, nor connect his specific misdemeanours diachronically with the state of today's Car Boot Britain. What did perhaps happen was that it presented a lightning conductor for forces that were until then no more than a vaguely moiling malaise, confirming the doubts many had about the shaky state of the nation.

A *scandalum* originally meant a physical stumbling-block, and there's no denying the Secretary of State for War enjoyed a most spectacular fall. He was by no means universally popular, and there were those in Westminster who considered him a lightweight character, unsuited to the job; there were others around the country who envied him his status, his wealth, his apparent cynicism, and his pulling power. Whatever the truth, he came a cropper for all to see, and this appealed instantly to that combination of voyeurism and *schadenfreude* in which this island race seems to specialize; and, though I am both weary and wary of the attitude that allows any goggling observer of manifest misfortune to feel there is some mitigating degree of sympathy as he hugs himself smugly and mutters, 'There, but for the grace . . .', none the less, as any dramatist knows, it can provoke an almost unbeatable *frisson*, and I am susceptible to it myself (though excuse me if I pass on this particular instance). Horace put it nicely in his first Satire: '*Mutato nomine, de te / fabula narratur*' – 'With a change of name, this tale might be told of you'. However seamy and murmurous its associations may be, something faintly folkloric now attaches to our hoary old family affair, an attribute upon which Patrick Skene Catling punned when he described it as 'the Western world's favourite twentieth-century bedtime story'.

In terms of political history, 'Profumo' is sometimes still held responsible for having brought down the Macmillan Government. Though the Affair incontrovertibly did not help matters much, this canteen-culture formulation really won't do at all. Despite the brilliance of Harold Wilson's performance in the Commons debate on the subject on 17 June 1963 – he spoke of the 'indolent nonchalance' of the Prime Minister's attitude – Macmillan still managed a vote of confidence (at 321 to 252, this gave him a majority of 69, which provoked some ribald comment), and he garnered a modicum of sympathy, although many agreed with the Liberal leader Joseph Grimond's assertion that the Government had generally forfeited the confidence of the country. Macmillan's claim that he was never 'party to deception' was widely accepted, though my own view is that he only saw as much as he wished to see, and that he certainly should have confronted his minister directly. 'I was too trustful', was the way he put it in the debate on the Denning Report (16 December), and he claimed to have been out of touch with the ways of the world; but when the sixth volume of his memoirs appeared in 1973, he admitted he knew that J was capable of behaving 'foolishly and indiscreetly', so there was little excuse for not double-checking the situation while it still might have been defused. I do not believe the suggestion, however, that my father thought the Premier knew for sure of his lie, but was sanctioning him to brazen it out anyway.

'He didn't want to hear any more rumours,' said J, 'not particularly about me, he didn't care a damn about me, but about anyone. He'd heard enough. Anyway, he was a pretty cold fish; he was too grand, and he didn't have many friends. The feeling was that he just hoped it would all go away. And his wife was of course having that affair with Bob Boothby.'

(Lady Dorothy was famously dishevelled-looking, and I don't suppose J had endeared himself to his leader when, emerging from

Downing Street with Macmillan, he had drawn the Prime Minister's attention to his wife waving at them from the back of the crowd – only to realize it was an elderly, gesticulating tramp.)

In the event, it was the Premier's prostate that proved the undoing of the Tories. A painful scare during a Cabinet meeting on 7 October led to his resignation (he lived another twenty-three years), but even so, Alec Douglas-Home very nearly won the ensuing election, and Wilson might never have squeaked in if Macmillan had stayed firm. It is true that the Profumo Affair caused some awkwardness to the Tory campaign, and I relish the account of Quintin Hogg being vigorously heckled on the subject at Eltham Hill School in October 1964. When he retorted above the hubbub, 'Let he who is without sin cast the first stone,' his interlocutor replied indignantly, 'How dare you talk to me like that?', whereupon the Minister for Science and Education conceded, 'I exclude you, you're not good-looking enough.'

I don't think Macmillan ever quite forgave my father for what he felt was the body-blow dealt their party's reputation, and his attempts to make light of the scandal were unconvincing: 'I'm the only man who's all right,' he joked in an interview a decade later, 'because every hour of my day is written down by the detective who never leaves me. . . . I haven't got the opportunity, alas!' On the only occasion I met him personally (in 1978) he invited me to sit next to him after dinner, was scrupulously polite about my father, and asked me graciously to convey his good wishes; elder statesmen seldom miss a trick.

My favourite among all the comments made at the time, though, was that of Christine Keeler on her release from prison: asked for her view on the collapse of Macmillan's Government, she replied, 'Why ask me? It's nothing to do with me.'

But – *retournons à nos moutons.*

VI

The House that Jack Built

THE DAY FOLLOWING my father's resignation, there was frenetic speculation as to our whereabouts. Literally hundreds of reporters around the world were said to be intent on flushing us out, and there were rumours that our little family unit was in hiding in Venice, or Sardinia, or Leeds Castle. Where else would a wily fox run to earth, though, but in the centre of his old ground, the heartlands of his former constituency? Here, in the Warwickshire home of my godmother Peggy Willis (after a brief spell with the Hares at Cottage Farm), we were secure for that first week. 'The reporters searched up and down the country, but could not find them,' wrote Denning, with some satisfaction. 'The folk of the village knew. But they did not tell anyone outside. They knew they wished to be left alone.' His approval of the prevailing decency of the traditional country people of England shimmers through those short sentences.

We had stayed often enough before at Ivy Lodge in the village of Radway so the circumstances appeared to me relatively normal. I had school work to get on with, under Laudie's supervision, and there was a succulent garden with an intriguing pond shaded by large-leaved plants I thought were rhubarb. My mother said we were just going to stay quietly there, as Daddy needed a rest – which was true enough – and I had no inkling that beyond the drive was a world turned upside-down. My chief concern was to avoid contact with Peggy's white-muzzled, drooling boxer Blitzy, of whom I was unjustifiably terrified.

Back in London, two loyal supporters were holding the fort. Stanley Brisco – who was offered a great deal of money by various parties – gave away not the slightest clue, nor did the young Chester

Terrace secretary Pam Plumb, who was left to fend off the media onslaught with precious little briefing, and had to deal with subterfuges ranging from journalists posing as private detectives hired by my parents, to a personal lunch invitation from the editor of the *Daily Telegraph*. She was then dwelling in a mews house nearby, and had an extension phone connected there, so was able to field all calls as if inside our home, but, to the perplexity of the waiting reporters, never emerged through the front door. (She went on to work at a very senior level in Whitehall, and received the MBE for her services, later returning to help run my father's domestic office life until his death.)

Before long, we had to move again, and this time the *metteur en scène* was Randolph Churchill – a man who loved a good crisis, and, however unpopular himself, knew what friendship ought to be. In what he called 'Operation Sanctuary', his house in Suffolk – Stour – was put at my parents' disposal, along with secret instructions to his staff (under the direction of his assistant Andrew Kerr) about how to look after 'OG's' – our guests, anonymously – and guidelines for leaving the country quietly, if they so desired. Randolph himself stayed with Aristotle Onassis aboard his celebrated yacht *Christina* but he still monitored his master-plan from abroad, and sanctuary was indeed afforded at Stour until my parents eventually returned to London. He was then one of the first to push through the crowds to their front door, declaring to the cameras, 'I've come to visit my friends – what the hell are you doing here?' J wrote to thank him for his help in 'our almost unbearable plight, especially in the face of my lack of frankness when you sought to help me earlier on'; and V added, 'I can only say from a very broken but still undaunted heart, "Thank You".' They sent Randolph a pair of embroidered slippers, and he replied that they would make him look like 'Bumpkin Pasha'. His reputation has not exactly been a record of such small acts of kindness – the next year, he underwent a lung operation and Evelyn Waugh recorded, 'A typical triumph of modern science to find the only part of Randolph that was not malignant, and remove it.'

Two things in particular I recall about that stay. On the outskirts of one town, as we drove to Suffolk, I saw huge advertising hoardings for the *News of the World*, with our name on them. 'It's just the papers with their tall stories,' my mother explained, and the words looked tall enough for a young aficionado of advertising posters to twig that this wasn't just some local difficulty they were going through. The other experience was altogether more pleasurable. One afternoon in the kitchen at Stour, Laudie gave me a piece of white bread spread with Lurpak butter: it's hardly a *madeleine* epiphany, I know, but almost every time I have eaten it since then, the pale taste, unsharpened with salt, seems briefly to conjure that early summer, the pastoral silence in a stranger's house, and a peculiar sense of safety which I did not then understand.

This was an astonishingly lonely time for my parents. Despite their later display of solidarity in public I know there was fierce emotional turbulence, and not as much in the way of stoical acceptance as may have been suggested. V certainly took legal advice about her position, egged on by several concerned female friends ('Val darling, it's just too dreadful; you must look after yourself, and those boys'), and a separation was not out of the question at this stage. She received more than one offer of a manly shoulder to cry on, and in the frantic heat of the moment when she first realized J's deception it may even be that she telephoned Tony (her ex-husband) and asked whether or not she should leave my father – an understandable reaction, though I doubt she seriously contemplated it for very long. J said he felt marooned like a castaway – one minute he had been up there on the poop of the Ship of State, with people saluting and following his orders, and doors being opened for him in every sense, and then he was adrift: 'I couldn't find anybody much to give me advice, even on the telephone. That was part of the problem, everybody was terrified. They had very strong feelings about not wanting to become involved, to be associated in any way. I can't say I really blame them. It was all my fault.'

There was one decision with which he needed help immediately. Denning recorded (just before dismissing J from the story in paragraph 222) that 'His name was removed from the Privy Council', but there was more to the business than that. On 13 June my father sent a handwritten letter to Macmillan – the MP initials on his letterhead sadly inked out – that read:

I am quite clear I can no longer remain a Privy Councillor – but how to divest myself of this cherished honour, I do not know.

I write to request that you take the appropriate action with Her Majesty the Queen.

He was advised by Iain Macleod and others that it would be better for him to resign, rather than be removed by the monarch (a situation almost without precedent), and so he took the initiative and resigned voluntarily. His name was removed at his request on 26 June, and the loss of this accolade was such a badge of dishonour that I think it upset him for ever.

On 18 June my parents returned to Chester Terrace with a police escort, and made their way through a large, initially silent, crowd. This was the hardest moment of their lives together. The *Sketch* described them as 'two broken people', but in fact my mother looked composed, with a headscarf and white gloves, and as they arrived she reached out with her right hand across the jostling morass and clasped her husband's hand in hers, guiding him to their front door. It was an image that moved a number of people to write in sympathy and admiration, though on the street there were inevitably jeers as well as cheers. There had been three decades when Valerie Hobson had sought out the flashbulbs, but from this moment on she never again enjoyed having her picture taken.

Running the gauntlet like this was something I was spared, as I stayed at End House in Kensington and only went home when things were a little less frantic. We then lay low for most of July in Warwickshire where both my Uncle Phil and my Aunt Betsy had cottages. J had to be interviewed by Scotland Yard about the case against Ward, and both my parents went to see Denning once his inquiry began – but it was on 8 July that my mother did something that showed her spectacular courage. In full view of the media, she honoured a previous commitment and went to open a home for the mentally handicapped at Dymchurch, in Kent. Wearing a great hat, and addressing a crowd variously estimated as between five hundred and a thousand (by the time it reached the Australian papers, there was a semi-biblical throng of three thousand), she sat on the podium next to Frank Longford during the speeches, and explained that although she had been in two minds, 'I hope you will understand that there are occasions when all personal considerations come second.' During prayers for the handicapped, she was pictured covering her face to hide the emotion of the moment, but she signed the visitors' book boldly – 'What a happy afternoon.' The next day, my parents flew to Zurich and stayed with Lilli Palmer and her husband, the actor Carlos Thompson, at their villa La Loma, which was generously offered to us all as a refuge on more than one occasion. After that, it was time to head for the hills.

On the last day of July, V drove her grey Zephyr north, with J following separately (on the day of Ward's conviction). I flew to Wick with my uncle, and we were tailed all the way from the airport by a small motorcade of photographers, along the switchback single-track roads of Caithness and coastal Sutherland until we all converged on a place called the House of Tongue. This charming, remote lodge was to be our haven for more than two months, over six hundred miles from the brouhaha of the capital.

The house belonged to Elizabeth, Countess of Sutherland, and her husband is said diplomatically to have given the resident housemaid temporary leave, as her name was Christine. The place was ideal, as the grounds were surrounded by a wall, and a wire fence was put across the drive to keep the press at bay. Inside this stockade we were quite private and secure – my aunt and uncle, plus my cousin Mary Ann, Mark, my parents, Mr White, Mrs Bivar, Laudie, my grand-mother – but any expedition outside the precinct was positively embattled. The idea, admirable in its way, was that our family should try to pursue a summer holiday which appeared as regular as possible; this involved boat trips from the nearby jetty (the house overlooks the Kyle of Tongue), forays fishing the lochs or Borgie River nearby, and, come the grouse season in August, shooting parties on the moor. Most of these activities entailed car chases between Donny Murray, the bespectacled keeper who led the way in his Land-Rover, and assorted vehicles containing what are now called paparazzi, who were often taken on wild goose chases by various members of the staff so that my parents could disappear somewhere for a few hours in peace. Having scant idea of the stress it was causing others, I used to find these car chases rather a thrilling game. 'Quick, get there before them,' I cried, as Donny, puffing, radish-faced with stress and overheating in his thick estate tweeds, struggled with the padlock to let us back into the drive. 'This is fun,' I said, bouncing on my seat in the shooting brake, as men clustered around our car and fired off flashes. 'Isn't it,' my mother agreed, flatly, shielding her face with a hand.

The atmosphere within the house was peaceful and insulated, and I loved the place from the very start (I think the entire family did, and they took it again the following summer). The enforced proximity bred what I now see was a kind of siege mentality among most of the adults, which must have been comforting to my parents in particular; in this Edwardian ambience, with its gunroom, tartan carpets, dinner gong and orderly kitchen garden, it seemed temporarily feasible to discount the outside world. If there was a television, I never saw it (Miss Lauderdale anyway regarded it with such suspicion that even in London I was only allowed to watch it once a week). At the breakfast table there were murmured discussions over the papers, but none of it impinged on my enjoyment of spending weeks on end with my family, having the run of the big gardens, and rare treats like chewing gum from the village stores − owned by a robust family called the Burrs, who often asked us in for tea − or the gloriously synthetic Cheez Whiz spread for tea, midnight feasts under the bedclothes with my mother, or my one-eyed granny singing me songs from the Edinburgh of her youth.

On Sundays we all trooped off to the little kirk in Tongue, and sat in the central, boxed-in pew reserved for the ducal lairds of yore, while the rest of the congregation ostentatiously refrained from staring at us.

One afternoon, when my Uncle Harold returned from fishing Loch Croker he spotted me taking more than a casual interest in the brown trout arrayed on a salver in the hall, and informed my father that, since I was all of seven, I should properly be initiated into the mysteries of angling. (Thus began an abiding obsession that has even spilled over into my professional life.) We two escaped to a little moor-land burn that was swollen with mahogany-coloured water from the recent rains, and for the first time ever my father and I fished together. It was elementary sport, lobbing a worm tackle and watching the yellow float as it twirled its way down the bonsai stream towards a ramshackle road bridge; but twice it dithered, dipped across the current, and bobbed under – at which point I duly reared back my rod and sent a diminutive troutling flying from the water and into the heather beside us. My father wrapped his arms about me in congratulation, and I sat triumphantly across his corduroy lap as he put his cap on my head and told me what a clever boy I was. (I made a pilgrimage to that spot eleven years later, but the burn had been cut into a drainage ditch, the pool had disappeared, and the water gargled blandly through a pipe beneath the road.)

In my spare time I haunted the lodge's gun- and tackle-room, scrounging transparent paper packages of hooks, picking up oddments such as rod-stoppers and twists of lead wire, frayed and discarded feathery flies, whatever might be going spare for my incipient collection, which I hoarded in one of my uncle's Dunhill cigar boxes. The room was redolent of citronella oil, with which we all had to dose our skins against the peril of midges on still days. Although I was much too young to take part, I became intrigued by the mighty preparations before a day's sport – the men in Savile Row plus-twos, the clatter of hobnailed shoes being donned for the hill, the thin reek of gun oil, the fat, shiny cartridges (a prime example of teleologic beauty, unless you are a game-bird), and the arrival of Jenny and Jolly, the unruly setters, their straggled coats the colour of ivory and gingerbread. There seemed something heroic about the military precision and self-confidence with which these expeditions were mounted, but perhaps subliminally I felt the family guns were breaking out through that cordon lurking by the gates, and the armed exodus in itself was liberating.

My other pastime was painting. My mother had an elaborate travelling easel with a selection of good oils in delicious little silvery tubes – *Burnt Umber, Vermilion, Rose Madder,* said the labels – and when the men were out ('they seem to like killing things,' she explained, never a fan of field sports) we would sketch together on pads, using flimsy sticks of charcoal. Some of her canvases were quite good: she favoured *nature morte* compositions in her derivative, but arresting, Matthew Smith style, and I used to marvel at the alchemy of her palette pad, with its oiled paper layers you could tear off and discard when the paint congealed. She explained that if you mixed all the available colours together, the result was always grey – a disappointing reflection upon the bright components of our universe, and one which I never could understand. I tested this one afternoon, having painted a garish songbird, and the mishmash was indeed a kind of grey, so I daubed some in the corner of my primitive composition and wrote the caption, 'An Egg Of It'. (I rediscovered this particular piece of artwork preserved in an attic portfolio, its pale brown underside crisping like Melba toast, after my mother's death.)

There was a brief phase when I enjoyed inventing elaborate maps, and labelling the imagined topography. One tea-time, when Mr White was serving the grown-ups Earl Grey and drop scones with bramble jelly, I thought to entertain them by declaiming the place-names I had made up for that day's island. Being a bit of a show-off I began to read aloud: 'Mount Monty, Ens Hill, Trout Bay, the village of Fuk . . .' There was a clotted silence, Laudie was summoned, and my career as an amateur cartographer was swiftly curtailed.

Maintaining the illusion of an idyllic holiday was a commendable performance by my parents, who daily had to put a brave face on things. They kept it from me, but a continual flow of mail and special deliveries was reminding them of unwelcome developments elsewhere – Lord Denning required access to my father's bank statements, proof copies of articles and books were being forwarded by lawyers, the press cuttings were voluminous – and there were the earliest of inevitable social snubs to contend with. (One Tory MP who had a house up there curtly cancelled a previous invitation for them to visit.) The episode my mother recalled as most wounding, however, occurred when she went for a walk alone with my Aunt Maina along the nearby beach at Coldbackie. My aunt had never really approved of Valerie Hobson – a glamorous, self-made divorcee from a profession known for its lax morals (acting, that is) – joining the Profumo family, but this was the first occasion when she made plain the extent of her actual dislike. She turned on her sister-in-law and coldly blamed her for everything that had befallen the family, which, she said, would never have happened if she had been the right woman for precious Jack, whom she clearly could not fulfil or satisfy, thus bringing disgrace to one and all. My mother was shocked and then livid (might she have felt there was a germ of truth in the accusation?), and for many years thereafter their show of friendship was never more than a veneer of verglas over cold stone.

Once the Denning Report was safely out of the way in late September ('Mr and Mrs Profumo are not prepared to see the press,' announced Mrs Cameron the housekeeper) it was time to head back home. On 4 October we arrived via the Inverness sleeper – J businesslike in double-breasted pinstripes, V with a camel-hair coat and scarf, me in a duffel coat and tie, and Laudie in her flat shoes. Explosive events in Dallas the following month drew the fire of the press, and the year finished quite quietly, by comparison. I have always liked Gore Vidal's reply, when asked what he thought would have happened if it had been the Soviet leader, as opposed to Kennedy, who had been assassinated: 'With history one can never be certain, but I think I can safely say that Aristotle Onassis would not have married Mrs Krushchev.'

That autumn, the UK box-office sensation was *From Russia with Love*.

———— • ————

More than once while working on my parents' story it has seemed to take on the astigmatic contours of some tainted fairy-tale. A common motif in folk tales of the *Märchen* variety – that is, the Grimm, rather than Disneyfied, versions – involves a central character undergoing a mutation or metamorphosis which is so intense that even after the spell is actually broken he or she can never entirely recover, nor quite readjust to the conditions of normal life. I have the impression that this happened to J and V, who, after years of assiduously building themselves up to be public figures, were spectrally transformed into pale inversions of their former extroverted selves – now avoiding people, shunning the limelight, having nothing they wished to say.

'It was as if we had been struck by lightning,' was how my mother once described it.

When they returned to Chester Terrace, the world looked like a grim and crumpled place. Faced with a dark swirl of alternatives such as exile, divorce, oblivion, they decided to stay together – 'She was very, very loyal,' said my father. 'Wonderful. Extraordinary.' To many, this was indeed how it seemed, though inevitably some commented that the very show of loyalty was a cynical piece of stage management; no doubt the same philosophasters would have criticized my mother for abandoning her husband in his hour of need, even if his dalliances and mendacity had driven a wrecking ball through their marriage. It is true he would have been helpless without her at that stage, vulnerable as a crustacean between moults, and for all her anger she felt protective towards him (he always showed this little-boy quality in times of trouble). He was subsumed with remorse towards his family and his constituents, and was scared and chastened by the experiences of recent months, but I do not suspect he was ever going to let himself be broken by any of it, nor was the guilt going to prove a shirt of Nessus.

For my mother's part, I believe she loved him despite the infidelity, which came as no great surprise – in some ways he was acting entirely in character. At the height of all the furore, a friend called to offer help, and V replied, 'It's all right. Really, I'll manage. It's not the first time, and it probably won't be the last.' (And I don't suppose it was – he was never going to be very good at monogamy.) She did not regard this as some momentary weakness on J's part, merely one consequence of living with such a man – 'the destruction that wasteth at noonday'. It was not the fling, but the protracted hurricano of relentless exposure that she could not so readily forgive. She may even have felt partially responsible for the marital circumstances within which this came to be. 'He got himself into such a frightful mess because he was shocked beyond endurance by the thought of telling me,' she wrote in a letter to me. 'But love, deep love, came to us through the dreadful tribulations that we shared later. We were under siege, but – perversely perhaps – these were to be the happiest years I ever shared with Jacket.' This was her verdict from the vantage-point of old age, but I doubt that's how it appeared at the time. In adversity, they clung to one another like Hansel and Gretel in the forest, at nightfall.

With certain honourable exceptions, they were instantly ostracized by former acquaintances *du meilleur rang*, and it was quite unusual for the so-called governing classes to turn on their own. 'I don't blame them,' J said, 'I had behaved shamefully, and they thought I was a bloody shit.' He resigned from his clubs – Boodle's, and the prestigious Other Club – as fellow members who were flywheels in the party machine would refuse to associate with someone whose behaviour had wrought such destruction to all they held dear. There was also widespread fear that, in the new climate of exposure, certain ancestral wardrobes might be found to conceal their own skeletons, so shunning was the best option. J and V lost their glamorous lifestyle, and became social pariahs. Iain Macleod, the Nuttings, the Douglas-Homes at Number Ten, and Randolph were among those who bucked the trend; the Queen Mother (whose guest they continued frequently to be at Clarence House) rang my father not long after his resignation and told him, 'So far as I was concerned, you were an ideal Minister.'

It fell to the redoubtable Miss Plumb to reply to all the letters my parents received, of which several thousand were kept in a box in the bank (the following is a brief florilegium). There were inevitably examples of obloquy and hate mail from outraged citizens who thought J had got what he deserved, plus lots of assorted cranks with only one oar in the water. 'What sort of woman are you to allow yourself to be tied to that Italian bastard,' wrote a Miss Lowe from Chiswick. 'He wants his dirty big prick cut off. The lying bastard is a sex maniac.' (For some reason, she went on to accuse my mother of having carnal relations with a black man.) Most of them were anonymous, of course. 'How can you stand him near you?' asked another charming correspondent. 'He's probably rotten with disease anyway. Where's your pride?' Opening the postbag must have been like Pandora's box.

Almost as disconcerting was the mass of religious advice from around the globe, with much urging of enclosed pamphlets and tracts. People wrote in Italian, French, German and Dutch, and letters came from America, Africa, the Antipodes, Japan and the Windward Islands. Some spoke of courage and survival – 'I admire you, my bonny lad,' began a Scotsman of eighty-five – others described tales of woe, similar experiences, chronic problems. It was a gallimaufry of opinions, some from close friends but the majority from hitherto unknown members of the public. 'I am just an ordinary housewife', is how several began; 'May I, a complete stranger . . .'; 'I felt I had to write to you'; 'Having been in trouble myself . . .' Reading through this mass of heterodox material, neatly and alphabetically archived, forty years later, impressed upon me perhaps more than any other experience just how high feelings were running at that time, and what lives of quiet desperation are really always out there.

The First Lord of the Admiralty, George Jellicoe, wrote in eloquent sympathy, and Bronwen Astor sent a most supportive note from Cliveden. The young Jonathan Aitken reckoned that nobody in the history of British politics had ever had to pay so dearly for a mistake. Lord Brabazon of Tara commiserated, 'Poor old boy. Just a line to tell you your friends remain as before . . . PS. Hope to see you at Bembridge.' Such old-world sentiments were appreciated.

From Slough, an Indian 'astrologer to the Princes' offered enigmatic advice; a lady from Rochdale sent in a postal order for half a crown; a Merioneth estate agent enquired if my folks would like any assistance relocating in a new property. An enterprising literary agent from Dean Street wondered if there was any possibility of a book in the offing, and enclosed a leaflet setting out his terms and rates of commission.

'Dear Sir, I, the undersigned, am writing at the command of God Almighty', began a man in Sedbergh (he was nothing to do with the publishing industry); a lady 'undergoing electrical treatment' in hospital suspected she had once been planted by the police to act as Miss Keeler's maid; also in hospital was a man who revealed that MI5 were employing thought-control techniques, and had deliberately ruined J's life because he was a Christian.

There was much mention of hypocrisy, suffering, storms in teacups and 'but for the Grace of God'. A letter from Ilford ran to forty-five pages. Several strangers offered my parents discreet use of their houses ('You could bring your own servants, too, if you wished', added an antediluvian chap from Devon). An ex-RAF mechanic was looking for a job as a handyman, one supplicant needed help paying his tax bill, and a businessman from Ealing wondered if the former Minister would now like to join his franchise distributing tape-recorders.

From her retirement home in Wembley, Nanny Bridgeland wrote to V: 'What a dreadful scandle it as turned into. I feel very sorry about the whole thing. I had a nice time down at Worthing and feel better for the change love to the children.'

One robust Yorkshireman chided J for looking so 'haunted' in the press stills; 'for goodness sake snap out of it – a man with your war record should have got out of the car and smacked the cameraman on the nose.' A well-wisher from Champaign, Illinois, confided, 'I've been through this sort of a mess, too, and I would have enjoyed a kind word from the trash man.'

From New York came a letter handwritten by Noël Coward: 'Darling Valise . . . I know you must be having a difficult and horrid time and this is just to send you my love as always . . . Beyond what I have read in the papers I don't know any of the ins and outs of the situation (This could perhaps have been more happily put!) but I do know this must be a bad patch,' concluding, 'Do remember that nothing ever matters quite as much as one thinks it does.' No wonder they called him Master.

———•———

Having shot the rapids, my parents needed to discover a quiet back-water where they could assess the damage they had sustained. While they decided upon what course their lives might next take, they required what is now known as some breathing space. Mark had just started at Eton (where, having a different surname, he endured some awkward moments with boys who did not know of his family connection), but I was still at home – eight, priggish, precocious, delicate and solitary. The obvious solution was to send me away too.

On 24 January 1964 – after rather a subdued Christmas – the Jaguar treacherously scrunched down the gravel drive between the rhododendrons and drew up beside the dour Victorian portico of Sunningdale School, in dankest Berkshire. It was not the same establishment my brother Mark had attended – that had to close down due to a sex scandal of its own – but Sunningdale was currently enjoying a good reputation among well-heeled parents due to the wisdom and kindliness of its headmaster and proprietor, Charlie Sheepshanks. He was a moustachioed, slightly dishevelled family man with a much younger wife, Mary (later a successful novelist), and that first afternoon the new boys were welcomed to tea in the private side of the school. There was Coca-Cola and home-made banana cake, and it all seemed reasonably *comme il faut* to the five neophytes with their pudding-basin haircuts and grey flannel trousers who eyed one another cautiously from sheltered positions extremely close to their valiantly grinning mothers. The swathed and pampered years were at an end, and Fauntleroy was about to undergo his very own transformation.

It would not do to claim that this was a place of hardship or oppression – the attitude was not quite as extreme as that of the Highland laird who, bivouacking in winter with his small son, reprimanded him for improvising a pillow out of snow: 'No effeminacy, my boy!' The school came as something of a shock, however, as its details bore just sufficient enough resemblance to one's home life to be bewildering – it was a slightly dislocated version of everything upon which one had come to rely.

At first, I was rather intrigued by the metal bedsteads, those ancient floorboards and the pocked and nibbled linoleum of my dormitory, but I could not quite believe I was going to stay there. Communal bath-time, lockless lavatory doors, unmaternal women, and the insalubrious odours – cabbage water, festering leather, sweat – all appeared domestic travesties, and there was an unsteadying groundswell of argot: going to the lavatory was called 'going across' (the main block was across a yard), 'brown rubbers' denoted, incredibly, a type of regulation, crêpe-soled shoes kept in wooden racks on the walls of 'The Pipe', a stony corridor where you were forbidden to run, and where footwear was polished weekly by 'Wally', a Maltese factotum who looked as if he was hiding from Interpol. The single feature of this inexplicably basic new environment which impressed upon me just how far I was from home – which practically came to symbolize my predicament, indeed, and has become an abiding memory of the place – was the bizarre nature of the food. Banana cake, I discovered, was never again on the menu, and the next time we'd see a fizzy drink served would be on Sports Day in June.

The kitchen was manned by a cook named Mary – a vast pundle of a creature, fearsome and permanently unthanked, whom before breakfast one might glimpse through the serving hatch sweating into her cauldron of eggs. Fish pie was probably the strangest of her concoctions, containing as it often did sections of fin and backbone, though she was a dab hand at bubonic milk puddings and Spam fritters, too. I have since had my fair share of outlandish dishes – from bats' blood soup to pig's pizzle in batter – but hers was the only cuisine that regularly stuck in one's craw. A jaundiced lady named Mrs Ball acted as housekeeper, and she would not remove your plate until you had finished. It was sometimes feasible to hide bits of food behind the hot-water pipe that ran down one side of the dining-room (eating to the roar of a hundred voices was also a novel and unappetizing experience) but your only hope of a meal that was actually familiar to the palate was to be admitted to the Sick Room, where the matrons were in charge of the catering.

Even by the educational standards of yesteryear, I feel it must have been a lousy example of the single-sex preparatory school of which so many then still flourished, offering harassed parents, in exchange for hefty fees, the chance to have their sons inculcated with the qualities needed for later life – servility, regular bowel movements, a working knowledge of seam bowling – and fit them for a military career, or service in the colonies. It was traditional rather than progressive (there was no gym or science teaching) and was regarded as a 'feeder' school for Eton; a television documentary was once made about it, entitled *Gateway to Eton*, and the local milkman was so incensed by some of the social attitudes expressed in the programme that he refused to deliver the school milk. In the little jerry-built chapel, where 'Sheepie' played the organ with crazed inaccuracy, one visiting preacher was pleased to explain that the purpose of such a school was 'to prepare you boys for death', though I'm not sure that this mission statement actually appeared on any prospectus.

You had to write home cheerfully every Sunday, unless it was one of the few weekends when you were allowed out. Precious little concerning one's travails made it through to the parental breakfast tray, of course, because of the time-honoured system of letters being read by a master before being sealed up. There was no chance of expressing one's own ignorant feelings, therefore, and instead you dutifully copied down details chalked up on the board, such as the dramatic 4–1 football victory against Lambrook, away, or the title of the film shown in the library on Saturday evening. My mother apparently kept every one of these letters, and my first, dated 26 January 1964, began: 'Darling Mummy and Co. It is so nice here I don't even want to think about going out. Yesterday, for lunch, we had venison . . .' (long pig, more likely). A little later – I had mastered the language of false re-assurance quite quickly – I insisted that 'I have settled down very well, and I could not even make myself feel homesick if I tried, and I did try and it didn't work.' I might as well have claimed the Easter holi-days were looking like an unwelcome interruption.

On the staff, there was a central triumvirate of Old Guard, most prominent of whom was 'Budgie' Burrows, a lean, stooping bachelor who had taught there for fifty years, and was rumoured to have been gassed in the Great War. He had parchment skin, a corncrake voice, and eyes like cocktail onions; with his neat white moustache, he might have resembled Mister Chips, but he was cantankerous rather than mellow, and doddering age had merely whetted his tongue. 'Remarkable', he would croak, whenever you got an answer wrong, blinking at you with saurian contempt; clearly, he found small boys infuriating in their habits, and his aim with the heavy board-wiper was still impressive. Budgie was master in charge of 'dorms', and would 'swish' you with his cane if you were caught 'ragging' (or so it was said); at seven each evening he chose a boy to take his Thermos down to the kitchen to fetch ice from Mary for his scotch, the enviable reward being a buttermint from his famous tin.

Running Budgie close in the venerability stakes was Mr Tupholme – always known as 'Teacher' – a benign, mumbling josser with pigeon-grey hair and eyebrows like oil-strikes, who would never have harmed a flea and was greatly beloved. He was a genuine polymath, teaching classics and maths to scholarship level, but he had a verbal tic which was to include the phrase, 'D'ye see?' in practically every sentence; during a single lesson, Faber Major once recorded over one hundred instances of this on the hand-held sheep-counter he had brought back from Hong Kong. The third of these Colossi was Mr Squarey, a florid and flamboyant historian with loud tweeds, trademark rose buttonhole, and the physiognomy of a benevolent sturgeon. He pursued ancient methods of teaching modern history – 'What was the date of the Battle of Bannockburn, write down, pens down, every fool knows, and the answer is, of course?' 'Who, me sir? Was it 1413?' 'Filth!'

The Dawson twins, Nick and Tim, were pretenders to the throne, and in due course took over the school: almost identical, athletic and handsome in their Greenjackets blazers, with their admirable black and brilliantined hair, they were the Tweedledum and Tweedledee of the place, the Rosencrantz and Guildernstern ('her privates, we'). Epitomes of glycerine charm, this brace of *faux bonhommes* specialized in soccer and geography – coincidentally, of course, two of the areas where I really sucked – and there was a deal of fine ivory in their youthful smiles.

Like most of its rival institutions, Sunningdale was a place where the emphasis was on games, at which (in the parlance of the boys) I was considered 'spastic' – I was also a 'swot' (making it into the Sixth Form for two subjects at the age of nine, Laudie's Bible sessions having really paid off) and a 'milksop', to boot. The latter appellation was for physically weedy boys, and it is true I spent much of the first couple of terms in and out of the Sick Room, with tonsillitis and various fevers. This was no great hardship because I began to read (bound back-copies of *Punch* were for some reason available, but I also discovered Mary Renault, Conan Doyle and Alan Garner) and I was virtually adopted by the formidable Matron, Pauline, who presided over the Paracelsian dispensary in her blue nurse's uniform. You were fed things like toast and warm milk if you were ill, and this state of segregation was much coveted, but malingerers were rapidly rooted out: swallowing toothpaste to give yourself a temperature, or faking a rash using hairbrush bristles, was never going to fool the starch-cuffed Irishwoman.

Pauline Doyle and her team of comely young deputies (there was a Christina, which was a near-miss) were chiefly responsible for our digestive health, which involved doling out matutinal spoonfuls of sticky Virol, Radio Malt or cod-liver oil, and checking that our bowels were fluently functional. Each morning you had to report to a matron whether you had 'gone across properly' or '*non*' (we were a polyglot lot) – and in the case of small boys she would sometimes go and check. This was a way of ensuring *mens sana in corpore sano*, I am sure, as was the insistence that we hold up a pocket hankie on the way down to breakfast, acquiring a habit that would save our faces in later life if overcome with a sudden urge to sneeze when in solar topee and inspecting the troops, or sitting down for tiffin in Swettipore. Never being careless about personal hygiene was a useful lesson in general. Once a week you were required to deposit your underpants into a communal linen basket, where the cleanliness or otherwise of one's garments might readily be observed by others in the queue, leading to some merciless teasing. Here, a terrible misfortune once befell me, because my mother had caused to be sewn into my Chilprufes some name-tapes that were originally hers, but with the 'Valerie' tucked back under the stitches; inevitably, the Christian name came adrift and disclosed itself, and for some weeks I was labelled a 'girl' – the *ne plus ultra* of insults.

By dint of being in the Sick Room, I escaped another of the fine old school rituals which was, on the third weekend of term, to harass and generally victimize any new boys who had proved themselves unpopular. This was known as Blub Sunday, a tradition the very existence of which was fiercely denied by the staff; fortunately (as a milksop) I was out of circulation, though I'm not sure much physical abuse ever really occurred. Besides, there was weeping most Sundays at evening chapel, when, after the uplifting strains of 'Abide with Me', Michael Tupholme in his lay reader's surplice would begin to mumble the gloomy prayers, and boys who had seen their parents briefly during the day would blub and snuffle at their renewed sense of abandonment. We were all in it together, and of course it wasn't the end of the world – not to the extent that it was for the Old Boys who fell in the world wars, whose names were listed on either side of the nave – but occasionally there were attempts to run away. (Spencer-Smith Major was legendary for once having escaped as far as Egham in his dressing-gown.)

So this was the world of enchantment, the baleful land of faerie, where I was to dwell for four long years. I don't suppose it did me any harm, but it certainly annexed my imagination for a time. I now see that the alternative would have been a home life which at that stage was fraught, and at least the school cocooned me from any domestic or public strangeness. In fact, Charlie Sheepshanks and his team managed an impressive feat of protectionism for which I am grateful – they kept from me, throughout my time at the school, any reference to the Profumo Affair. The boys were sternly lectured about this before I arrived (I don't suppose many of them had the faintest notion of the matter anyway), and the newspapers discreetly failed to arrive in the library on certain days, also. Given the popular currency of the story, this was quite an achievement, and it may have been a case of Stockholm Syndrome but I became eerily attached to this other-worldly place; at least I'd begun to understand how it worked.

Now that I was spending more time away than at home ('School is really where you live now', as one doctor so helpfully put it), there was no longer much need for a governess, and Laudie left us to go and look after the daughter of a Greek shipping magnate. I am clear when this exactly happened, because her last duty was to take me to the school train at the start of my second term, and she had dressed me in my smart blue uniform. The Sunningdale tradition, however, was that you travelled in your grey Sunday suit, so I was the only boy incorrectly attired. Although these schools were always said to be fostering your sense of independence, they were really all about conformity; that was the first time in my life that I definitely wished to die.

I never quite got the hang of being a team player, either, though I was desperate to succeed. I longed to have my picture in the great line-up of First Eleven teams that stretched down the corridors, recording the lofty Corinthians of past years, right back to Victorian times. Somehow I knew it was never to be. In due course I became what was charitably known as 'the backbone of the Second Eleven', but to start with I was spindly and scared and no good at running (though, with two chaps suffering from chronic asthma, I was never quite last in the agonizing steeplechase). In break-time, when boys chose teams for 'kicking around' or the peculiar school game called 'hot rice', I would be loitering by the fence until there was no one else to choose from. In the summer, I operated the tallywag while the real athletes got padded up and ran about, or else I lay on my rug alongside the other spectators and incinerated ants with my magnifying glass. Sports Day – when real-world food was trotted out for the benefit of visitors – represented an especial ordeal, not just because I never won anything but because my father (still incredulous that he had sired a son who was patently an athletical dunce) insisted on filming my every awkward move with his cine-camera (the same one he had taken to Russia before the war). I went simultaneously in fear of my mother's spectacular hats, the appearance of which made me want to combust spontaneously with needless embarrassment.

Although I could scarcely tie up my plimsolls without falling over, I had learned to swim well, and there was salvation in the pool, where eventually I won a cup for the breast-stroke. Nude bathing before breakfast was a feature of the summer terms, an exercise designed to invigorate us with chlorine and stiffen our resolve – perhaps having a similar effect on some of the masters invigilating this activity, a couple of whom, hands in pockets, seemed to volunteer for the chore with cheerful frequency.

On the work front my progress was better, and my nickname (quite an important thing, in such a community) was, fortunately, 'The Professor' – though I was never mistaken for a Balkan dignitary. In fact, the academic feedback began to be so favourable – forgive me, while I treat us all to a fanfare on the auto-trumpet – that my father, in his wisdom, decided to bowdlerize my reports for fear any approbation might turn my dizzy young head. I only discovered this recently, and for some reason it made me absurdly indignant. His habit was to read the reports aloud to me in his study, and when I was recently riffling through a cache of these I saw that for years on end he invariably toned down every single term of praise – for instance, by removing 'extremely' from 'he has done extremely well', inserting a modifier 'quite' into 'he produces intelligent work', or simply pencilling in alternative versions; thus, where Sheepie generously wrote 'once again David has defeated all the opposition', the paterfamilias substituted, 'This is good – he continues to show promise.' The practice continued until I was in my late teens, and although it's a minor matter, and was presumably conducted *con amore*, this petty deception suggests that my parents had a lopsided notion of what was likely to prove damaging to me. A modicum of praise and encouragement at this stage – especially, perhaps, given the delicate state of family affairs at large – was hardly going to make me dysfunctional (the headmaster, who saw rather more of me than they did, felt it might be positive), but I suppose they could not risk a son, wildly *entêté* from having come top in Latin construe, starting to wet his bed or beginning to light small fires in the corner of the room.

Jack and Val may not have been shrewd educationalists, but they were no fools. It may be they had come to dread the very signs of pride, however youthful, after their own experience of an almighty Fall. Perhaps deep and recent disappointment had cauterized the natural flow of congratulation, so that, for years, there was too much 'hurt' there to allow them to say a heartfelt 'Well done'. I simply do not know, but – oh, for Heaven's sake, man, take a grip, it never upset you that much at the time, you're a big boy now, stop strumming your emotions, this is all most unseemly, what will your family think, we've all got our crosses to bear, stop dwelling on the past, go and build yourself another pink gin. You know, I think I shall.

My one hope of joining any roll of honour seemed to be the varnished wooden board that dominated the library, and recorded the names of those who had won scholarships to various public schools. We spent so many hours waiting 'on silence' in this room that the surnames on this list remain quite familiar even now – Parsons, Impey, Tinsley, Gascoigne, Hogg – fine minds the school had ushered forth. Sitting through the roll-call or eagerly awaiting our turn to collect the sweets ration from the 'grub trolley' (whereon, one Easter that fell before the end of term, Pauline smashed with a hammer all the elaborate chocolate eggs that mothers had sent to assuage their guilt), there was plenty of time to memorize these names, though few could compete with the cosmopolitan splendour of some of those on our current school list, which hung on the other wall – Beelearts van Blokland, Montagu-Douglas-Scott, Earl Grosvenor, Von Hounighen Huene, Chippendall-Higgin, and of course, *primus inter pares* in this concourse, my own.

Even more exotic than the boy who was to become the richest man in Britain was His Highness the Maharaja of Morvi, an understandably arrogant and indecently handsome prince who was idolized by some of the staff because he was also a lethally fast bowler. On his birthday, he broke all precedents and entertained the entire school to a tea party at which he was enthroned at one end of the dining-room, whence he doled out presents to every boy, and hewed into a gigantic cake that was an iced facsimile of his family palace. No doubt Pauline would have liked to have taken her hammer to that, as well, in the interests of equitable distribution. I remember big Mary peeping around the door in wonderment – and I wonder, in turn, if she would have been capable of such a confectionery *masque*, had her lot been that of a Mrs Bivar rather than the perpetually unappreciated mass caterer for the spoiled young denizens of a drear academy just off Dry Arch Road.

The last tea I ever ate in that room was when I returned at the age of seventeen to play in an Old Boys' football match. I actually managed to score a goal against the little Sunningdalians, and – as was the ceremony – our former Captain of Games marched up and put a cap on my head and cried out, 'Well played, Profumo!' So, to satirical applause, the milksop became the oldest boy ever to be awarded his soccer colours. '*Gaudeamus igitur*', as I expect they still say in the Common Room.

Meanwhile, my socially benighted parents had to decide on their new *modus vivendi*: were they going to change their names and live abroad, or retire to the shires and go into the antiques business, or tough it out in town? Moving to the country had been discussed in the pre-lapsarian period, and now it did seem to be on the cards. They had the signal advantage of financial independence, so they were not constrained to peddle themselves on game shows or give jocular addresses at company conventions. In January 1964, my father made a very substantial 'marriage settlement' of £97,000 which included provision for Mark's education and maintenance, among various other contingencies which were no doubt causing my mother anxiety. It seems to me that this signified the striking of a deal, and from that moment the groundwork was laid down for some familial reconstruction.

In September of that year, amid considerable excitement, they bought what was to be our new home – the Dower House, near Westmill in Hertfordshire. A pretty, Queen Anne *villino* set at the end of a long drive with several acres of neglected garden overlooking tumbledown pasture and parkland, it appeared to be exactly what they desired, especially as it would require quite extensive conversion work to meet their needs. The design and rebuilding of this house preoccupied them for at least a year, and it became the ideal focus for their distracted energies; this was something they both adored, and the result was a labour of love that brought them a timely and subtle satisfaction. Putting things together, in a world that has tended towards disintegration or threatens entropy, can of course take many forms, from collage and sculpture to the fusion or accumulation of words, but the achievement of harmony after discord is surely a fundamental aspiration of the spirit. I will not pretend the Dower House was a work of art, but as a project it engaged them with passion, variety and the vital sense of making something.

Like Winston Churchill, my parents were easily satisfied with the best; as their architect they engaged Raymond Erith, a Classical perfectionist and painstaking historian of period detail, whose assistant was the young Quinlan Terry. Planning the new footprint of the building, suggesting ways its living space could be reconfigured, and the design of an entirely new façade (complete with specially baked bricks) and the numerous site visits once the work actually began, became a major diversion from what now seemed like the inhospitable circumstances of their London life. Preparing their new home also involved ancillary expeditions in search of furnishings – the antiques shops of the Home Counties were scoured in a way that seemed a throwback to my mother's childhood forays with her papa, and days out from school were often combined with visits to various (deadly dull) Berkshire dealers, or to the nearby nurseries of Jim Russell, a fashionable horticulturalist who was based too close to Sunningdale for my comfort. Gardening was to become the new passion of my father's life, but there is only so much time you would wish to spend on a precious day's exeat sitting in the back of a raindroppy car re-reading the *Eagle* while the adults ambled enthusiastically through those expensive shrubberies.

On 15 October 1964, the day of the general election, V put on J's breakfast tray a card that simply read – the text surrounded by kisses – 'I vote for *you*.'

But, for all the prospect of a rural retreat, my father was not envisaging a life of leisurely retirement; it no longer seemed an option. He had been brought low, but he was not entirely down: he needed to prove that, and at the same time to put something together in public to set against the damage he perceived he had caused there, too.

From the *Bulawayo Chronicle* to the *Northwestern Evening Mail* (Barrow-in-Furness) it had been reported on 23 April 1964 that John Profumo was venturing from the shadows, to begin volunteer work at Toynbee Hall, a slightly moribund charity in London's East End. Some of the coverage was understandably a bit vague about what went on there, and plumped for 'working in the slums'. In fact, it was the first of the Universities Settlements, a movement founded in 1884 by Canon Samuel Barnett originally to offer students (who had included William Beveridge and Clement Attlee, in their time) subsidized lodgings in return for some voluntary assistance with those in conditions of poverty – Irish and Jewish immigrants in particular – in the Whitechapel area that was forever to be associated with Jack the Ripper. The movement had spread around the world, but in 1964 the original charity (named after Arnold Toynbee, the Victorian social reformer and economist, not his more celebrated namesake) was an unprepossessing centre offering legal aid, meals for the destitute, old people's clubs and a host of other services. Its chief claim to fame was as the place where Marconi had given the first British demonstration of his wireless, but now it was urgently in need of funds. My father had never even heard of the place until he was contacted by the Dowager Marchioness of Reading – mother of his old Oxford friend Michael – who said she had just spoken to them and they assured her they would turn away nobody who offered to help. He rang them the next day, out of the blue, and he was still working there in his ninety-second year.

There were those who regarded all of this as a stunt, a penance that was no more than a gesture. History has proved them wrong, but one can see why, at the time, it was hard for some people to reconcile a sudden devotion to good works with the still-recent and lambent image of a man supposedly associated with the fleshpots of the *haut monde*, in whom the philanthropic impulse had not notably been identified. My feeling is that the ex-Minister's instincts were not going to let him down again; he felt the time was right to make his move now, when the inevitable publicity would benefit his place of choice just as surely as some of it would reflect positively on his own determination to make some kind of new start. He did not want to look as if he was licking his wounds. This display of guts and repentance has rightly been admired over the years, and one should not underestimate the bravery required in showing that he could soldier on, even though decades of comment upon it have come to seem hackneyed. 'I was terrified on that first day,' he admitted, 'going to this strange place after my disgrace. My political background meant some of the socialist workers would have nothing to do with me, on principle, and there were others who feared my presence might attract adverse publicity. But I was pleased to be just warmly greeted by an old lady with grey hair, who turned out to be the bursar; and that was my introduction to Toynbee Hall.'

My father started taking in washing from the residents, making himself useful around the kitchen performing basic tasks, and maintaining the lowest of profiles. Many who remembered him from those first days – such as Doris Greening, the bursar, and Olive Wagstaff, another of his earliest mentors – agreed that he was extraordinarily modest and shy; it did not take long for others who worked there to see that his motives were genuine, and that he was willing to turn his hand to anything, from dancing with old ladies during tea parties to coping with meths drinkers (I remember his shocked description of addicts who mixed boot polish with puddle water, to get a 'high'). The warden was Walter Birmingham – 'a Pacifist and a Quaker and a man of honour', in J's words – an academic and intellectual who had just returned from Africa, and whose background could hardly have been more different from a Conservative Secretary of State for War. My father shadowed him, learning the ropes, beginning to attend to small matters of detail. Against all the odds, he found his new milieu. A less glamorous counterpoint to the Court of St James could scarcely be imagined, yet it became a lifeline. Icarus, it turned out, could swim.

His affection for the people of the East End, many of whom knew what it was to be down on their luck, was plain for all to see. You can't fool such folk with gleaming Tory charisma, but in time they became his new constituency. As a boy, I could not see what all the fuss was about over his 'new job' – I still had no idea of the deep background – but there was no mistaking his pride when he told me that Benny, the news vendor by Aldgate East tube station, used to give him a free paper every day, or how welcome it was, walking through the market in Petticoat Lane, when some of the stallholders began to greet him by name. The Toynbee team would have no truck with the media intrusion, either, which was persistent for a while: one undercover reporter from a French magazine, posing as a social worker, was soon twigged by Doris, who treated her to a tediously long tour of the various buildings, before settling her down to do some nice basket-work with the pensioners. Once it was clear he was no opportunist – no fair-weather friend – Jack gradually won the right to such protection, and there's no doubt this feeling nourished him. In return, there came a generous spirit – one that, in his previous walk of life, might have remained stoppered up for good.

On their tenth wedding anniversary, New Year's Eve 1964, when we were still living at Chester Terrace, my mother wrote him this letter:

> My beloved Husband – The whole of time would not be long enough to tell you of my joy in being married to you. Joy is not measured just by lovely things: the birth of babies, the song of birds heard together, the fun of holidays – the lyrical-love of lying with you.
>
> Joy is to be found, too, in the relief after pain shared, in the good news following bad, in the knowledge of greater closeness after disaster. And so it is for me, with you. These have been some of the fullest

most wonderful years of my all-too-short life. If I live, your devoted
wife, *another* ten by your side, I shall have fulfilled a dream.

I love you, and forgive me my trespasses . . .

Valerie

Although they skilfully sheltered me from the real problems with
which they were having to contend, children can be intuitive enough,
and I became aware, on odd occasions, that for some reason we were
not quite going along in sync with the rest of the world, like the
moving handrail in a subway that sporadically judders at a different
speed to the escalator itself.

At the age of nine, I began to suspect I had been adopted – a
common enough phenomenon, I gather, but my conviction sprang,
illogically, from the absence anywhere of wedding photos, and the fact
that, when questioned about their marriage and how they had met,
my parents seemed evasive and unamused. I now think it was just that
they were intent on not looking back, and had no wish to venture
down memory lane. After what must have appeared otiose wheedling,
my mother did produce some photographs of their big day, and that
must have placated me. Still, I was beginning to feel that my parents
were keeping some secret from me, and it was to be a while before
my innocence was definitively ended, like that moment when the first
pustule appears on your previously smooth complexion.

We spent Easter of 1965 in Aberdeenshire, where my uncle owned
a stretch of the River Deveron. It was my first experience of spring
salmon-fishing, which involved hurling out a metal spinning lure into
some extremely cold water, and winding it back towards my feet. I
caught nothing, and my mother spent much of her time untangling
'bird's nests' of nylon line which had jammed up the reel as a result
of my botched casting. We stayed in the Meldrum House Hotel,
owned and run by a family friend named Robin Duff, a queenly
gentleman aesthete who had once acted as private secretary to
the Maharaja of Bundi, had a penchant for all things balletic, and was
a flamboyant but uneven cook. (My aunt claimed once to have discovered a rook feather in her game pâté.) One night, his staff all

walked out when the restaurant was fully booked, so the four of us stood in as waiters. While the culinary laird, shouting and swigging and scorching himself in the kitchen, prepared the meals single-handed, we fetched and carried. Some of the diners were a little sur-prised to find that their *sommelier* had been a member of the previous Government, but all went well and I received half a crown tip – the first money I ever earned.

The problem came not in the hotel but when we were on the way to the river, and my father pulled into a lay-by to look under the bonnet because the engine was pinking. An army lorry was already there, with a couple of soldiers leaning against the tailgate having a fag. I don't remember how, but some scoffing took place – I'm sure these squaddies didn't recognize J, it was just unhelpful jeering at an older man who was having mechanical problems. He banged down the lid, and drove off, and it was the first time I had ever seen him dangerously lose his composure; he was slamming his palm on to the steering wheel, cursing their behaviour – 'Not long ago, I was in charge of the bloody lot of them' . . . 'Jack, Jack, *calmes-toi*. The chil-dren, you know, please?' Their uniformed insolence, the slovenliness, the rank insubordination, had piqued him dangerously. After a few miles, he fell silent, and when we reached the river he took himself off a long way downstream, alone, for the rest of that morning.

Although the building work was still going on around us, we moved from London down to Hertfordshire shortly after my tenth birthday, just in time for Christmas 1965. The Dower House was elegant and comfortable and had a happy atmosphere, but for some reason I never quite loved it. My parents did, though, and the place acted as a cata-lyst, accelerating their renewed interdependence. They were both fiercely determined to make a go of it – 'nothing was going to be allowed to get in our way' – though this like-mindedness, which was more than tinged with defiance, meant there was not much mental room for others in their gorgeous cocoon. (I was later reminded of Plutarch's description of the exclusive lifestyle of Antony and Cleopatra: an *Amimetobion*.)

Although she was much taken with the idea of a bucolic retreat, and the house itself was certainly a peaceable enclave, filled with their precious things, my mother was not really a country girl at heart. She admired the views, appreciated the fantails and tumbler pigeons my father installed in his home-made dovecote, enjoyed painting and flower-arranging and walking her yappy spaniel, but she was happier indoors than out. She luxuriated in the privacy of her own sitting-room, with its burnt-orange walls, the hi-fi playing Fauré or Bach, and – above all – the absence of others. She spent hours on the phone to her female friends (plus Tony, who remained a close *confident*), bluish Gitanes smoke scribbling the air, and composed copious letters, writing on a clipboard with her Shaeffer pen, a long, loping script that I would identify gratefully on the envelopes that arrived almost daily at school. In the holidays, she tried gamely to play cricket with me on the lawn, or escort me fishing on the stream nearby, but these were not her idea of a pastime. There were frequent shopping trips to the local market towns, however, and I happily went along with those, having inherited from her (to my father's astonishment) that unmasculine passion.

It was in his library that we tended to spend more time, for there the main television was located. The room – where he worked at the desk, with his defunct ministerial dispatch boxes still proudly on display – was not much used for reading, except for his daily diet of six newspapers (the fascination with politics never curdled). His literary taste extended little further than the ditties beloved since childhood (he had Leary the Lamplighter's lines by heart), so the majority of books on the shelves had been purchased by the yard – you always know something's awry when there is more than one incomplete run of the collected works of Walter Scott. The exceptions were those volumes inscribed to him by their authors (in which case he might look himself up in the index) or the various manuals on horticulture. The redesigning of what had previously been a market garden became his chief recreation for a dozen years to come, and he developed a conspicuous talent for it. He came to relish not just planting and pruning, but a new-found pleasure in taxonomy and nomenclature – *Agapanthus*, *Frangipani*, *Acer rubrifolia* went his new litany of delight, as he took visitors on what was called his Cook's Tour of the flower-beds. I think the harder physical work also provided a focus, and he was as enthusiastic about rotavating the derelict orchard or mowing the several lawns as he was prodding his way around the greenhouse.

Until we left Chester Terrace, I had rarely seen my father in clothes so scruffy as to appear quite *déshabillé*, but now his worn cords and polo-necked shirts became a familiar mufti, though whenever he drove to London the formal suiting was still in order. We began to spend time together, and to discover each other's company. He had set up a workshop in the basement, with a good carpentry bench and tool rack; he was a keen handyman, and hours would be spent here, making mirror frames, cutting out and painting Perspex, faking tortoiseshell boxes. He jigsawed miniature display stands for my mother's collection of geological specimens, and fashioned tight-fitting covers in a dozen differing colours of velvet. During the holidays, I appropriated it as a laboratory for my chemistry set – it was an amalgam of cooking and alchemy, really, because we had as yet no science teaching at school, and I was more attracted by the kit and caboodle than anything else. Experiments of the prescribed kind (heating copper sulphate, testing for oxygen with a glowing splint) were soon augmented by minor alembic procedures that were not in the enclosed Merit booklet, and involved ingredients that were definitely off-menu. I persuaded my mother to acquire a small bottle of sulphuric acid on my behalf, which produced a one-off stink bomb that was not appreciated (I had no idea what I was doing with such dangerous stuff), and thence I graduated to the making of rudimentary gunpowder. My friend Jamie used to come for a short stay most holidays, and one of his London pals had shown him the recipe for 'flare', combining crushed charcoal, sugar, and dry weedkiller. We dug this into trenches as a fuse trail leading up to molehills, which we filled with flare, so that, when lit, they went up like volcanoes, leaving a heady smell of caramel in the air. I doubt this achieved much in the way of talpicide, but it certainly incited the displeasure of the melancholy old gardener, Mr Fitzgerald.

Apart from five acres of garden, we did not own the parkland in which the house was set. This belonged to our neighbour, a dog-and-stick cattle farmer named Teddy Livermore, whose attitude to husbandry was – fortunately for me – so *laissez-faire* that, for a peppercorn consideration, we had the run of his land with rod and gun (and later with my first car). He was elderly, white-stubbled, and lame, with a wife of nervous disposition who seldom ventured out of doors, and two daughters – one a voluptuous young woman with cornsilk hair and a complexion like butter-milk, the other somewhat less so.

There was no arable, and little dairy work, so the place was relatively quiet, and we had herds of cattle to grace our view. Thinking to initiate me into the rites of the natural world, my parents took me up one afternoon to watch a cow give birth. It was the most horrifying thing I had ever seen. The calf was breeched, and the mother in loud distress; the vet explained that he was just going to give her a drink of chocolate to make her sleepy, but tried in vain to shift the wretched thing, despite much squelching and squirting, which I witnessed with a rising gorge. The calf had to be pulled out of the cow with a rope attached to the ancient Massey Ferguson, and it seemed as if the mother would split entirely in two, so gaping was the rupture, her nearside flank convulsing like a windsock. They both perished, and that was the last time I saw an act of parturition until my own children were born.

The River Rib is an obscure chalk stream, and an overgrown stretch ran through the furthest part of the farm. Unlike the classic angling waters of the southern counties, with their barbered verges and tamed willows, this was jungly and unkempt, and nobody had fished it for years. The water was vodka clear, however, and if you crept up gingerly towards the little pools, braving the nettles and thorns, you could occasionally see a great, wild brown trout suspended as if in isinglass, beneath the shelter of arthritic tree-roots, or finning contentedly in the filtered sunlight. I have never since seen brownies like them – lean and long, with greenish backs and treacly-looking sides, not exactly handsome, but most desirable to a boy just discovering the world underwater. Although my mother disliked the killing of anything, she sat patiently with her book while I laid siege to them, with bungling techniques at first (you only got one chance before they lunged away), but learning as I went. It took me several summers, but eventually I succeeded in catching all but one of these mighty creatures, the alluring images of which – even in middle age – still glide sometimes through my sleep.

By the age of eleven, I was also proficient with a shotgun, Mark and I often walking the woods and hedgerows with J, in pursuit of rabbits, pigeons or crows. There was a makeshift hide where we could wait for flighting ducks, and in the winter months a ragamuffin syndicate used to shoot a few pheasants around the coverts, our local window-cleaner doubling up as gamekeeper for the day – a Barbour jacket over his boiler-suit, the tops of his regulation wellies turned down. Each shot I took I found thrilling, and by the time I was a teenager I had become a passable marksman. Many companionable hours on the farm in search of the odd woodcock pelting through a copse, lurking on the lip of a rattery at dusk, or trudging across the dark corduroy of plough-land to track a hare, were enjoyed by this particular father and son and proved an ideal antidote to life at boarding school.

Our holiday expeditions tended to be family-based, too, and I think this was arranged largely for my father's benefit, to afford him a sense of security. There was little contact with any of the scattered Hobsons, but we often visited Aunt Betsy in Warwickshire, who was childless but nephew-friendly; she sported a spectacular head of dyed black hair, and had an expensive weakness for clanky bracelets and a wardrobe of silk blouses and trousers of garish hue. She loved Jack Russells, painted alarmingly caustic cartoons, and was the worst driver anyone knew – she once came to London in her new car, complaining of a strange smell, and hadn't realized the gears required changing manually. Whenever in town, she stayed in the same rooms at Claridge's and quaffed Dubonnet-on-the-rocks.

It was End House in London that continued to act as the family lodestone, and this influence was extended in 1967 when, for a decade, Uncle Harold acquired his own sporting estate up in Sutherland. Every summer, and sometimes at New Year, too, we would put the car on the night train at Olympia and travel to Inverness. There, after porridge and kippers at the old Station Hotel – where those travelling with gun dogs could leave them on their leash with the porter at the front desk while they breakfasted – we would pay a ritual visit to Graham's, the tackle shop, and then drive on up to Lairg, dropping back east through Strath Fleet, past Muie, to Rogart, where the Balfours' house overlooked the sinuous spate river. Tressady had originally been built as yet another of the 'shooting boxes' for the Dukes of Sutherland (now chiefly commemorated for their supposed pioneering of the Highland Clearances), and was a gloomy, gabled, asymmetrical structure, where few birds sang and the branches of a monkey-puzzle tree tapped on your window-pane at night. I adored it.

These trips were ordeals for V, however, but for the most part she endured them as cheerfully as she could. The entire place was devoted to seasonal sport – 'blood sports' was the preferred term, in her diary – her King Charles spaniel was gun-shy, there was only one gift shop less than an hour's drive away, and she was forced to spend polite time with her sister-in-law Maina. For us – 'my menfolk' – it was bliss. The head keeper was another Mr Murray, but he was no russet-faced stereotype from Central Casting, with dour demeanour and breath tartan from scotch: he was droll, friendly, communicative and hard-working, and it was George Murray who became my mentor, with his rakish deerstalker, Silk Cut cupped in one palm, that naughty gleam in his eye. His wife Jessie was a quiet and slow woman, who did the housework in socks and sandals; she had painfully thin, oily hair, and there were lumps like bunions all over her head. With Mr Murray – never 'George' to me, and 'Murray' to the adults – I shot my first grouse and landed my first salmon, and he was always encouraging, gentle in manner, and quick with his chuckle. He was, in my uncle's archaic but admiring phrase, 'one of Nature's gentlemen'.

From the moment I entered the heavily furnished gunroom every August, with its racks of nobly scarred rods, winders festooned with line, the tray of miniature Bell's bottles for your hip-pocket, and photographs of my uncle with various trophies (including an African tarpon that was beyond big), I was in thrall to the sporting history of this house; but what made it snag the memory so keenly – I now see – was the essential frivolity, the determined party spirit, to which I was then unaccustomed.

My cousin Mary Ann, more Mark's age than mine, was really the *agent provocateur* here: her effervescent style, 'groovy' clothes, and underlying kindness of heart meant that she was often urging evening diversions on those who might otherwise have subsided over the bridge table. She was devoted to my father, and Uncle Jack knew how to rise to an occasion, especially when it involved a pretty girl. In his old element, cheek by jowl with his sister, he was called upon to be extrovert and entertaining, an aspect I had thitherto not really seen. Always one to respond to an audience, he excelled at the frequently risqué charades, sang a repertoire of Jack Buchanan tunes, did throw-back comic turns from Harry Lauder and Stanley Holloway, took house guests on 'Hellfire Rides' across the moorland roads at great speed ('I was taught to drive like this by my old friend "Sev" Sevelode'). One Hogmanay when the staff were all admitted to the drawing-room and drams were freely circulating, he improvised some conjuring tricks that would not have disgraced his idol, Tommy Cooper. My mother smiled valiantly throughout this rehearsing of his innate, premarital persona. (On evenings like that, there was certainly no sign of any hair shirt beneath his smoking jacket.) For my part, always by far the youngest, I could only cackle from the sidelines, and aspire one day to join in.

The Tressady years laid a trail for many Highland holidays to come. My father and I later stayed at the Loch Maree Hotel, site of one of the most notorious outbreaks of botulism in British history; we caught no fish, but befriended a gillie with a wooden leg. Another summer saw us back on the Borgie River, where the proprietor was an iconoclastic retired major who declared salmon-fishing didn't give him a 'cockstand' any more, and urinated against his rose bush every evening to make it flourish; he lost a son in a wildfowling accident, then took to the bottle and – so I heard – set fire to himself. In that hotel I was introduced to a general who had taken part in a cavalry charge during the Great War, and a former gamekeeper who had amassed a fortune by devising a superior type of dog food. As the saying runs, 'There's more to fishing than just catching fish.'

In September 1968, just before my thirteenth birthday, I became an Etonian. Those who grumble about how miserable they were are perhaps even more tedious than chaps who regard their schooldays as the best of their lives – I don't think I fall into either category: I disliked my time there largely because I disliked being a teenager. It was an antiquated place, not barbarous but unruly, with several notoriously perverse housemasters and a heavy reliance on unregulated government by senior boys. Nineteen sixty-eight was arguably just when the so-called 'sixties' were at their apogee, and even a place so congealed with traditions had felt the drumbeat of the popular bands and caught a whiff of 'reefer'. There might have been some 'beaks' on the teaching staff who remained convinced God was an Old Etonian (like Captain Hook), and there was still plenty of fagging, beating, homosexuality and casual anti-Semitism, but much of this changed during my five years there – we saw the first day girls and several black African pupils (one wrote a book about his experiences, *A Nigger at Eton*) – and though the drift towards modernization may have been continentally slow, there were signs of an uneasy shifting of tectonic plates.

I had failed the scholarship exam, but was young enough to try again in the summer. Accordingly, I was admitted as an ordinary 'Oppidan', my housemaster being a well-meaning but uncommunicative languages beak called Bud Hill, who was on the brink of retirement and ran a pretty mediocre ship. We dwelled in a building next to the chapel called Baldwin's Bec, which had just been physically modernized and was one of the few to have new-fangled central heating (the others relying on coal fires). The house matron – called the Dame – was a burly woman with the androgynous name Leslie Millar, a short-haired basso profondo with the forearms of a mule-skinner, but a skilled nurse none the less. Bud's eternally anxious wife hovered in the domestic background, and was known to us as 'Screech'. On the first day, I was awoken by Mrs Ransome, the 'Boys' Maid', who drew back the curtains and and announced (inaccurately on two counts), 'It's going to be a lovely day, Mister Proforma!'

For me, the concept of sexual intercourse actually began in the autumn of 1968. I was childish and innocent in crucial ways when I went up to Eton. Our leavers' talk at Sunningdale – where we all anticipated the secrets of those Eleusinian mysteries known as 'the facts of life' – had not been very elucidating, warning us somewhat vaguely against becoming too friendly with older boys, and the little

I had ever heard tell about sex was from preposterous locker-room rumours along the lines of turning your willy inside out until the blue bit showed. More disadvantageously, I had as yet no idea of another fact of life – that my name might be associated with a 'sex scandal'.

In medieval legend, swallows were said to blind their offspring to prevent them from coming to harm by trying to fly the nest too young; when the time came, their sight was restored by feeding them on the sap of the celandine, from which that flower gets its name. My parents had hitherto done a pretty good job of keeping me in the dark for my own good, but for reasons I have never quite appreciated they launched me into the public-school world without that celandine moment. It was not a good decision.

On that first day, I became a eunuch. This was the slang for a member of the College Chapel choir; my voice was an uncertain alto, but Eton had just disbanded its Choir School, so anyone who could sing semi-straight was being co-opted. I took my place in the venerable *cantores* stalls for morning chapel, and introduced myself to my neighbour, a tiny scholar who immediately enquired, 'Oh, are you anything to do with that Profumo who sold information to the Russians?' I politely replied that I was not.

Later, during that busy day, there was more to come. Among the assorted slubberdegullions inhabiting Baldwin's Bec there was a ginger-haired shitweasel of a boy in the year above me, whose affectionate sobriquet was 'the Butcher'. He was a corpulent, befreckled southpaw, whose estranged father was an airline pilot, and his Antipodean mother looked like some cartoon tabby. Anyway, I feared and hated him long before I knew anything of his pedigree, because that afternoon I encountered him on the stairs (where he was swinging apishly around a newel post) and the conversation went roughly as follows: 'You're Profumo?' 'Yes.' 'Christ, the Profumo Affair?' 'What's that?' 'Fucking hell.' 'Is it something to do with *The Man from UNCLE*?' 'You've got to be kidding. You better watch it.' 'I don't know what you're talking about.'

'Well,' began the Butcher, taking a deliciously deep breath, 'there were these two tarts . . .' And so I soared, blinking and swooping from my nest, into the sharp light of day.

He'd got one or two details wrong, as I was shortly able to ascertain by visiting the school library. This was an unusual way to discover details of your father's sex-life, but I could see perhaps why my parents had not wanted to tell me about any of this in person. However, it became one of the few things for which I could not readily forgive them. I confess I was bewildered. Here was a family secret, and I appeared to be the last person in the world to know. So it goes. For those first few weeks there were many other novelties to accommodate – I was suddenly in an adolescent world of Brut aftershave, Corona bottles, furtive cigarette butts, psychedelic posters, shag spots, flared Levis, Disraeli Gears, and all the preposterous peculiarities of Eton piled on top – so I did not have a lot of time for home truths to preoccupy me. When you have to learn abstruse details about your new community, such as the colours of the cap worn by the Master of the Beagles, or the precise location of Queen Anne's Flower-Pot (to say nothing of Tuesday's test on third-declension Latin nouns), worrying about the image of your father in bed with a young woman can hardly be allowed to take precedence.

Broaching this directly with my parents never seemed an option. I assumed that their silence on this matter simply meant it was something they did not want to talk to me about, and I was at least correct in that: not until the following year did they make any attempt to discuss it, and it was hardly a sacramental moment (I merely affected bravado and helped them get it over with). Of course, I began to regard them in a different and curious way, and if I had been gutsier I suppose I could just have confronted them and demanded some kind of explanation. I loved my parents, and had always had every confidence in them, but I must say this did come between us.

I might also have spoken to Mark, who was in his last term (or 'half'), and in the same house, but I had become instantly nervous about the whole subject, and felt instinctively that I should let sleeping dogs lie (I now know, of course, that they will tell you the truth if you wake them). My brother Mark and I had never before overlapped at school, and the five years that separated us had always just been sufficient to keep us quite distant in our interests. It was not just this intervening lustrum, however; we shared a mother and a home, but our teenage temperaments were distinctly different, and although we were pleasantly fraternal we were not then exactly kindred spirits. He was quiet, industrious, stalwart, meticulous, and intellectually a late developer; keen on fencing, numismatics and photography, he was not the sort of elder sibling to have the latest Guevara poster or tie-dyed girlfriends with libertarian attitudes to hygiene. The years have brought us closer, even though today he has become a fearsome, distinguished and bearded Barnaby Rudge who, at the drop of a parking ticket, will have you sent down to Van Diemen's Land to break rocks. Had I gone to him for counsel, it would doubtless have been forthcoming; but I did not want to look as if I were making a fuss.

In her book *Memory* (1983), Mary Warnock considers the philosophical conundrum of whether or not you are substantially the same person you were forty years ago, and uses the analogy of a trusty old bike that lasts for ages; by now, practically every part has been renewed, but there was never an observable moment when the bike was replaced wholesale with another one. That autumn, I was definitely equipped with a new set of gears.

The following year, a fine thing happened: in May, I sat the scholarship exams once more and, when the results went up, there was my name at the very top of the list of elected candidates. My father felt strongly that it would be better for me to continue as I was, and not to go and live in a separate house with the King's Scholars, so I remained an Oppidan. Bud Hill left, and we moved to another building, Angelo's, where the housemaster was Robert Hardy, a learned but unassuming classicist. Erected in 1790, it was a disgracefully dilapidated house infested with rodents, woefully under-plumbed, and regarded as being one of the most undesirable of all residences. One of the few practical skills I acquired at school was how to lay a decent fire, but the coal allowance was so meagre that in winter I often slept in my clothes; one longed for the tradition (prevalent in Gladstone's day) of the Dame issuing brandy to boys as a nightcap.

Towards the end of September 1969, there was a great deal of media discussion about plans by the *News of the World* to begin serializing Christine Keeler's memoirs. There were a number of vociferous complaints – the remarkable Frank Longford being to the fore, as often – citing the fact that my father had suffered enough, paid his debt to society and so forth, but some of these efforts at support only had the effect of friendly fire – an 'Establishment' blue on blue. Motives were anyway varied. The *Daily Express* editorialized, 'He has long since paid the price, which many think an excessive one, for his indiscretion. It is an affront to the standards of British journalism that he should now be pilloried again in such a way.' Serialization began on 28 September with the gleeful announcement: 'The establishment is mad about it' (it has never been entirely clear what this signifies); continuing, 'We agree with Lord Longford that Mr Profumo should be FORGIVEN . . . But the part he played cannot be FORGOT-TEN.' The new proprietor of that paper, Rupert Murdoch, replying on radio to accusations that he was a money-grubbing muck-raker (my words, for brevity's sake), said, 'The Profumo story will never be dead. It's a part of history. This is a story of great public interest.' There was much discussion of a Privacy Bill and Freedom of Speech, and the Press Council censured the *News of the World* (circulation six and a half million) for its decision to proceed.

This hue and cry once again drove my family back into the public arena, and was a difficult time all round. There was dramatic television debate, with David Frost interviewing Murdoch (who stormed off afterwards) and the BBC cancelling a programme with Miss Keeler at the last moment 'for editorial reasons'. The *Daily Mail* wondered what a foreign visitor might imagine J had done that was so terrible: 'They would probably decide he must have done something like setting fire to St Paul's or mowing down a troop of orphans.'

With all this newspaper speculation for me to digest, I was beginning to wonder myself. I confess I failed to take it well. By now I was anyway a paranoid teenager whose moods were impelled by a hormonal cyclone; I had been smitten with a plague of boils (in some ways, murrain would have been marginally less awkward). Irrationally, I was convinced the world was unfair. The press were a bunch of ephemeromorphs, below biological classification, and some of my peer group were not much better. One episode of no doubt good-natured teasing resulted in me slugging one housemate full in the face, something I have never bothered to do since. It was a somewhat lonely experience – in that stark Australian analogy, 'I felt as solitary as a bastard on Fathers' Day' – and there wasn't much back-up from the home team, either. Consistent with the parental philosophy that if you discuss things they will only get out of proportion (or whatever the muddled thinking was) it was merely assumed I would quietly get on with my work. The subject was never directly raised, even then. I now realize they were still at it with the school reports, too; my tutor Robert Hardy at the end of that term suggested my morale was reasonable, 'despite everything that could have downed him', which the ex-Minister translated as, 'despite the change in accommodation'. Good grief.

All I was having to contend with, of course, were sniggers and nudges and the occasional bout of name-calling ('Keeloid' was the Butcher's exceptionally witty nickname for me, at that time), but the unwelcome attention was generically worse for my parents, who habitually referred to such intrusion as 'really too boring'. Their exemplary behaviour, which was to pretend nothing got to them, was hard enough for them to maintain, and it was naturally expected that I would emulate it. 'None of that matters,' my mother liked to say, after an especially boring episode, 'it's just water off a duck's back.' I found this brave but unconvincing talk. So far as I was concerned, as an immature, papuliferous fourteen-year-old desperate not to stand out in the crowd, I had been ladled a big bowl of stone soup, and I was planning on crying into it if I felt so inclined.

One side-effect of this tiresome period of our lives was that I began to be unduly sensitized to certain words, and found the very appearance of them a cause for concern.

Some words seem attractive irrespective of their lexical meaning. I'm not talking here of sale-rail poeticisms such as 'footfall' or 'twilight' (though this may be how they acquired that patina), but those that strike one as somehow intrinsically beautiful, that possess a *frisson* factor. Compton Mackenzie once listed 'apricot', 'shadow' and 'forlorn' in his personal list, whereas A. E. Housman claimed there were certain words that made him shudder with such ecstasy that he dared not mutter them while shaving. We cannot shear them of all associations, of course, but my choice would include 'paradise', 'melancholy', 'gossamer', and 'fountain' – 'Just reeling off their names is ever so comfy', as W. H. Auden wrote sardonically of lacustrine terminology, in his poem 'Lakes'.

A converse effect can be produced by the register of others. The logical empiricist Wittgenstein (who for some years subsisted largely on a diet of cornflakes, reasoning that if once you had discovered something suitable there was little sense in changing it) applied himself to what he called the problem of 'aspect seeing', whereby we don't all perceive the same thing, and this leads to the scrambling of language. Neutrally considered, the word 'scandal' might have a euphonious, kinetic quality to it – as does 'Christine' or 'Cliveden', both elegantly rhythmic in their way: but for some years any surprise encounter with them gave me a slight physical jolt, a cold flush, a metallic taste in the mouth. I could often spot a page where one of these verbal incubi lurked, and I came to dislike the sound of other, unrelated words, which were freighted with mnemonic irrelevance – 'Kilner' jars, 'kilos', 'Keiller's' marmalade, and 'keel-hauling' transmit a clangour to me that is quite unjustified, while 'scalding', 'sandals', and even, absurdly, 'candle' have surrendered any music and become bruised. The Estuarine pronunciation of scandal – 'skan-dooh' – sufficiently approximates the Gaelic '*sgian dubh*', that handy little dagger which Highland Scots thrust into their stocking-tops, so that sometimes I wriggle my shoulders when I hear it. (Dear God, how much simpler life would have become if it had just been something he could have stuck down his sock.)

On their wedding anniversary, 1969, V wrote J an admiring letter:

> My own *dear* Beloved – For these wonderful years of gaiety, fun, romance, luxury and laughter I thank you! Never once since I met you have I been bored; never once have I not wanted you. And never once, even for a moment, have I not loved you with all my heart. I believe that somewhere somehow I must have loved you all my life . . .
> Your happy wife Pidge.

My parents' public show of resilience was of course not all it seemed. The admirable façade concealed frustrations, not least because my father's progressive involvement with his life as a social worker was offering him a new identity, whereas my mother's role was increasingly domestic. There were suggestions that he had become a changed man – kinder, more humble – and certainly he now had more time for other people (he went to visit Bill Astor in hospital just before he died, and Bronwen wrote to say her husband had slept well for the first time in years). But I feel that, a few years after his Fall, J had pretty much forgiven himself for his sexual infidelity, and the penitence that was so remarked upon, while genuine enough, was not for having deceived the mother of his son, but for having lied to the Mother of Parliaments. He was scrupulous in avoiding any social offence, feeling still *maudit* in political circles. My parents attended Randolph Churchill's funeral (in 1968), for instance, but avoided the reception, in case their presence embarrassed Macmillan; Jock Colville later wrote to assure them that Mac 'bore no animosity at all, and much wished you had come'. J told me that for a long time he 'felt like a criminal' – but there is truth in Joseph Fouché's phrase (also attributed to Talleyrand), '*C'est plus qu'un crime, c'est une faute.*'

As well as his help with the day-to-day chores there, Jack was helping Toynbee to think big. An indefatigable networker, he unashamedly tapped for funds every contact he could, and simultaneously began to raise its flagging profile by inviting visitors who would draw attention to the new projects the Toynbee team were devising, which, over the years, addressed everything from education to domestic violence. Clem Attlee became President, John Hare – now Lord Blakenham – the Chairman, and as early as 1965 Harold Wilson came to inspect some building works (he assured reporters he had been given permission to use a spade by the appropriate union). The Archbishop of Canterbury came, as did Ted Heath, who toyed with the prospect of playing the rather good piano there. Impresarios Bernie Delfont and Lew Grade made handsome donations. It was not by any means a one-man show, but the positive publicity was often due to my father's presence.

Since 1968, he had also been a Visitor at Grendon Prison, near

Aylesbury, a psychiatric institution with one hundred and sixty inmates. James Callaghan, then Home Secretary, had invited him, and this was seen as a first step towards official rehabilitation. On his first day, he was told not to approach the parrot perched on one prisoner's shoulder as it had been trained to peck your eyes out. Another inmate told the former politician that it was he who should be inside, after what he had done to the country. Opening an exhibition of pictures by Grendon prisoners in November 1969 – in his first public speech for six years – J spoke feelingly of the need for proper after-care: 'Rehabilitation is a long, lonely, hard haul.'

There was worldwide coverage on 18 November 1971 when the Queen came down to open the new social welfare centre known as Attlee House. (My father had suggested that a Foundation be set up in Attlee's memory, and at one stage during the fund-raising for this, a man had turned up at reception, asking for J: it was Attlee's old batman, who said, 'If he'd been alive he'd have wanted to thank you at this very difficult time, so I've come instead.') In what was interpreted as a symbolic moment, the monarch made sure she was seen and photographed talking to J, and there were numerous headlines about 'forgiveness' and the end of exile – 'And the Profumo Affair was dead,' concluded the *Daily Mail*, though it appears to have forgotten that almost every year since.

Toynbee occasioned another *rapprochement* when Tom Denning – Master of the Rolls – attended a celebratory dinner to mark seventy-five years of free legal advice, and was seen chatting amiably to J at Gray's Inn. The next day he wrote a charming letter about my father's voluntary work, adding, 'How nice it was to meet your wife – it recalled her most memorable performance in *The King and I*.' Sportingly, there was no reference to having interviewed her for his report.

As J began to rise through the chain of command with his charity – in time, he became Chairman, and eventually President – it no longer mattered if it was a clanking merchant ship rather than an aircraft carrier – he was preoccupied, and part of a team, and he was up there again for all to see. Although few were aware of it, a shadow now fell on V's outwardly refulgent spirits. For four full years (1971–4), the only time in her life, she kept a brief daily diary, and more than anything else these suggest an encroaching *Weltschmerz*, a sense of frustration at the narrowness of her horizons, and a smoored recrimination at what had happened during the previous decade. No longer a star, and now denied the subsequent glamour of the political stage, she had lost her audiences; her children were away most of the time (all year, in the case of Simon), and her husband was again so busy that she was left to her own devices. They had established their new fastness, and feathered it idyllically, but she had not perhaps envisaged how often his work would make him late back from London, or require him to spend the night in town; the occasional notes from an anonymous well-wisher claiming that he was seeing a girl in the East End did not help the situation, either. V was in her mid-fifties. 'How often have I written – My family is my only life?' read one entry, the devotion perhaps fringed with regret. She began to fuss over J (never a good idea), and fret over minor causes, the accumulation of which, over this period, began to be toxic. As a self-absorbed teenager, of course, I rarely spotted any of this, and – when I did – was not yet man enough to be sympathetic.

The diaries are clogged with domestic trivia of the type that enervated her, and also fed her ambivalence about creature comforts ('I must sound like a dreadful spoiled bitch'). She knew my father expected her to run a household and maintain the sort of staff he had never been without (neither of my parents had cooked so much as a piece of toast since they were married); we were fortunate in having the continuity of Brisco, who remained scrupulously fond of V although his latent misogyny saw off any number of temporary housemaids. For a time, we had a Methodist cook, Mrs Waller, a widow who had started her career in the kitchens at Windsor Castle; she was temperamental, so came and went several times, but was a passionate humanitarian and became a soul mate to my mother, accompanying her on visits to see Simon.

My parents had never got used to living in each other's pockets and my impression is that J needed to cut himself a little slack with his London commitments. He was a difficult person to humour in those days, and was such a creature of habit that V was often exasperated – 'I am exhausted with trying to please him'. Having become accustomed to the role of *seigneur*, he expected everything to be tidy, staff to know their place, food to be properly presented, and no smell of cooking to permeate from the kitchen. He had been brought up to realize that sometimes 'I want, gets'. His moods when they were in private also exhausted her – of course, diaries often magnify the proximity of cohabitation, but this aspect was repeatedly pronounced. There were recurrent spats, suggesting anything but equanimity on both sides: J 'goes beserk' about a bathroom leak; he was 'testy and difficult all day'; he was 'in a rage all night' when I rang from school and said I wanted to study drama. In May 1972 there was 'a violent explosion' about something that went wrong with his flowers, and he 'went mad', so that V slept in another room, though slipping back to their bed in the early hours so Brisco would not suspect anything was amiss when he came to wake them.

Unsurprisingly, there were periodic records of 'depression'; she developed chronic insomnia, and began to take pills. There was a list entitled 'Little Deaths', suffused with menopausal *tristesse*, lamenting the supposed end of physical attraction – 'the lost power of one's brilliant, shining eyes' – and one entry even speculated on what it would feel like to open one's veins in a bath ('people would think I was just being theatrical'). I don't believe she was actually suicidal, but there were moments of acute unhappiness, and some evidence that she was gradually withdrawing into a later version of that lonely 'bubble' she experienced after the birth of Simon.

With so much time for introspection and emotional stock-taking, V compensated for what she saw as her self-indulgence by giving voice to empathy for the beleaguered and dispossessed. As many of us are, mid-life, she was in search of some spiritual direction; this would not have been a subject to discuss with her husband, whose stolid Anglicanism continued to support him (even when the ice was so thin he was on the verge of treading water) by being resolutely unexamined. The power of love and prayer now featured regularly in her diary, and assorted jottings, coupled with expansive schemes for uniting the peoples of the world, divagations on the sacrosanct life of animals (not helped by my passion for 'murder'), and a restlessness about the catastrophes besetting the globe. Night after night she recorded details of the news that appalled her – the cholera epidemic in Pakistan, the Irish

Troubles, napalm, the killing of Sharon Tate – worrying that she could do so little to counteract 'so much sadness and horror'. Towards the end of May 1973, she dreamed she was a deaf mute in nineteenth-century Mexico: this kind of agitation was never properly stilled.

Some of her attitudes were undoubtedly manufactured – rhetorical exercises in selflessness that forced her to adopt a charitable perspective. She frequently championed the underdog, but with little sense of conviction: it became her fault that a jobbing gardener and his wife did a runner one night, stealing some of her property, and there's no doubt she adopted people's causes when they were lame ducks. But she had the courage of her convictions, and also organized sterling work for charities such as Mencap and LEPRA. Religious faith arose to embrace her: she was briefly taken with the 'charismatic' movement, and even had a brush with Catholicism (again, unlikely to play well with her husband), visiting the Holy Land, Lourdes and Iona. Her diary remarks are frequently dulcified by a dusting of benevolence, but I suspect she knew that beneath all this warmth of expressed intention there remained – stubbornly, as it had been there from childhood – a temperament as beautifully gelid as cucumber sorbet.

The version of God she conjured has always struck me as a peculiarly unforgiving one, and more than once she scourged herself for letting Him down and wasting the talents He had given her. There was guilt at not having taken better care of her physical body: she used the analogy of a Porsche that she had failed to keep topped up with oil, and then 'leaving the lights on'. This wasn't all entirely in her mind. On 11 August 1974 – when J and I were up north together – my mother collapsed with pains in chest and arms, and was admitted to the cardiac unit of St Mary's, Paddington.

If the very act of maintaining the mask of sang-froid was contributing to her real stress and distress, it was not because she was fed up with her husband. Earlier that summer she had written to him reaffirming 'my deep and true admiration and love – with the exception of yourself alone, *no one* but me knows of the suffering and steadfastness, and absolute iron determination with which you have tackled these last (many) years. I've seen, and watched and wondered.' They seemed to enjoy arguing away over many paltry things, and sometimes fought like cat and dog (though never in front of children or servants), but this merely diverted them. Making caustic comments about people on the television was a favourite pastime, and I remember when Barbara Castle was once pontificating on the evening news, and J said, 'Listen to that terrible woman; she's slept with practically everyone in the House of Commons', V's instant riposte, delayed only by a dismissive exhalation of Gitanes smoke, was, 'Well, that's the pot calling the kettle black.' There was never any danger that they would enter that stultifying, deep-frozen state of matrimony where both are bored and ignored. In disputes, V tended to be acidulous and dismissive – she was capable of being very cutting – whereas J was a practised shape-shifter, hard to pin down, yet stubborn, cunning, and petulant if crossed. Thus they continued to strike sparks from each other, and there was plenty of fire in the flint. They were mutually protective: helpmeets who had clung together, united *contra mundum* (for all their temperamental differences) in an attitude where the instinct for survival was not unalloyed with contempt.

For a while as a teenager I was secretly riled at my father for visiting on me what I saw as the fall-out from his ridiculous lust. I think they had decided that if they made a fuss about the consequences of his disgrace, then I might take this as a licence for scapegoatery. Most of the time I went along with this, accepting that the Profumo Affair was one of the family *tacenda*, and that when any reference to what J called 'all my troubles' (or 'those events') became unavoidable, a state of armed neutrality would supervene. Even through adolescent lenses clouded by the usual cocktail of neuroses and misapprehensions I could see that they had both been hurt, and if, when it came to expansiveness with his son, my father might prefer to bury his head in a volume of sand second only to the Sahara, then I would go along with it *pro tem*. Besides, it was hard not to like him, with his air of unshakeable confidence and irreverent humour – life-saving qualities which allowed him to appear unscathed by almost anything.

My mother was volatile, strong-willed, and prone to dealing in abstractions; she was intolerant of certain weaknesses, but seemed drawn to the apparently helpless. Charity did not begin at home, however, and she could be a stern taskmaster. With the arrival of puberty, I had become somewhat estranged from her; she resented this (especially since both Mark and her husband had developed prophy-lactic stratagems for avoiding emotional discourse), and, by an understandable process of displacement, the sense of isolation she felt encroaching was somehow my particular responsibility. I'm not quite saying she blamed me for not being the daughter she never had, but my alarming descent into the male world must have left her feeling slightly outnumbered.

Even allowing for the usual teenage stuff, I did not just then cut a very prepossessing figure. Avid not to lose out on the mild noncon-formity exemplified by my public-school peers – with a few exceptions it was in truth a predictably superficial affectation – at the age of fifteen I went for the swinging look. In the hope that it would camouflage my lack of self-confidence, I acquired a wardrobe of moleskin bell-bottoms, grandad T-shirts, velvet jackets with large lapels, Indian silk scarves, polo-necks of vomitous Paisley fabrics, Mohican-fringed suede boots, elaborately studded belts and an Afghan-style coat (worn inside out). Above the beaky nose, and epi-dermis like a plate of M&M's left out in the sun, I contrived to part my straggly dark hair in the centre, and (to complete the absurdity, which I mistook for a rangy machismo) I began smoking a small clay pipe. At parties, full of mulled wine and lurking around the crisp-bowls, too shy to introduce myself to girls, I must have looked sarto-rially like an unemployed pirate.

'Very dirty and non-communicative' was my mother's glib diary verdict on my appearance (2 July 1972), and she did not refrain from upbraiding me for my deliberate dishevelment, and the hangdog air she could see I was cultivating. Perhaps to match my misguided new image, she began to address me as 'Dave'. I walked with a stoop, and had developed an incipient stutter, and I must have presented an in-furiating spectacle. 'Why don't you hold yourself upright, like a fine young man?' she asked. 'People won't understand, they will think you are ashamed of something. Shoulders back, look the world in the eye.' This was precisely what I was attempting to avoid, being preternat-urally self-conscious. I felt like a freak, some scaly boy in a raree show; I conceived of myself as a leper with his bell, wandering the medieval lanes in search of a kindly *parabolanus*. I expect my parents wondered, in the usual way, where they had gone so wrong.

One of my favourite entries from V's diary is dated 16 May 1974: 'Saw Chagall – disappointed.' They had been staying, as they often did, at the Colombe d'Or hotel in St-Paul-de-Vence, when she was finally introduced to her hero. I don't know what he did that was so disillusioning, but it is indicative of how their social life had recovered some of its former *soigné* quality. Apart from stylish holidays – they saw Gracie Fields when in Capri, the Puccis in Florence – there were modest weekend parties at the Dower House, though generally when their son and heir was safely away at school. They entertained Margot Fonteyn and her quadriplegic husband Tito, Selwyn Lloyd and Ted Heath, Henry Moore (a near neighbour), Kenneth Clark, Lilli Palmer, Leslie Mitchell and his wife Inge. On another occasion, the logical positivist A. J. Ayer was staying, with his wife Dee Wells the broadcaster, and my mother roped him in to helping me with my school holiday quiz – a bit like getting Archimedes round to help with the maths homework. The author Paul Gallico, a smooth and tedious raconteur, used to rehearse fencing manoeuvres with Mark on the lawn.

Another frequent visitor was Tony Havelock-Allan himself, then living blissfully with Viv Wannamaker, a rich and glamorous American lady. His film career had finished in 1970, with *Ryan's Daughter*, which was not a critical success though it won Johnny Mills an Oscar for his portrayal of the village idiot – V saw it in April 1971, and her diary notes, 'It is *so* slow.' What impresses me now (and merely perplexed me then) was how my father could put up with such a situation, but the fact seems to be that he had no respect for Tony, and never regarded him as any kind of lingering threat; he coolly tolerated his continuing presence in my mother's life only because contact with him diverted some of her pent-up, emotional pressure. Even when Tony married again, in 1979, a younger and rather tiresome widow, he continued to entertain the proprietorial ministrations of his first wife (V was, it must be said, not entirely sensitive to the implications of this for her successor) and was, to the end, a plausible, patrician, and impeccably egocentric man (he was ninety-eight when he died). 'People say you truly cannot love two men,' she wrote to me, 'but you can – and I have. They were so different, perhaps that made it easy for me.' Frankly, I think my father deserved another medal – with bar and oak-leaf cluster, this time – for his marital forbearance.

Following a police raid on a pornographer's shop in Soho in May 1973, when a book of addresses was obtained, the papers were full of the events surrounding the resignation of two other Tory grandees. Lord Lambton (Under-Secretary of Defence for the RAF) was found to have been in a compromising situation, as they say, with prostitutes, thus exposing himself to the possibility of blackmail, and he applied for the Chiltern Hundreds. He was already noted for his Epicurean tastes, and, commenting later on his preference for simultaneous congress with girls of different skin colours, he remarked that everyone liked a little variety. Ann Fleming once said of him, apparently, 'If Tony didn't make love four times a day, he suffered a nosebleed.'

In an unrelated episode – and, by bad luck, a confusion over names – Lord Jellicoe (now Lord Privy Seal) felt constrained to admit that he, too, had consorted with a call-girl, and also resigned, before he could be exposed. Learning in part from the mistakes made a decade earlier by his former colleague, he owned up to Ted Heath before too much damage was caused either to the party or to his own reputation (he was widely respected, and had been a celebrated war hero). The field-day the press had with what was known (because of the central female figure) as the Norma Levy Affair had a depressing effect on my mother, as the media celebrated the tenth anniversary of 'Profumo', and I'm sure it contributed to the stress that made her unwell.

By now I was becoming senior enough in the school to feel safer whenever a new rash of name-checking broke out, and there were certain members of the staff to whom I could turn if I wanted tea and sympathy, though I seldom felt the need. Although disappointing my father by refusing either to be confirmed or to enlist in the Corps (Mark, like a regular guy, had done both), there was some evidence that progress was being made with my studies. Both J and V were leery of this – they harboured a mutual and ingrained antipathy towards the idea of the swot, and seemed convinced they were landed with a cleverclogs, though in truth I was as lowbrow in most tastes as my father. One of Eton's fortes is its tutorial system at the Sixth-Form level. Here I was blessed with the intellectual encouragement of two great teachers. David Evans (then a young history guru) and Michael Meredith (a former English don) refused to allow my scuffed, shirty, lethargic persona to dampen their enthusiasm for culture and learn-ing. I think they each divined that the potential slacker who, in his spare time, would evidently prefer to read *Exchange & Mart* over a packet of Chipmunk crisps rather than bone up on the early frescoes of Ghirlandaio, would require jump-starting on a regular basis if his mental banger was ever going to make it to the racetrack, let alone compete.

Ours was a sporty house, and ball control continued to elude me until the end of my sentence. The pre-eminent alfresco diversion, it seemed to me, was angling before breakfast on the college stretch of the Thames, where Izaak Walton had fished with the then Provost while preparing a book that was destined to be one of the most reprinted titles in the history of our language. This made me happy, but the achievement of capturing an occasional pike that could be dished up did not really signify when athletic honours were being dished out, and when compelled to lend my footling efforts to team-work on those playing-fields where Waterloo was said to have been won I had to skulk, dowdy and unadorned with colours, like some subfusc tench amid shoals of fleet and glistering perch. To the con-sternation of my parents (I never quite discovered why) there was lots of acting to divert me. I fondly considered my co-editorship of the school's 'Chronicle' was a nice appointment, though conceivably they thought even such ur-journalism bore the stigma of Fleet Street. Still, I was in the first ever group to take cooking as an option, and what more could a son do to gladden his parents' hearts? Somehow or other, I eventually became president of 'Pop', the self-electing élite of Eton prefects that gets to swan around in fancy waistcoats, and, on 13 December 1973, I crammed my belongings into the back of our Austin Maxi, and left. (Five days later, I learned that Magdalen College, Oxford, had awarded me a Demyship in English Literature.)

That Christmas, I was given my first car – a VW Beetle, finished in astonishing orange. For several unrepeatable months, I criss-crossed England going to parties and wallowing in what I conceived was the high life. My attempts to appear louche were perfervid. There was the obligatory elephant-hair bracelet, an occasional earring (clip-on: I was a deep phoney), and yellow hair dye brushed into the forelock; I must have resembled some pox-doctor's clerk. The pipes had been ditched in favour of rare and costly Balkan Sobranie Imperial cigarettes – complete with integral filter tube and maize-paper wrapping – which, themed with a fake-fur Russian hat, and an extravagant Kashmiri scarf interwoven with (as I thought it) strobelight-responsive silver threads, was designed to attract numerous, but temporary, mates. Even taking into account the prevailing mores of that era, this was perhaps not an epigamic display to rival the peacock's shuffle and sway, or even the sudden scarlet of an amorous stickleback's livery, but in the event I did persuade a few girls to spend the night with me, and, at long last, I felt as cock-a-hoop as some Pathan tribesman who had just been handed a hard-boiled egg.

On 9 March 1974 I left London for a three-month Grand Tour of the East, with my close friend since Sunningdale days, James Sassoon. Any hippyish inclinations I may have harboured at school were now renounced in favour of travel from one salubrious hotel to another, toting tropical-weight luggage rather than backpacks. Our families' contacts were also shamelessly exploited, and in Jaipur we were invited to stay with the Maharaja in one of his palaces. 'Bubbles' (Bhawani Singh) was the son of my father's late polo companion, 'Jai', and his mother Ayesha – an imperious beauty, and a formidable politician – was also in residence. It was my first taste of royalty, and it went to my head. We drove to the annual Polo Ball in Bubbles's crimson Thunderbird, and the crowds draped garlands over us all. We were admitted to the city arsenal, issued with antiquated Purdey shotguns, and taken to shoot sand grouse among the dunes. The actor Jimmy Stewart was also staying, and I developed an unreciprocated *tendresse* for his daughter, Judy. One night, carpets were spread on the lawn, a cocktail chariot was wheeled up, and I drank my first glasses of whisky (a rite of passage, indeed). We left for Udaipur by train, in the Jaipur family's private wagon-lit, and later visited the ruins of Fatehpur-Sikri, where it was bitterly hot and the desert guide, on hearing my name, uttered a sprightly croak: 'Ah, Christine Keeler!'

In Thailand, despite our contact list including two sensational girls – memorably named Toy and Pong – we managed to make some kind of history by spending a week in Bangkok without enjoying any dirty work at the crossroads (I'm not sure what the Nomad Boy would have made of that). For a while, I did feel I was retracing my father's steps, because in Tokyo I too stayed in the Imperial Hotel, visited Hiroshima, overdosed on temples in Kyoto, and saw the summit of Mount Fuji clear from the passing train. Our itinerary also involved the Trans-Siberian Express, with its disconcerting, pervasive aroma of plum jam and burning plastic; I trudged through *Middlemarch*, and made myself feverishly ill by eating home-made yoghurt purchased from a peasant lady on the platform at Khabarovsk. Photography was still restricted, and a Soviet citizen who tried to pass us notes in the dining car was removed by police at the next station. In Moscow we dined with a consular official, who made mocking remarks to the KGB bug he knew was in his apartment, and a bottle-blonde knocked on my hotel-room door inviting me, in broken English, to fix her broken ball-point (I obliged, to the limited extent of my penmanship). On our last night we blew all our remaining Intourist vouchers at a rooftop restaurant where I drank White Grizzlies (vodka topped up with Caucasian champagne), danced exuberantly with an ursine companion who turned out to be a policewoman, and, staggering back through Red Square, fell to my knees into the snow and was sick in several languages. It had all been most educational.

There was once a *Spectator* cartoon in which an anteater in a zoo was loudly complaining that, however hard he tried with good works and other activities, he was only ever remembered for one thing. *Bonum nomen, bonum omen* – if you're not happy with your name, you may not be happy with yourself; and if I claimed to have been entirely comfortable with mine, then it would be another case of The Thing Which Was Not. Having left the confines of a decade of boarding schools I soon realized that the world was going to be full of guides from Fatehpur-Sikri. By any standards, ours is what the Scots would call a 'kenspeckle' surname, that tickles the antennae of the curious. It has become notorious and glaciated – it is verbal *firn*, last year's granulated snow that is compressing into ice. By a process of antonomasia, 'Profumo' in some circles signifies certain general associations, and functions as shorthand for scandal, intrigue and what has subsequently been called 'sleaze'. Notoriety is the flip side of celebrity: it involves widespread recognition, but it won't get you the best table in any restaurant where you'd really want to dine. At times, ours has seemed an unfortunate byword: if I'd wanted a household name, I'd have settled for David Domestos.

Reviewing *The Pendulum Years* (Bernard Levin's excellent study of the sixties), Anthony Powell remarked, in a feline aside about the Profumo Affair, 'how much less memorable if the protagonist's name had been "Wilson" or "Brown",' and, faced with yet more pabulum in the papers, my mother once exclaimed, 'It's all because of that fucking surname.' It seems true that 'Profumo' is just too handy a yardstick to discard, whenever certain parliamentary foibles recur, and even when the press is in rare, adulatory mode, there are usually just enough column inches available to rehash the past. John Aubrey told an excellent story of Edward de Vere, beginning, 'This Earle of Oxford, making of his low obeisance to Queen Elizabeth, happened to let a Fart, at which he was so abashed and ashamed that he went to Travell, 7 yeares. On his returne the Queen welcomed him home, and sayd, "My Lord, I had Forgott the Fart." '

Now that I'm older, I flinch less often at the almost myoclonic reaction some folks have to the announcement of my name. I used to have a Kryptonite antipathy to the presumption of strangers, but I have become a disciple of Hanlon's Razor – 'Never attribute to malice that which is adequately explained by stupidity'. A Fulham car mechanic enquired if I was a spy, a restaurant manager asked if I would be arriving with any call-girls, and a New England pastor said, 'Hey, that's some name!'; I assured him, in the spirit of Christian fellowship, that back home quite a few folks were called David. A typical, everyday exchange might go like this: 'Oh, any relation?' 'To whom?' 'You know – *the* Profumo.' 'Yes, he was my father. Did you know him?' 'Oh, no.' 'Well, then, I'll just have my card back/room key/dry cleaning/double pre-frontal lobotomy, thank you.' People can be quite strange, but I have never had to contend with anything like Nicholas Mosley's enquiry from fellow officers during the last war, 'Not any relation of that bastard?'

At times I've fancied avoiding the verbal birthmark by embracing the Icelandic system of patronymics, whereby I'd be plain old David Johnson. The desire for anonymity (or at least starting with a clean slate) must be countered by what I call the Toupee Syndrome: sooner or later, your new wig is going to slip, and the reaction to your real baldness is going to be commensurately more awkward. Anyway, the fact is that I have seldom felt ashamed of my father's name (many are the times when I regard it as a badge of honour), and, once you start resorting to disguises, people are inclined to be suspicious. An especially dense plantation of *Cupressus leylandii* presupposes a desire for exclusion, but may suggest there is something to hide: if you're snug and busy inside your house, you can always get used to that view and the snarl of the motorway.

When I was a columnist with the *Daily Telegraph*, my father often joked that people used to ask him if he was any relation of mine. Another reason not to adopt a *nom de guerre* when attempting a career as a writer was that here, perhaps, Profumo *fils* had a proper chance of making a name for himself. Sometimes this attempt is tantalizing. When the *Telegraph* diarist reported my helicopter crash, no mention was made that I had once done a stint of almost a decade writing for the paper – 'the son of the disgraced former War Secretary' was the best description they could muster. I sometimes think of T. S. Garp, John Irving's superlative fictional creation: an aspiring literary novelist (whose mother is a media darling), even when his book comes out he is still recognized as 'the bastard son of Jenny Fields'. After a while, I came to accept that all of this went with the job of being my father's son – the knack is not to let yourself be defined by it.

On 9 October 1974 I went up to Magdalen, where I spent three fleeting years reading English and pursuing two loves. The first was an historian from St Hilda's – Helen Fraser – whom I met on 11 October. I clove to her, and, following the precedent of Wittgenstein's cornflakes, have been cleaving to her ever since (we were married in 1980). We met at a freshers' audition, and drama became my other passion. For two years I went at it hard as an acting hack, playing anything from Donald Duck to Prospero, until it was even saunter-ing across my mind to attempt it as a career. Both parents were appalled – possibly realizing my lack of brilliance would only result in misery – and were brim-full with disparagement; my mother wrote me a number of letters casting aspersions on her own former profes-sion, stressing that 'it is simply no kind of life for a real man', and even set up a dinner with Alec Guinness, who had been primed to endorse her sentiments. It didn't help that in my last year I shared a former bargee's cottage in beyond-Bohemian squalor with Jamie Chatto, who spent much of his time playing the saxophone and writing scripts, and was heading straight off into show business. For my twenty-first birthday, my parents funded a fancy-dress party at the Randolph Hotel: the dress code was Hollywood, and Valerie Hobson very stylishly came as herself.

When I decided to apply for a post-graduate course – instead of drama school – it was therefore considered to be the lesser of two evils. I needed to get a First, and worked quite assiduously, but suf-fered from such pre-exam nerves that I almost funked the papers (for-tunately, my saviour from St Hilda's was there to help me along). I was duly called for a viva, which lasted an excruciating half-hour during which it was made plain to me that I was considered a bor-derline case, and that pretty soon I needed to conjure an intellectual bunny out of my academical hat. I was saved by a dead Duck. One of the examiners was a kindly cleric named Reggie Alton, who asked me a simple question about Stephen Duck ('The Thresher Poet'), a woefully obscure versifier I had mentioned in my eighteenth-century paper: my convoluted reply seemed to satisfy the assembled dons that my studies had indeed been esoteric enough to warrant the degree I craved. Duck became my pet poet, my scholarly ace, a talisman: I later acquired at auction a copy of his seminal work *Poems on Several Occasions* (1736), and I gave it to our son James when, in 2005 while

I was finishing this book, he in turn achieved a First in English at Magdalen.

It is said that one of the reasons the medieval Church disapproved of what we now call the Mystery Plays is that everybody wanted to play the wicked roles – Cain, Herod, the Devil – as they were more glamorous and dramatic. Novelists, too, frequently find it a much greater challenge to make their benevolent and morally worthy characters convincing or engaging – one only has to think of the anaemic Brownlow, as opposed to Fagin or the Dodger, in *Oliver Twist* – because the problem is that good deeds tend to appear dull: they simply 'write white'. So it is that J's impressive commitment to Toynbee Hall was a long round of Adult Literacy Schemes, Housing Associations, and fund-raising appeals, during the course of which he remained deliberately self-effacing, except when it was vital to some project that he take centre stage. He had been instrumental in getting the Community Service Volunteers their first office in Toynbee, and had helped set up the Workers' Education Centre for Asian and African immigrants (there is a large Bangladeshi community in the East End), as well as being an enthusiastic promoter of the Toy Libraries Association.

One Toynbee worker was quoted as having said, 'Everybody here worships him. We think he's a bloody saint.' Legend has it that Saint Denis of Paris, having been decapitated, bent down, picked up his head, and walked the two leagues to his burial place. My father's middle name was Dennis, and of course I'm not suggesting he was any kind of martyr, but he did astonish people by the way he walked back to face the world. His behaviour, though by no means saintly (and I don't even subscribe to the concept of atonement), appeared heroic, and made his family proud. Well, I would say that, wouldn't I?

His industry was not going unnoticed, however. In June 1975 – on a list of names 736 strong – he appeared in the Queen's Birthday Honours with a CBE in recognition of his social work, and on 2 December we went to the Palace for his investiture.

There were congratulations aplenty in the papers, and many references to 'coming in from the cold'. The *Daily Mirror* called it 'his passport to respectability', and, according to a breathless account in the *Express*, all along Petticoat Lane there was cheering – 'Barrow boys left their stalls to pound his shoulders and pump his hand', and he was unanimously crowned 'A Cockney by adoption'. The ever-magnanimous *News of the World* informed its readers that this was 'one of the hardest-earned CBE's in history'; it had been a Downing Street recommendation, guided by Harold Wilson himself, and I rather agree with an acerbic comment which appeared much later in the *Sunday Times*, to the effect that nothing short of an Order of Merit would ever repay the debt the Labour Party owed my father for his previous role in politics. This attention was all very gratifying, for once, and J was as pleased with the positive reaction as he was with the gong itself. (Only Maina demurred, telling my mother she didn't think he should use the initials, as he was still in disgrace.) In an adulatory *Daily Mail* piece (14 June), Lynda Lee-Potter noted shrewdly how the life-rebuilding metaphor was already becoming hackneyed, but praised the example J continued to set, concluding, 'His son may well have cause to be prouder of his father than the son of any Prime Minister has ever been.' We might as well leave it at that.

I never did return to continue my studies at Oxford. Out of the blue I was offered a temporary job teaching English back at Eton, and before taking this up I disappeared to a house in Tuscany, where I fancied I would dash off my first novel. For a couple of months I lived on my own – itself a novel experience – and the solitude began to work on me, though counterproductively; it was a cold, lonely prospect across the valley, and I began to talk to myself, eventually conducting dialogues in Italian and English, fuelled by flasks full of the estate's own wine. Helen and I were then estranged, and my parents came out for Easter, read the situation, and advised me to come home. I wrote precisely three pages of a book, but at least I had learned that it was not the way I was going to get things done.

My career as Captain Grimes lasted less than two years, but I was surprised at how much I enjoyed the classroom side of teaching (I had a fairly cushy billet, of course, and never had to brave the state system). At Eton, I was by some way the youngest 'beak', and was pleased on my first day to be challenged for using the staff photocopier by an elderly and rebarbative colleague, who mistook me for a pupil. I stayed just for the summer, then taught for a year at the Royal School, Shrewsbury, where I had been lured by Tom Wheare – formerly a young Lord of Misrule on the Eton staff, then a Salopian housemaster, and later to be the distinguished Head of Bryanston. I shared digs with three other bachelors, and we had an exhausting time of it (in Shrewsbury, there is said to be a different pub for every day of the year). It was here that a learned colleague in the English Department taught me the recipe for a cocktail known as Death Comes for the Archbishop (I became familiar with the drink, but never got round to the Willa Cather novel of that name). By purporting to have a heavy drama commitment, I managed to dodge most of the sports duties, but, through an administrative misunderstanding, I ended up helping to coach the Second Eleven cricket team, umpiring matches, and eventually even playing the game. At that stage, I felt it was time to move on.

My parents had bought me the lease on a little house in London, and by now I had effectively left home. Practically on a whim, they decided the Dower House was now too big and difficult to run, and they sold up; V had become more uneasy spending time alone there, especially after a couple of burglaries (one of which was partly an inside job), and the indomitable Bustie was wanting to retire to Dulwich, grow his whiskers, and move in with his long-standing pal, Pat. In the summer of 1979, while J and V were still house-hunting and I was about to begin postgraduate research, Helen and I got engaged; the Frasers have a Hebridean retreat on the island of Harris and there, one evening, I came over all romantic and tied a piece of wool around her finger, St Kilda-fashion.

We were both twenty-three, and (to resort to one of my least favoured words) our 'relationship' had been thrillingly 'on–off' and embattled for long enough for us to realize that a decision was needed. My parents patently thought us too young – V might well have been speaking from personal experience, I concede, while J's own protracted bachelorhood was never a topic he mentioned with regret. There was probably something else. Three years previously, Mark had married a younger girl whose family circumstances were such that she clearly needed and welcomed my mother's attention, which suited both women (though that marriage did not survive much longer); the Frasers, by contrast, were so evidently such an accessible and attractive clan unit, that from the start I think my parents were a little wistful about my easy affection for them.

It is not often you see a chap composing a paean to his in-laws, but they deserve more than a brief mention in dispatches, because my parents' suspicion was spot-on: this was indeed the sort of family I'd wanted to have. At the time of our wedding, Alasdair Fraser was a consultant at St Mary's Hospital, Paddington; a Highland Scot, with all the dour, Presbyterian moodiness that sometimes entails, his fondness for literature and fishing meant we had enough in common to overleap the existential chasm between us – namely, that I had spirited away his firstborn lassie. Most unusually, he became one of my best friends, supportive of my writing ambitions, and nicely competitive when out on the water. At the end of an Alaskan angling foray together, I even finagled him into a mildly provocative Anchorage striptease joint, where the star turn was a comely ecdysiast divesting herself of fishing vest, waders and tackle; he sat patiently through it, nursing his single malt, but when our lascivious cabbie later enquired if he had enjoyed the spectacle, the good doctor grimly replied, 'I'm a Harley Street gynaecologist.' His wife Elaine, a Swansea bluestocking who went on from Oxford to Harvard on a scholarship, was a *femme savante* who had combined a career in advertising and journalism with bringing up four children, and looked like her daughter's older twin.

Our married life began with me once again a student, and Helen working for the BBC. At King's College, in the Strand, I began to research the dark and unpopular poetry of Jonathan Swift, to do a little teaching in the English Department, and to review books (though I preferred to think of myself as a 'critic', and not some Johannes Factotum, who would write, like a *Scriblerian* hack, on any subject that presented itself for money). I was aspiring to a doctorate and a university career – something my in-laws understood better than J or V. To combat what she saw as my weakness for unnecessary erudition, my mother would offer me her paperback copies of Jean Plaidy or some nice, slim volumes of verse by Rod McKuen, or Pam Ayres, as an antidote to what she called (in moments of spirited literary debate) my 'fussy-fanny attitude to writing'. By now, my father must have given up all hopes that a proper vocation – the military, or the law – would catch my fancy, and was resigned to having Dr Dryasdust as a son, though he was canny enough not to be quite so contrary and obstructive as his wife. In the event, I did not complete my doctorate, but jumped ship and became a freelance journalist.

By now, my parents had moved to the Hampshire village of Upton Grey, which seemed to suit them admirably. They were less remote, and the area's population of retired, affluent minor gentry proved comforting as they grew older. They spent the middle of the week in their London mews house, and J was thoroughly occupied with his Toynbee business by day and dining clubs or parties in the evening. My mother came to dislike such gatherings, complained that Jolly Jack always had to be the last to leave, and preferred quieter evenings with just one or two friends, with whom she liked to attend the theatre. J only liked it if there was singing and dancing ('folderols'), or if they were going backstage. Cabaret and the circus were really his preferred dramatic forms, as both tended to feature girls with spangled kit and feathery appendages. On a visit to the Folies Bergères in Paris when I was still a schoolboy, it was all I could do to restrain him physically when a couple of the more determined, betasselled artistes sashayed down the aisle and tried to lure him up on stage.

The fact is that J once again came to rather enjoy being recognized and making a slight exhibition of himself, whereas V increasingly shunned any public attention. In her late sixties, gently ageing but still beautiful, she began to loathe being photographed, and became despondent about her looks. She was moody and could be short-tempered. She suffered from gallstone problems, and in 1981 underwent a pancreas operation after which she told me she never again felt entirely well. Never one to malinger, she turned her very considerable attention towards those she decided were definitely in trouble: Laudie, dying of cancer alone in her flat because her faith proscribed medical help; Aunt Pat's marital and financial problems; Simon, Tony, Mark. Her generalized spiritual fervour was evident, but did not seem to bring serenity: she surrounded herself with palm-leaf crosses, Hands of Fatima, rosaries of wood from the Mount of Olives, bookmarks inscribed with uplifting thoughts, and other *bondieuserie*, but she remained tense and driven. Still sleeping badly, and finding food and drink a chore, she seemed to take little pleasure in her physical sur-roundings, though two spaniels gave her comfort, and she restlessly patrolled the shops (her Christmas presents were generally all wrapped and ready by the end of October). My mother's personality was so enduringly forte, however, that you might overlook the essential fragility; the last thing any of us wanted at this stage was for her to feel for a second time struck by lightning.

'All sentences that begin "God Forbid" describe something that is possible' – so runs one of my favourite Yiddish proverbs ('The dumplings in a dream are not dumplings, but dreams' is another). Rumours of film versions of the Profumo Affair being prepared for both the big and small screens began to reach the papers in 1984; Palace Productions was said to have put both of 'Les Girls' under con-tract during script development, and a television project ('High Places') was under way from Central TV's Zenith. Whenever there was a setback, claims were made in the press that the 'Establishment' was blocking progress, under the guise of the Independent Broad-casting Authority, MI5, or its Uncle Tom Cobleigh division. Dirk Bogarde reportedly declined the role of Stephen Ward out of defer-ence to his friendship with my mother, and then David Bowie was also mentioned as having expressed an interest.

Gossip about such projects tends to rise and fall periodically, like the ghost net, affording a brief glimpse of the contents before drift-ing away. I wanted to assume that nothing of the sort would ever make it to the production stage, and I still then entertained a vague notion that in some way such films would not be allowed, by law. Whenever approached by the media, J maintained a policy of not reacting, so that he personally could not be associated in any way; even an objection can act as a bellows to smouldering, mouldering rubbish heaps, and most developers are understandably well-briefed on our idiosyncratic laws governing libel. (Besides, having had his bluff notably called on two previous occasions, J was inclined to be cautious.)

Fortunately for the various entrepreneurs, interest in the early sixties was enjoying something of a resurgence. In February 1986, after a three-million-pound refit, Cliveden reopened as an hotel, with a predictable degree of coverage; I felt unable to accept the *Daily Mail's* generous invitation to review it for them, and in the event they secured the services of that other, obvious journalistic choice, Christine Keeler. In April, Mandy was photographed shaking hands with Princess Anne at the première of *Absolute Beginners*, the culty sixties film in which she appeared; she also published a novel – 'I might have won the Booker Prize,' she purred, 'instead of the Hooker prize' – which gave Bron Waugh, ever a fan of hers, the opportunity of putting her surname and mine together on the front cover of *Literary Review*, the magazine he edited, and to which I was a regular contributor. 'It was too glorious a chance to miss,' he told me, 'and anyway I assure you it will only add to the gaiety of the nation.'

Our family was anyway feeling low in the water that year because my father's younger brother Phil died suddenly at the age of sixty-seven, and their oldest sister Betsy followed him just a few weeks later. (My grandmother had made it well into her nineties, but now the 'Mafia' was becoming perilously depleted.) My uncle had a heart attack in a friend's London house while my parents were abroad, and I had to go round and deal with the body; it was the first time I had been alone with a corpse, and for several hours I sat in a cramped bedroom staring at the sallow soles of his feet, his mouth twisted agape as if in an eternal snore. The undertakers eventually hustled him vertically down the narrow staircase in a black-draped container, knocking all the pictures off the wall as they went. I did not contact J and V with the news because they were flying back from Venice that evening and I thought it would be less of a shock if I went round to tell them in person. Death in the family notwithstanding, I hastened professionally off to a lunch appointment with the deputy literary editor of the *Sunday Times*, Nigella Lawson. That afternoon I received a phone call, 'This is John Grigg from the *Times* obituaries desk. I just wanted to say how sorry we were to hear about your father . . .' This is how it ends, I thought. I could see, instantly, the sudden tumble from a lurching water-taxi, that despairing hand disappearing beneath the glaucous surface of some canal – but no, wires down at Wapping had become crossed: it now transpired my uncle was the one they meant. Still, it wasn't a good moment.

When, that October, allegations were published concerning Jeffrey Archer and the prostitute Monica Coghlan, there was a lively pretext for the recycling of old newsprint; one feature about 'wronged' Tory wives observed how not many of them wore leather miniskirts.

May 1987 suggested the net was now being swept along on vigorous new currents. References were being made to 'Profumo, the Movie', and the actors Donald Pleasence, Michael Elphick, and John Suchet were all being mooted as candidates for the role of the Minister, in what the *Star* called a 'celluloid version of his disgrace'. It was all becoming hard to avoid. By now, Helen and I had two small children, and I was feeling keenly protective of all three generations; to make matters even more immediate, Nik Powell, the Palace Pictures producer (who was married to shoeless *chanteuse* Sandie Shaw) lived practically opposite our house near Marble Arch, so most days I had the pleasure of seeing him scamper off to work on his latest project.

May also saw the publication of two related books, which were serialized head-to-head in rival newspapers. The *Sunday Times* (where my own work then appeared each fortnight) ran excerpts from *An Affair of State* by Philip Knightley and Caroline Kennedy, which is on balance one of the better books on the subject; it is less hysterical about conspiracy and cover-up than some of the others (though convinced that Ward was 'framed'), and the journalistic style is concise. John Carey, reviewing it in the same paper, concluded, 'It's like having the plot of a le Carré novel explained to you by several different narrators, all of whom are probably lying.' Over at the *Mail on Sunday* they were concurrently treating us to excerpts from *Honeytrap* by Anthony Summers and Stephen Dorrill, an altogether more provocative and extravagant 'exposé' of our supposedly corrupt Establishment;

its vertiginous style made it eye-catching enough, though with disclosures such as Tom Denning's home being on 'a trout stream where Izaak Newton himself fished' one wondered what else had bypassed their fact-checking department. The books were widely reviewed together, too, and newspapers across the land were loud with the squeaking of little wheels as commentators scooted around on their favourite hobby-horses. In the *Observer*, Anthony Burgess (widely remembered for his own acts of kindliness and charity) had this to say of my father: 'As "poor Jack Profumo" he was granted the opportunity to repent and be purged by doing social work': how easy that makes it sound.

In the event, the film called *Scandal* started shooting in June 1988, with Ian McKellen in the part of John Profumo. Jim Thompson (then Bishop of Stepney) wrote to the actor, asking him to reconsider his involvement; his reply insisted that the hypocrisies of those times needed representing. In fact, McKellen had recently 'come out' as a homosexual, and I believe he wanted to show – by accepting to play a man he described as a 'raging heterosexual' – that this need not involve typecasting. The line about hypocrisy became standard humbug for the makers of this film: I don't believe a single person working on that picture cared a *foutra* for the fate of Stephen Ward, but, against a perceptible rise in public sympathy for my parents, anyone interviewed played the Dead Scapegoat card. There was a lively cast. Deborah Grant played my mother, Leslie Phillips was rather an absurd, predictable Astor, and the 'girls' certainly looked their parts: Peter Fonda's daughter Bridget was Mandy (her most recent film having been *Shag*), and the beauteous Joanne Whalley-Kilmer made a humdinger of a *femme fatale* as CK, though when actress and former showgirl actually met it was evidently not a success. John Hurt starred as Ward, sleekly coiffed and every inch the clergyman's son (they both were, as it happened). There was a microcosmic scandal when, during filming, he abandoned his American wife, Donna, and took up with Jo Dalston, assistant to the producer. In their long and cunning build-up to release, the publicity people seldom missed a trick.

The charity première of *Scandal* was on 2 March 1989, at the Leicester Square Odeon. There were some favourable reviews, and it did good box office: the coverage was widespread, and it had become impossible for us to dismiss or ignore it. No longer able to regard developments with the studious equanimity of some *tricoteuse*, I have to say that my sense of humour failed, and the whole thing made me want to go off and get dog-sucking drunk. Somehow, my parents retained their composure, but they witnessed this latest, high-profile, reanimation of events with mounting disbelief and increasingly heavy hearts. They did not see the film, but such was the publicity that titillating stills were widely reproduced, and the comment was unavoidable. They felt re-exposed, as if living in a formicarium. As a family, we referred to it but obliquely, refusing to let it block out the sun; but just the knowledge that they were being mimicked in some nearby cinema really pistol-whipped their elderly *amour propre*, and it was beyond us all to laugh it off. For J and V, it was the worst kind of *déjà vu*. They were bewildered that things could have come to such a pass that, even after so much time, there was apparently not a stage where people might decide enough was enough. I never felt sorrier for them in my life.

I went to see *Scandal*, to stop imagining the worst, and tried to reassure my parents that it was all a fuss about nothing. It was still a disconcerting experience, of course. McKellen's portrayal of J was unlikeable, but not vicious, and (no doubt for legal reasons) the part was downbeat from a creative point of view – Joe Boyd, the executive producer, claimed they had had to 'tiptoe around his characterization' because nobody really knew what he was like. Luckily, the great man looked so absurd in his wig that there was little uncanny resemblance. (Johnny Edgecombe wrote to *Time Out*, 'I sympathize with John Profumo if his portrayal was as bad as mine.') The period detail was otherwise quite sly, with particularly good use being made of the background music: when the girls get dressed to kill for a night out on the town, it is to the Shadows' 'Apache'; the (apocryphal) scene wherein the Minister and the Spy almost coincide at the Doctor's home plays out to Sophia Loren telling Peter Sellers, 'Doctor, I'm in Trouble'; and during the resignation sequence we are treated to the Beatles singing, 'Listen, do you want to know a secret?' – though by that time, frankly, I did not.

On Comic Relief Day, just after the film went on general release, I found myself up in Norfolk, facing serried ranks of disconsolate sixth-formers wearing exotic neckties and red noses; as part of the King's Lynn Fiction Festival, I had agreed to give a reading from my first novel, *Sea Music*, which was about to appear in paperback. 'I assume the name helps?' asked the young English teacher presiding. 'No relation, obviously?' My plangent and finely modulated prose having been received with busy silence, I slunk thirstily to my billet, only to find that the well-meaning landlady ran a teetotal and smoke-free household, and kept a largely Alsatian pet which lunged like a honey badger if you attempted to enter the bathroom. My hostess apologized for her daughter's absence, but explained she'd gone to the movies to see – well, I was planning on an early night, anyway.

Despite other distractions, 1989 was quite a busy year for me professionally. My novel had won the Geoffrey Faber prize (which had given me the chance to make a mildly sarcastic acceptance speech in their boardroom, teasing Faber and Faber for having turned it down); I had another book appearing in the autumn; there was my column in the *Daily Telegraph*, and I had been invited to be one of that year's Booker judges. It was the twenty-first anniversary of the prize, so we were involved in a certain amount of publicity, and over the course of that summer I had to read a total of 26,424 pages of fiction – a task that had proved a welcome distraction. By the time the shortlist brouhaha was over, and the televised dinner ceremony was approaching, I had begun to feel I had attained a little literary stature. Hotfoot from our final deliberations (Kazuo Ishiguro was to carry the day), I changed into black tie, made my way, nodding and smiling self-importantly, through the crowd, and took my place at a round table. Several publishers caught my eye, but I splendidly betrayed nothing, savouring my moment of power. 'It's been quite a day,' I confided to the delightful lady next to me, pursing my lips into what I fancied was an enigmatic pout of exhaustion. 'Really?' she enquired brightly. 'So, are you some kind of literary person, then?' Well, at least she didn't ask me if I'd seen any good films lately.

The events of 1989 did nothing to ease my mother's encroaching sense of redundancy. She had long since, I believe, forgiven J his original sin, but the sheer effort that had gone into reshaping their post-lapsarian world seemed to have been mocked by all this Technicolor mummery. Rather to her surprise, the experience had exhausted her reserves of stoical resolve – the bell curve of her fabled imperturbability seemed to be on the downturn, and she was fed up with putting a brave face on things. Men had often let her down – her picaresque father, the winsome first husband, then Jolly Jack – but V had always managed to look strong; she had convinced herself (and others) that she could still take the initiative. Now, she felt marginal-ized. The days were gone when my father was described as 'husband of Valerie Hobson', and increasingly frequent references to her merely as something like 'Profumo's wife' were reducing her to the level of just another of the walk-on parts in a cheap show perpetually in rep touring the provinces. I remember the white-hot indignation with which she told me that a tourist had recognized her in a London book store, and had come up and asked her to autograph a book by Christine Keeler. You can have too much of a bad thing.

She had even toyed with the idea of resuming some film work. There were still occasional enquiries, but it was generally assumed she was no longer available; reasserting her identity in such a way had its attractions, though, and there was serious discussion of (among others) a script that involved playing opposite Paul Newman. Several factors held her back, I think to her regret. She had quit while a leading lady, and most of the approaches were understandably for cameo roles; she was also anxious at having lost her looks – in fact, she might still have appeared magnificent on screen – and, more tellingly, she felt out of practice and out of touch with the requirements of the medium that had altered, perhaps unrecognizably, over thirty-five years. There was concern, too, that any career revival might attract unwanted attention to the family, and that film work would almost certainly have to take place in America, which J had vowed never to visit again. There was no question of her going without him, it seemed.

None of these obstacles to acting seemed to apply to writing, however, and to this she turned with an enthusiasm which one might lazily call cathartic, except that the process never seemed to assuage itself, and developed into a veritable *cacoethes scribendi*. Commonplace books, stories, prayers, poems and hugely long letters came racing off her clipboard as she sat up fitfully into the early hours; many of them were headed my way, since this was not an activity with which J could engage, though he condoned it for keeping her occupied. She also embarked upon her life story, a project which he emphatically did not endorse. An entry in her diary for February 1973 shows she had already mooted it back then, but – in a most discouraging sentence – 'J says, "You'll never finish that, either."' In the event, he flatly refused to discuss it with her. Although over the next eight years she never progressed chronologically much beyond their marriage, he felt it was bound to lead further into areas of fallow he saw no good reason to disturb. V applied herself with great energy to this undertaking, pro-fessing no desire to seek publication – it was 'just a lot of dosh really, that might amuse the boys one day' – but he and I suspected other-wise. The prospect appalled him, and he did not read it.

Selfishly, embroiled as I was in a second novel plus the distractions of our own family life with two smallish boys (James and Tom), I was not overly generous in my feedback, either. Having worked as an editor on a magazine where friends thrust their precious manuscripts unsolicitedly into my in-tray, I already knew what a thankless task it can be to appraise the work of those you love, but here I was given little choice. The style was open and abstract and breathless, which did not appeal to me (a slow and costive prosaist), though I tried not to regard this as a turf war, and kept my powder dry on the verbiage front, despite characteristic sniper-fire ('Dave, you agonize so much over every word. Dash the story off lyrically, and it will flow . . .'). What concerned me more was the extensive airbrushing of personal history, the verbal evocation of a big happy family which I knew was not authentic, and the constant, hectoring Pelagianism, that insisted on excusing the shortcomings of most of the characters in her saga. Early drafts of the manuscript (entitled *A Day Too Soon*, echoing the circumstances of her birth) were so full of the milk of human kind-ness that I think my mother would have had it churned, if she could, the better to spread it around.

None of this was doing any harm; mine was only one opinion, after all. Just as much hard work can go into producing a poor book as a fine one, and writing can be troublesome enough without someone leaving boot-prints all over your immaculately poured concrete. She sensed my coolness, of course, and took umbrage. To this period – the early nineties – therefore belonged some of our more vigorous disagreements: I was the nearest sounding-board, and several times a week I would receive letters challenging the way I was bringing up the children, my views on nuclear weapons, what I was writing in the papers (mostly about other people's books), the Rushdie Affair ('that disgraceful friend of yours'), the importance of correct footwear for women, and my lifestyle, such as it was, in general. I called these her 'God's Lungs' letters, because the most protracted and homiletic of them all was about the abuse I was visiting, through smoking, on the wonderful body He had given me – and quite right she was, too. Another refrain was the iniquity of the class system and inherited wealth – again, a perfectly reasonable topic to broach with your privileged son, though the arguments were more a hangover from her theatrical days, and the spurious egalitarianism then fostered by Equity members to accommodate the also-rans of that profession.

In compensating for a lot of understandable uncertainty – we can all fall prey to that – V became fiercely dogmatic and confrontational, safe in the knowledge that, unlike most of her other menfolk, I was so similar in temperament that she could rely on me to rear up and give battle. She felt that her time was running out, and what she could not bend to her will she would merely deny; easygoing chats about family relationships as we strolled between the lavender beds with tankards of Pimm's were therefore a pitifully rare occurrence, though the odd jolt of alcohol did often help us through the trickier weekends. We were seldom incommunicado for long, and though the mother–son relationship was often fiery – explosive, even – giving vent to our feelings was probably better than the two of us merely smouldering away on the lip of the family caldera like a couple of huffy old profumaroles.

★

279

On 31 January 1991, Simon Havelock-Allan died, at the age of forty-seven – 'after a lifetime's disability borne with patience and humour', as his mother's words so succinctly expressed it in the *Times* announcement. Because he had always lived in a Rudolf Steiner home since I first went to see him when I was a teenager, Simon occupied an unusual place in my affections; I saw him just a few days a year, but he was constantly talked about at other times, and never once did I find visiting him a chore. Some who have Down's syndrome are harder to manage than others, and of course the childishness factor can vary from day to day, as it can, in practice, for us all; but, by the time I got to know him, my half-brother was noted for his cheery disposition, and the abiding innocence – absence of malice, really – for which such boys and girls are now well known was in him so luminous a feature that he was curiously inspiring to be with.

'Henry', as he was known by the other boys (there were several Simons), was not without guile, and always had a knack for mischief and stringing people along, until that time when his final illness – incipient Alzheimer's – began to close up the doors of his perception, like some Advent calendar in reverse. From his father (who scarcely saw him) and his devoted, but absentee, mother, he inherited a talent for histrionics that came in very handy for the Nativity play, but could make more mundane matters a bit of a performance (he doubled up as his own audience, much of the time). He was a delicate, fastidious boy, with none of the physical clumsiness that sometimes goes with such disability; I am sure his marked Havelock-Allan family resemblance made it all the harder for his buttoned-up progenitor to relate to him. In his heyday Simon was talkative, quite capable (he could write his name, play instruments, throw pots) and had a pronounced sense of the absurd. You could never afford to take your eye off him when out in public, as he had no idea about self-preservation; he had a passion for hoarding colourful commodities such as bubble-bath bottles and aftershaves, to which he would methodically help himself as one herded him around Woolworth's. These walkabouts of temporary shoplifting became so familiar that the assistants greeted him by name, and, king in the country of his own imagining (and accordingly carrying no cash), he acknowledged their obeisance with gracious bows, until nothing more would fit into his basket, and we had to begin diplomatic negotiations about what could really be exported from the store.

Simon minded greatly about his sartorial appearance, and seldom came out for lunch without tweed jacket and tie – his godfather Noël knew of this fondness for neckwear, and sent him splendid examples each Christmas. For such a slender chap, he had a wolfish appetite, and eating out was regarded as a paramount treat. As these expeditions were usually at weekends, when most hostelries are at their busiest, our mother had worked hard over the years to find places where such a guest and his family would not be considered an anomaly, and I don't mind admitting (despite my supersaturated cynicism) that it was a tribute to her willpower and optimism whenever our boy was conspicuously received with such affection. The kindness of relative strangers tends to be forgotten; but in this respect it has always impressed me. The Butcher's Arms at nearby Priors Hardwick, for example, was run by Lino and Augusta Peres, a young Portuguese couple who had turned a modest pub into one of the most popular restaurants in the region, packed out with well-heeled, big-spending punters. Our mother had been quietly taking Simon there since their earliest days, when you could barely get a sandwich to eat around the fire, but ever since then they treated him like a VIP – Coventry nabobs, and their retinue of shiny-jacketed clients, would be left goggling at the fancy menus while Simon was installed at his usual table, and served up at once with his customary beaker of squash ('Orange wine'). Once, when I took Simon out on my own, they opened up just for him, even though I had forgotten it was their day off.

In the springtime of 1991, V wrote J a letter that began: 'Yesterday we dropped into the earth the remains of my first, beloved, ever-baby son Simon.' She thanked him for years of 'support and sympathy, all through those heavenly weekends in Paris when we were first together – always, always, were you tender and caring.' The text goes on to stress how alone she felt –

Can you imagine the relief, when I told you? I even remember the small café where I did so. At last, I had someone to share and, even

better, to help. You were wonderful. You accepted my little handicapped one into your heart, and your family. Tony is only too right
when he tells everyone, 'Jack is the *most wonderful* father – what would
Simon have done without him?'. I can never repay you, I shall not try.
You will *feel* my gratitude, and love till the day you (too) die. I love you
so much. – Valerie.

The period of profound disequilibrium which characterized the last
few years of my mother's life was not provoked by the loss of her son:
having seen his entire life through as best she could, there was, instead,
a sense of peace, and an end to the insubordinate guilt that so often had
risen to overtake her rationale. She began to have weekly discussions
with her friend Alan McGlashan, an author and psychiatrist whose
gentle and sophisticated company quickly became indispensable to her
routine. His letters to her suggest that the restlessness from which she
was suffering had been caused by suppressed feelings of grief and anger
that had gradually formed a 'shadow side' that had broken through into
her consciousness; she had to accept them, and stop feeling guilty at
their existence (though he did admit that it was probably not worth
trying to share them with her husband at this late stage). This certainly
meant something to her, and his counsel gave her some solace.

Resentment at the way her life had been hijacked – that would have
been my own analysis. Another flash flood of distressing publicity
descended on her in April 1992, with the publication of *The Naked
Spy* by Captain Yevgeny Ivanov, a preposterous rodomontade of a
book that was given undue prominence by the decision of editor
Andrew Neil to serialize these scurrilous memoirs in the *Sunday
Times*. My parents decided to take action, for once, and consulted two
of the most formidable legal brains in London (Richard Rampton QC
and Lord Goodman) to challenge the libellous allegation which was
the chief selling-point for the publisher.

The gallant Captain (who, some say, had been demoted to a ferry
boat on the Black Sea, and was a terminal alcoholic) was finally speaking out about his role in the events of 1963, which he mendaciously
claimed had involved him visiting our home in Chester Terrace one
day at my mother's invitation, bringing with him some bottles of

vodka and a Minox camera. 'Come in, Captain. Glad to see you. How are you?' he remembered her saying, and while she was making him a nice cup of tea (presumably all the staff were in an opium den, or lying murdered in their beds) he nipped along to the Minister's desk, which was naturally piled high with top-secret papers, and slipped some into his pockets. On another occasion (this housewife's taste for vodka must have been insatiable) he was able to make off with plans of Polaris missile bases, and his damaging and entirely insupportable assertion was that the Soviet Government were just about to black-mail J when he resigned in the nick of time.

It is amazing what people will believe if they read it in certain papers, and this was too serious to let pass; the publishers had to apologize in open court and agreed to cease distributing the book in that form, and the *Sunday Times* printed a grudging retraction. My mother took it very badly, and, this time round, was distraught almost beyond words. It did not help that this was also the year when the sexual indiscretions of both Paddy Ashdown and David Mellor were revealed – neither was the real deal, but the associated coverage was decidedly unattractive. There was also another addition to the hard-back library – David Thurlow's *Profumo: The Hate Factor*, a charming title, I must say.

When our daughter, Laura, arrived in February 1992, she was the first Miss Profumo to have been born in Britain for more than eighty years. It was perhaps an index of how perverse V's emotions could be that she – who had always longed for a daughter, just as her own father had wanted a son – now scrupulously avoided making much of a fuss over her first granddaughter, and seemed to be holding herself in check. (Mark was by now married again, to a fellow bar-rister, and they subsequently had two daughters and a son; but I don't think our mother ever found it easy playing the role of Granny.) She was critical of my wife Helen (now an executive producer) for decid-ing to go back to work, insisting that a mother's place was in the home – a plain case of displacement and wishful thinking from someone who, for various reasons, had spent too little time with her own children. At times, it almost seemed as if she was irked by our great good fortune. Part of her therapy, perhaps, was to reorder the past in her mind, and this involved present-day configurations some-times being adjusted to conform to a new reality. Unwitting revi-sionism is a common enough concomitant of increasing age – I may well be indulging in it myself – but there were times when it smacked of desperation, as if she had retreated into some hinterland from which she refused to be drawn.

Helen and I had begun house-hunting in Scotland – a place for which V had professed affection over forty years, and where she had even said she'd like her ashes scattered; now she insisted, however, that this was an idea that would be ruinous to our future ('Dave is just becoming escapist, he doesn't really want to live up there, it's a holiday idea, and it's simply not on'). Under an assumed name, she started getting particulars from estate agents in the West of England instead, in an attempt to steer us towards somewhere notionally 'closer to home'. Such domineering tactics, though doubtless adopted with the noblest of intentions, could be exhausting, but my mother was becoming impatient with the world. At the end of 1994, J and V cele-brated their ruby wedding with a brief ceremony in St Columba's: among my mother's papers, I later found her Order of Service card, on the back of which she had carefully drawn up a family tree which showed, beneath 'Us', three boys conjunctly – Simon, Mark and David. Her universe had become an uncertain place.

'I shall never make old bones,' wrote V to me that year, 'and I can think of nothing worse than being a drag on everyone.' On two occa-sions she suffered what was known as 'a turn' (I suspect these were TIAs, transient ischaemic attacks) when momentarily she could not speak and was partially incapacitated, but her letters continued to be full of concern about my father's well-being instead, despite the fact that her own health was deteriorating. Something was awry in her metabolism, and she often looked chalk-white, haggard and distant. She was seventy-eight, wore a feathery wig, and walked with a stick. After an accident when she fell in the kitchen, her arm was broken and she never fully regained her strength, despite an operation to replace the shoulder joint. 'It's called getting old, Dave,' she said, 'and I don't recommend it.' There was never once a complaint about pain.

Her arm was still in a sling when, in October 1995, she gamely attended the seventieth birthday party given by Margaret Thatcher at Claridge's. There was a great deal of media coverage for this event, and both my parents knew it was significant because J had been notified in advance that he was going to be sitting next to the Queen. 'To my horror, she sent me a note saying she wanted me to sit on her right-hand side,' he related, 'and the meal itself went well, but I'll tell you what: after the dinner itself, in one of the other rooms, I found myself walking past Prince Philip's chair, and I said, "Look, Sir, I just want to take the opportunity of thanking you for letting me sit next to your wife tonight." I thought that was pretty bold of me, and he just replied, "Nothing to do with me." He wanted to make it abundantly clear that it was not with his approval.' One wonders why – when Her Majesty, plus the Queen Mother, Prince Charles, and even the late Princess of Wales, all supported this disgraced Minister's efforts by turning up in the East End – the Duke of Edinburgh remained so entrenched in his disapproval. Perhaps there was some lingering moral issue, after all.

If V was increasingly reluctant about their social life, J was in some ways reverting to a man-about-town. She felt worn down and vulnerable, conscious that her psychic armour had slipped, the protective scutes were no longer safely overlapping – whereas he was energetic and frisky, having decided, by contrast, that the world had thrown its worst at them and there was nothing much to be lost by brazenly ogling women in public places, holding hands with the restaurant manageress on his wife's birthday, buying a copy of *Penthouse* to take on the train, and sundry other traits of the *vieux marcheur*. His concept of fun had scarcely diminished, nor his fondness for what Dean Swift called '*la bagatelle*': he was standing, suited, in the china department of Harrods one afternoon when a tourist mistook him for a salesman, enquired about eggcups, and was treated to a conducted tour of several rooms. At the age of eighty, he took me for dinner at Boodle's, then suggested we drop in for a nightcap at Les Ambassadeurs, the private club off Hyde Park Corner; he hadn't been a member for years, but he cheerily greeted the doorman, signed the book, and asked if Mr Mills, the owner, was in. He was apparently in a private room elsewhere, but sent his compliments. We sat at the bar swigging scotch in the company of various superannuated boxers, until I felt the paternal chutzpah had been sufficiently proved.

Although at times my mother could be witheringly contemptuous of this brand of masculine behaviour, she tried not to be a killjoy, and was aware of the discrepancy between her preferred recreations and those of her more ebullient husband. In one of her last letters to me – the valedictory *timbre* was becoming common – she unfairly castigated herself 'for being a dud all these years', lacking the energy to travel and live it up with J. She resolved, 'I must somehow pull myself together for these last years, for his sake. Because I love him', signing off with her mantra, 'Where there is love, anything is possible . . . Mother.'

On Thursday 12 November, 1998, attempting to reach the front door to meet her doctor, she vomited, collapsed and lost consciousness. An ambulance took her to the London Clinic, and in the early hours of the following morning we gathered round her bed while a locum priest, a retired missionary, was summoned to say prayers. Her eyes never opened, but it may be she knew we were there. Her chest rose and fell, but it was just a mechanical remembrance of the brain. She was already far away from us all when her heart failed, and it was over.

At the funeral parlour, where I went with my father to see her laid out, it was the only time I have ever seen him cry, and that was the worst moment, knowing he was to be alone. Alec Guinness read at the service, and there were some fulsome obituaries of Valerie Hobson, the actress. She would have been proud of her final notices, with perhaps the best send-off coming from the *Liverpool Daily Post*: 'No wonder Profumo had lied to Parliament, you could see them thinking, he would not have wanted to lose a wife like that.'

'*Que reste-t-il?*' Who knows what will survive of us?

VII

Waiting for the Sun

THE DAY AFTER the funeral, my father suffered his first stroke, and was admitted to the Wellington Hospital in St John's Wood. He recovered his mobility and powers of speech, but was no longer allowed to drive, and lost some of his physical independence. We stayed with friends in Perthshire that New Year, and took him to see the house we had just bought nearby, on a small hill farm overlooking the Vale of Atholl. Our new neighbour had been a contemporary of his at Oxford, and a veteran of the Italian landings, and the two old warhorses began to ravel up the past together.

Early in the next year, his sister Maina also had a stroke and died. During a holiday convalescing abroad, he slipped and injured his hamstring, and never again walked without a stick. In March 1999, he sent me a lovely letter saying he had not felt well enough to write 'since we lost Valerie', and signing himself for the first time, 'Jack'.

'Boys do not grow up gradually,' wrote Cyril Connolly. 'They move forward in spurts like the hands of clocks in railway stations.' Something similar happened to my father in those first few months of 1999: the dapper old beau was by no means helpless but had become a more tentative figure, stumping along the corridor with his wispy white sideburns, for all the world like the Yoda. His sense of balance deserted him, and later a night-time haemorrhage caused him to lose most of the sight in one eye. There was another, more serious, stroke, and I found myself at his bedside in the Basingstoke hospital, where he stared at me apparently without recognition. As they examined him, I looked at his body, suddenly frail – the plucked-grouse torso, his twisted and unspeaking visage – and thought, 'Can this really be the same chap all that fuss was about?' I sat there for hours, until, in a threadbare whisper, he informed me, 'I don't like that man who brings the food.'

We decided it was time to move him back to town, and find a flat where he could be nearer to our London home. I began to go through my mother's voluminous papers, tentatively, as if she might at any time come in upon the process. They included collections of cuttings about life after death, a small archive of articles about the Princess of Wales, an anthology of favourite religious writings, a portfolio of neatly typed prayers she had composed, and box upon box of Christmas and birthday cards sent to her by the family, carefully trussed within rubber bands, arranged neatly by year. I also found letters to various people to be opened after her death, dating back as far as 1975, including one (from 1996) to me: 'How will you read this? Where will you be? (Where will *I* be? – oh, I know somewhere marvellous.)' It goes on to attest to the happiness of their marriage: 'We had a truly happy time together. Nothing can ever un-do that. He made so many silly things happen, but they have been from human failing. I know you are very angry with Daddy, but he is a brave man. See that he isn't alone. He needs an un-empty bed, in time . . .' She concludes with this: 'The world needs courage and intellect. And heart. And love. You have them all in abundance. May God bless you till we meet again. My love *always*. Mother.' In the bottom drawer of her desk, in a little wooden box that had contained crystallized plums, there was a single conference badge – treasured, I'm certain, because it expressed a rare conjunction: 'Mrs Profumo. Actress'.

My father had no intention of lapsing into the role of slippered pantaloon, however, and on moving to his London flat he rallied again. Toynbee, where he was now President, continued to occupy much of his time, and there was every sign that he intended (as my mother put it) to 'drop in harness'. The forty years' service he completed there was far longer than his entire parliamentary career, and he continued to be recognized for it. He was made an Honorary Fellow of Queen Mary College, was awarded a Beacon Prize for 'exceptional contributions to charity' (the evening his underwear threatened to fall down in Downing Street), and had a building named after him, that was opened by John Major. Modest as his demeanour remained, though, I think Jack Profumo always regarded with wry detachment many of those who had survived the obstacle course of public life unscathed.

'The wind in one's face makes one wise,' ran one of George Herbert's proverbs, and Jack Profumo had certainly become a wise old bird; in an interview with his coeval, Bill Deedes, he said, 'There's so much unrequited loneliness. Society has become compartmentalized, so that although people occupy the same physical space, they never interact.' For all his gregariousness, he well understood what it meant to be lonely.

In these later years, I became my father's keeper. He knew exactly when to be charming and grateful for my help, and to acquiesce to my cajoling, but little would divert him from the course of his social life. His fondness for female company seemed unabated, and a number of lady-loves passed in shadowplay across the scene; but so habituated had he become to the clandestine manner in this area of his life that even now, when the coast was clear, he preferred to work in mysterious ways, and his activities were not easy to monitor. But I do not think there was ever again a serious contender for his heart.

We held a Service of Thanksgiving for Valerie at St Paul's, Covent Garden –'the actors' church' – and a silver ciborium was consecrated in her memory by Jim Thompson, then Bishop of Bath and Wells, who spoke of her 'bright flame of human talent'. In this grand finale, my boyhood premonition of a scene with full episcopal trappings was eventually realized. Mary Soames and Paul Scofield gave readings, and Johnny Mills – being too blind to read – recited 'Johnny in the Cloud', from his role as a fighter pilot in *The Way to the Stars*. Outside were the usual autograph hunters, and one said loudly of Edward Heath, 'I bet he's signed more of those here today than he did copies of his autobiography.' It was gratifying to see that the spirit of show business prevailed.

My mother's wishes had been to be cremated, with half her ashes to be interred in the family vault in Hersham next to her husband's, when that day came; the rest should be scattered somewhere wild and beautiful. On New Year's Eve 1999, my father and I sat alone in front of the television in a cottage on our Scottish farm. Earlier in the day, he had suffered another little stroke, and he was shaking under a woollen blanket, finding it hard to speak. I had slipped a disc changing a wheel in the snow, so we made a sorry pair, and the rest of the family had gone out to a Millennium party elsewhere. Sipping at our scotch, we watched the river of fire fizzling along the Thames, and listened in silence to all the manufactured sentiments about the century's end. It would have been their forty-fifth wedding anniversary. It was very cold, and all the stars were out.

Up on the moor behind the house is a big, pale stone where I often sit and watch the glen. Just before noon, on the first day of the new year, I drove my father into the field below, so he could see clearly where we were going to stand on the brae above him; I poured him a flute of Dom Perignon ('Miss Hobson only drinks champagne'), then Mark and I went up the hill through the smirring rain, and stood either side of the rock. We had no elaborate cinerary urn – just a plain plastic container. For a brief while we stood there, waiting for the sun. It was chill and clear, but it appeared as if on cue, so that she was perfectly lit as the ashes whirled up into the grey wind, towards the peaks of scree and the snowfields above, a last, swirling signature in the air.

In the field below, my father managed to raise his glass in a salute.

The clouds pass, but the sky remains.

Acknowledgements

My thanks go to all those who helped me during the writing of this book, with comments, encouragement, or advice. In particular: Geoffry Adams, Nikki Barrow, James Bevan, Jane Birkett, Michael Blakenham, Joanna Breyer, James Chatto, Ros Chatto, Simon Corbett, Bill and Pam Doyle, Simon Ellis, Bill Forse, Alasdair and Elaine Fraser, Sandy Gordon, Geordie Greig, Mark Havelock-Allan, Marie Karpinska, Josine Meijer, Neil Patterson, Pam Plumb, Michael Samuel, Nick de Somogyi, Valerian Wellington, Sebastian Whitestone, and Rowan Yapp. Clearly, this could not have been written without the co-operation of my parents, either. Some other individuals have preferred not to be named. I have received invaluable assistance over the years from the staff of the London Library and the British Library. My stalwart agent, Gillon Aitken, has certainly earned a mention in dispatches, and honourable mention must also be made of my editor Roland Philipps (to whom I commend the Mexican proverb that runs: 'With patience – and saliva – the elephant rogers the ant').

My vocabulary is insufficient to express the gratitude I feel to my wife, Helen, for her years of loving support.